A Player for a Moment

Notes from Fenway Park

Also by John Hough, Jr.

A Peck of Salt
A Two-Car Funeral
The Guardian
The Conduct of the Game
A Dream Season with Gary Carter

JOHN HOUGH, Jr.

A Player
F·O·R A
Moment

Notes from Fenway Park

HARCOURT BRACE JOVANOVICH, PUBLISHERS

San Diego   New York   London

Requests for permission to make copies of any part of the work should be mailed to: Permissions, Harcourt Brace Jovanovich, Publishers, Orlando, Florida 32887.
"Night Game" from *Collected Poems of Rolfe Humphries*, reprinted by permission of Indiana University Press. © 1947

Designed by G. B. D. Smith

Printed in the United States of America

Library of Congress Cataloging-in-Publication Data
Hough, John, 1946–
A player for a moment.
1. Boston Red Sox (Baseball team) 2. Fenway Park
(Boston, Mass.) 3. Hough, John, 1946–   —Biography.
4. Authors, American—20th century—Biography.   I. Title
GV875.B62H68   1988   796.357'64'0974461   88-3006
ISBN 0-15-172033-9

First edition

A B C D E

For Mary Kurtz Hough
In loving memory

And after the ninth, with the crowd in the bleachers thinning,
And the lights in the grandstand dimming out behind us,
And a full moon hung before us, over the clubhouse,
I drifted out with the crowd across the diamond,
Over the infield brown and the smooth green outfield,
So wonderful underfoot, so right, so perfect,
That each of us was a player for a moment,
The men my age, and the soldiers and the sailors,
Their girls, and the running kids, and the plodding old men,
Taking it easy, the same unhurried tempo,
In the mellow light and air, in the mild cool weather,
Moving together, moving out together,
Oh, this is good, I felt, to be part of this movement,
This mood, this music, part of the human race,
Alike and different, after the game is over,
Streaming away to the exit, and underground.

From "Night Game" by Rolfe Humphries

Contents

I would like to thank the Boston Red Sox for enabling me to write this book. My thanks to Public Relations Director Dick Bresciani and his assistant, Josh Spofford. I'm especially grateful to Jim Samia, also of that office, for his help and understanding. I would like to thank Ken Coleman for kindnesses extending beyond the baseball season. Thanks, finally, to Rubin Pfeffer for the idea, and to my editor, B.J. Robbins. She's still the best.

A Player for a Moment

Notes from Fenway Park

One

The Sorrows of October

IN THE PRESS BOX AT SHEA STADIUM A LEATHER-SKINNED MAN in a powder-blue sport jacket sits with his elbows spiking the counter, his chin against his knuckles, studying the ball game. He isn't jotting notes or keeping score, but it would be hard anyway to take him for a reporter. He is rawboned and sun-fried as an old wrangler, and he watches the game with a critical squint, pulling on a cigarette and blowing smoke through his crooked nose. He's the next person down from me, and I keep looking at him, trying to place him. A ballplayer. Bald, gone more to stringy lankness than fat.

"I hit a home run out there one time," he says suddenly, speaking to a young man who came in with him and is sitting on his other side. He points to the fence in left, stretching the longest of arms. "Only home run I ever hit to left field."

The voice is a rusty growl.

"How many home runs *did* you hit?" the young man asks.

1

"Thirty-five."

There's a lift in the voice, an air of pride. This has to be a pitcher. Who but a pitcher would be proud of thirty-five home runs over a career?

The May night is warm, and they've thrown open the press box windows, admitting a sweetish odor of cigar smoke from the lower grandstand and the roar of the big crowd. It's a happy crowd. This isn't a game so much as a celebration. The Mets and Red Sox, winners and losers in the recent World Series, have reconvened to play an exhibition game. The victors and vanquished, come back to fight a mock battle. It has been a mean, wet spring, but this night, May 7, is as warm as summertime.

"Who's the umpire behind the plate?" the tall man asks his companion.

"You got me."

"Say"—the old ballplayer leans my way—"you know who that umpire is behind the plate?" Sad eyes, down-slanting. Canny, too, like a fox.

Of course: Warren Spahn. He was always bald. He was bald in the late fifties.

Spahn and Sain: Then pray for rain.

"Doug Harvey," I say.

"Harvey, yeah," says Warren Spahn.

I don't remember Johnny Sain, but Spahn was still pitching when I got to college. I got the jingle *Spahn and Sain* from my father. The old Boston Braves, my father explained, had had two great pitchers and a collection of bums. The Braves had left for Milwaukee, and since I followed the Red Sox, I wasn't too concerned with Spahn and the Braves, who played in the other league. Still, he was one of the giants of baseball, and commanded a certain reverence.

A memory bobs up, Spahn on the cover of *Sports Illustrated*. He is winding up, cranking his arms way back, rocking, staring in with dark, burning eyes. The magazine lay on the oval table in the bay of Buddy's parents' kitchen. Buddy was my pal from next door. His father, unlike mine, subscribed to *Sports Illustrated*, with its slick color photographs, velvety, glowing, exciting as the games themselves. My father took *The Sporting News*, fuzzy newsprint with endless hard news and fast-fading little pictures. It wasn't just a question of cost; my father was a newspaperman.

The Burroughs' kitchen table was as yellow as the inside of a peach. I was at home there; I sat down and gazed at the magazine. *A Look at the Left-Handers*, it said. *Warren Spahn the Best of Them All*. I wanted it. It would go in one of my scrap-books. Buddy would want it, too, but I could take care of that. I was—what?—ten. Buddy, then, was eight, the soul of ami-ability, amenable, putty in my hands. He had freckles on a pug nose, a sunny smile worn off-center, slopped on like his clothes. I talked him out of the magazine, though he kept scrapbooks, too. I could talk him out of, and into, anything. The picture of Spahn went into a scrapbook, smoothed down with the fragrant liquid paste my father brought home in quart jars from the newspaper office. I have that scrapbook still; it is somewhere up there in the clutter of the attic, just one of many, a whole library of baseball scrapbooks that still exhale the sweet smell of liquid paste.

I'm on my feet, notebook in hand. "Mr. Spahn?"

Spahn turns and regards me with baleful curiosity, as if I were a new face sent up to pinch-hit against him. Down below, Wade Boggs, the world's best hitter, strikes out, and the crowd hoots a derisive cheer. When last seen in this ballpark, Boggs was sitting on the bench with his head bowed, weeping.

"I'm writing a book about the Red Sox," I say. "Could we talk?"

Still measuring me, Spahn says, "I don't see what your book has to do with me."

"It isn't *just* about the Red Sox," I say. "Can I sit down?"

Spahn exchanges a look with his companion and shrugs. I wonder if it's my blue jeans he dislikes. His friend wears a coat and tie.

"I guess so," Spahn says.

I lower myself into the plastic chair. Spahn's eagle gaze has returned to the game. He drags on his cigarette.

"You a sportswriter?" he asks.

Thinking he wants credentials I say, "I wrote a book last winter with Gary Carter."

Carter is out there, playing first base for the Mets. Spahn says nothing.

"Can I tell you a story?" I ask.

"Sure." He watches the game.

"I went to college near Philadelphia," I say. "I used to go to a lot of games at Connie Mack Stadium."

Spahn smiles faintly. "Old Connie Mack Stadium," he murmurs fondly.

"When I was a freshman," I say, "you joined the Mets. The night before my final exam in Latin, a friend of mine came bursting into my room. 'We're goin' to the ball game,' he says. 'I can't,' I tell him. 'I've got my Latin final tomorrow.' 'The Phillies are playing the Mets,' he says. 'I can't,' I say. 'Twi-night doubleheader,' he says. 'I know it,' I say. 'I can't go.' 'Warren Spahn is pitching,' he says. That did it. Off we went to the ball game. We didn't get back till after one in the morning."

Spahn gives me a look. "So I'm responsible for you flunking Latin?"

"I didn't actually flunk," I say, and regret it immediately.

"Oh," Spahn says, grunts it dismissively and returns his attention to the game. *What the hell's the point of the story if you didn't flunk?* says his face.

"My grade dropped ten points," I try.

"Is that right?" he says.

From a ninety-two to an eighty-two, the difference be-tween hitting .330 and .280. Warren Spahn, who pitched beau-tifully that night, lights another cigarette. I remember the ancient seedy ballroom of a ballpark, loggias hanging out over the field under an oval roof of sky. I remember how the air was blue-dyed under the lights by the smoke of cigars and cigarettes. I think, *Why does he smoke?*

"You shut them out that night," I say.

He looks at me. "No, I didn't."

"I'm sure you did."

"I didn't shut out anyone that year," he says.

"Well, you pitched the whole game. I'm sure of that."

"Maybe," he says.

"You don't remember?"

"Who pitched for them?"

I rummage back. Chris Short? Jim Bunning? "I do remem-ber that Ed Kranepool hit a home run for you guys."

Spahn still shakes his head, no. How could he have for-gotten? It was, it turned out, his last good game. At least, that's how I remember it. The Mets released him that season.

"How old were you then?" I ask.

"Forty-four."

"Is it hard," I ask him, trying to be gentle, "to know when to retire?"

He fixes me with smoky eyes. "What are you after?"

Do you remember your last game? I want to ask. *Do you re-member the last pitch you ever threw? Did you know it was your last?*

"Well, Gary Carter said . . ."

"What would Gary Carter know about it?"

"I don't know. He's thirty-three. . . ."

"Thirty-*three*," Spahn scoffs, as if no age could be more callow.

"I'm forty-one," I say. "Maybe that's why I wonder about this."

Spahn rubs out his cigarette.

"Look," he says, "if you're asking me if I have regrets, the answer's no. Most guys think about retiring when they're thirty-seven, thirty-eight. Hell, I pitched two no-hitters after I turned thirty-nine. I had some damn good years left in me."

He watches the game. Mookie Wilson shoots a ground ball to Boggs at third, easy out. Mookie was the last man to bat in the tenth inning of the sixth game of the Series, played right here. One of baseball's legendary moments. Mookie jumped the rope of Bob Stanley's inside slider; the ball glanced off Rich Gedman's mitt and flew to the backstop, a free trot home for Kevin Mitchell, poised at third, the tying run. Then, with Ray Knight at second, Mookie pulled the ground ball to Buckner.

"No matter how old I got," says Warren Spahn, "there were days when I threw the ball as well as I ever did. I just couldn't do it as often."

He won't admit a thing, won't give in. It must have been a great asset, this stubbornness, a form of courage on the mound. Don't admit you're beaten. Pitch as long as you can, as long as they leave you in there. As many innings. As many years.

"It doesn't look like the Red Sox are going to repeat," I say, after a silent interval.

"Teams don't repeat any more," he says. "They used to, but not any more."

"Why?" I say.

"Complacency," he snaps. "There's no pride anymore."

Spahn's Braves won pennants in '57 and '58. In '57 they won the Series against the mighty Yankees, who *always* repeated. In those days the Series was played in the daytime, riveting the country through the warm, yellow afternoons of early October. Radios snarled the play-by-play in the stores and barbershops up and down Main Street. My parents refused to let television into our house. We were the only family in the neighborhood—in all of America, as far as I could tell—without one. So I watched the Series in the dark paneled den of the big house down the road, Buddy's house. On school days the games began without us. We would leap down out of the bus and run all the way, Buddy puffing behind me with his shirttail pulling out.

"Your Braves repeated," I say to Spahn.

"Yeah, and we should have won four in a row, not just two. In '56 we had a one-game lead over Brooklyn going into the final weekend. We played the Cardinals three games, and they beat us two out of three. They played way over their heads. In '59 we finished in a tie with the Dodgers. We lost the play-off when Mantilla booted the ground ball."

He watches the game stonily, as if his mood had been poisoned by thirty-year-old memories of a pair of losses in St. Louis, and an error by a reedy young infielder who said afterward the tension had gotten to him.

"We were a hell of a ball club," he says suddenly. "Talk about pride. Listen: We didn't need management to get on us when we were goin' bad. We got on each other. We chewed each other out. Red Schoendienst wouldn't *let* us lose. 'Make 'em hit the ball to me,' he used to say. 'Make 'em hit it to me.' That was the attitude."

It is the top of the second inning, and Bill Buckner is ambling to the plate in his ankle-hugging high-top shoes, his trademark since the Series, when he was crippled by a damaged Achilles tendon. He couldn't run. All heart, he went creaking around the bases, flailing his elbows like an old man. Now a cheer is building, and when the PA announces Buckner, the crowd stands, giving down a whistling, jeering roar. In that deathless tenth inning Mookie Wilson pulled the ground ball to Buckner, who leaned over stiff-legged with an eye, perhaps, on the lightning-swift Wilson. The slow ground ball climbed over Buckner's glove and trickled into right field as Knight galloped around with the winning run. Who in America has not seen a replay of Buckner's error? Now the mocking ovation finally spends itself. Buckner digs in, takes a stride, then knocks a lazy fly ball to right field. Another shrill cheer.

Warren Spahn watches silently, apparently unmoved by the treatment given Buckner. I can see he's had enough of me, but as I begin to push back my chair he says, "Some of these guys never even played in the minors. They never rode the buses, or lived in the cheap hotels. It makes a difference."

What difference? I wonder. *Can anyone really know?* I get up, collect my pen and notebook.

"Thank you," I say.

He nods.

"So long," I say, and offer my hand.

"So long," he agrees, and reaches up. His hand is long and knotty.

I keep going down the curving Formica counter till I'm out of his sight. I sit down, a stranger, among the beat reporters. The Mets have grabbed the lead, 1–0. There's no hope: they're going to win. You know it, the way you know it when kids fight, old playground enemies, their relationship defined forever by their first battle. The Red Sox seem listless, as if they have no stomach for this. I can't say I'm enjoying it, either.

It ended here. Game six. Game seven. Our heroes fell in an alien land far from home. As they left Shea Stadium, Mets fans threw beer bottles at them. A bottle gashed the silvery head of Jack Rogers, the traveling secretary; Jack came home with his skull wrapped like a mummy's. Queens is a world away from the Back Bay, where Fenway Park snuggles; the Series wasn't a war of ideologies so much as a random clash of alien cultures.

Queens is a one-hour plane ride from Martha's Vineyard, where I live with my wife and stepdaughter in a house built by a whaling man, surrounded by woods and dirt roads. The wooded hills stagger down to Vineyard Sound, which stretches six miles to the town I grew up in. From the air the Sound is lime-green over the sandy bottom, dark blue over the shoals. As the little plane wheels toward New York, you can see my home town, Buddy's and mine, spreading off the southwest corner of Cape Cod. The plane's shadow skims along below like a sparrow.

Long Island Sound looks darker from up here, muddier, than the waters of home. By and by the Manhattan skyline spells itself out in the brown smog piled over the city. As you buzz over Queens, dropping for LaGuardia, you get a good look at the gaudy horseshoe of Shea Stadium, blue as fingerpaint in the gray sprawl of the city. Mets blue, turned up loud. They like noise down here.

The journey, to this point, is old hat. In the winter just gone by I made it four times, continuing to Long Island, where I was working on the book with Gary Carter. Gary would send a friend to meet me, or would meet me himself, and we would zoom off on the expressway past Shea, which was decked out in the most enormous banner proclaiming 1986 WORLD CHAMPIONS! I thought the exclamation point was unnecessary, but didn't say anything. Gary loved seeing the banner. He would gaze at it as we drove by, rapturous, as if he'd sighted a vision in the sky. Certain friends of mine, Red Sox fans, wondered how I could stand it. Traitor, they kidded me. Benedict Arnold. None of them was trying to earn a living as a writer.

The Series ended here, so this is where I begin. I take a taxi from LaGuardia, and instead of zooming away to Long Island, we veer down off the expressway to the whitened asphalt desert surrounding Shea. My heart is thumping by the time I pay the driver. I've never been in a big-league clubhouse or on a big-league field.

"Are you a ballplayer?" the driver asks.

I stare at him. He isn't kidding.

"No," I say, "but thanks."

I tip him big and head out across this vast, bleaching parking lot. It is a couple of hours before game time. Here and there a van or station wagon sits with its back end open, spilling barbecue paraphernalia. Picnickers stand around drinking beer. A couple of guys are playing catch with an old hardball. A tape deck squats on a car roof. Noise. Subway trains rattle by on elevated tracks. The expressway traffic growls along. Gulls cry, banking down to scavenge bread crusts, potato chips, chicken bones, shreds of pizza. The biggest noise comes every few minutes when a jet coasts into LaGuardia. The planes fly in so low you could almost hit the silver bellies with a stone. Their roar lags behind them, scorching your eardrums and tickling your clavicle. What a place to build a ballpark.

A city cop and a stadium attendant are guarding the press gate. The cop stands with his hands clasped behind him, deep in thought. The attendant sits by the turnstile, an old man with a scowl, rubbing his face. I have a press pass, I tell him. He says nothing, just gets up and scans some cubbyholes. He finds my pass, a cardboard tag on a string. I loop the string around a shirt button and push through the turnstile.

Now what? The place to begin, I decide, is the Red Sox clubhouse. Tell me I can stroll into the Oval Office, the Senate Cloak Room, a party at Frank Sinatra's house, and I'll believe it more easily than I believe this. Someone else is walking these high tunnels, this warren under the grandstand; not me. I ask a photographer, hurrying through with a couple of cameras slung around his neck, where the visitors' clubhouse is. Easy. Down on your left. The tunnel is lit by wan, intermittent bulbs, like a subway. I come to a varnished door guarded by another cop. The cop looks vexed, as though the job here were distasteful to him.

"Can I go in?" I ask him.

He lifts my pass, tilts it to the dirty white light. He jerks his head at the door. I open it.

The first thing I notice is that no one looks at me. The

door bumps shut; nobody glances over to see who might have come in. I stand rooted just inside the door of this small, close room, gazing around at Marty Barrett, Dave Henderson, Glenn Hoffman, and Wade Boggs himself. None of them seems aware of me. A radio swamps the room with pulsing rock. Dressing stalls honeycomb the walls. I can smell chewing tobacco, like stale and pungent brown sugar. I enter in a few more steps. Still no one looks at me.

Hoffman is stepping into his game pants. He is young and leggy; there is a delicacy to his reedy build and pointy face. He missed last season, heart trouble, of all things. He barely made the team this spring.

At a varnished table sits Dave Henderson, sprawled back reading a tabloid newspaper. "Hendu," we call him fondly, one of last autumn's heroes. Hit one of the biggest home runs in Red Sox history. He'd come off the bench in the fifth game of the play-offs when Tony Armas, the center fielder, sprained his ankle. With two out in the top of the ninth, the California Angels were opening champagne in their clubhouse. Hendu was at the plate. The Sox trailed by two. Two strikes on Hendu, a man at first. Already this inning Baylor had blasted a home run, bringing us closer but raising the odds against Hendu. How could lightning strike again? The home run was no accident, though; Hendu continued to bash the ball in the Series.

At the other end of the table sits Marty Barrett, the doughty second baseman. Barrett perches forward, idly shuffling a pack of cards. He is compact, solid, with a square-jawed, honest face. Another Series hero, though he did whiff to end the whole thing, cutting hopelessly at an inside slider as New York erupted in celebration.

A spindly youngster sits in front of his stall, staring down at the rust-brown carpet. He wears only shorts and a jersey; his legs are thin and very pale. He is vaguely blond, with a wisp of mustache. He doesn't look like a ballplayer.

Boggs is in the far corner, briskly pulling on his uniform.

A reddish-gold beard, new this spring, wraps his angular jaw. Boggs's face is all clean, straight lines. Classic. With his beard and straight-edged face he looks like Saint George.

Hendu tosses down his newspaper, rises, and goes to the bat rack on the wall by the door. He passes a few feet from me; I can smell soap and chewing gum. A full-length mirror shimmers beside the bat rack. Hendu yanks out his bat and plants himself in front of the mirror. He cocks the bat. His chest bulges like a bulldog's. He inspects himself in the mirror, looks himself up and down.

"I ain't been hittin'," he announces, as if the man in the mirror hadn't heard the news.

Boggs slaps on his hat, snatches up his glove, and glides around the table to where the skinny blond is sitting. Wade gives the kid a bracing clap on the shoulder and thrusts down his hand.

"Welcome," he says. "Good to have you, man."

The kid manages a smile as he takes Boggs's hand.

"Thanks," he says.

Boggs wheels, bustles out of the clubhouse. The door shuts with a bang. All this time I've been standing in the middle of the room, writing some notes, trying to look at ease. I don't know what to do yet with my freedom. I *am* free, I remind myself, and so I follow Boggs.

The tunnel to the field is dim and melancholy. A plywood ramp has been built, climbing and sloping down again like a bridge. Brown puddles stare up from the concrete below. It is cold, as if spring still hasn't flushed out all of winter.

Boggs's spikes clump loudly on the plywood. The ramp shelves down to a square of light, to noise, music, and voices and the pretty *plock* of wood on a hardball. Boggs emerges, pulls a bat from the rack without breaking stride, and climbs wooden steps to the ballfield. I stop at the end of the tunnel, the throat of the dugout. The field stretches out slightly below eye level. The Sox are taking batting practice to the accompaniment of loud, loud music.

I step up into the dugout. Right there, right beside me, stands Jim Rice. His arms are folded and he is contemplating the field. He smiles, as if at some private amusement.

"Excuse me," I say, and walk in front of him.

Rice's gaze flickers sideways, then back again to the field. The mahogany face is flat and handsome and moody as a sullen sea. He says nothing to me, and I climb the spike-gnawed steps that run the length of the dugout. The piped-in music seems to pour down from all directions, too loud, too insistent. Ricky Skaggs, Ritchie Valens, the Bee Gees. The grandstands are nearly empty; perhaps a crowd soaks up the music, takes the stabbing edge off it. A small gaggle of writers is watching batting practice from behind the cage. I walk out, mingle with the writers and ballplayers. Game six, game seven. On this very spot.

Dwight Evans is in the batting cage. Bill Fischer, the Sox' pitching coach, is throwing. Fischer is fat and burly, and his face is as hard-bitten as if he'd spent his life on the docks. I remember seeing him pitch in Fenway Park for the old Washington Senators.

The air around the cage is sweet with the reek of chewing tobacco. The lone source of this seems to be the Sox' hitting coach, Walter Hriniak. Hriniak at the moment is crouching on his haunches, studying Evans through the netting. A glove is wadded in his hip pocket. He bounces to his feet.

"Swing too hard this time, Dwight," he says. "Swing from your ass."

Evans nods, then drives the next pitch low and hard into left field.

"*Okay*," snaps Hriniak.

Evans scoots out of the cage, Boggs scoots in. Time is precious. Hriniak studies Boggs without speaking. Hriniak has bright yellow hair shooting down out of his cap. The sun has burned his face pink. He is sweating hard.

Boggs sprays the ball all over the outfield. With his final swing he catches a high pitch with the meat of the bat, lifts it to deep right field, high and lazy and out of the ballpark.

"Oh, *yes!*" he sings, and spins out of the cage with his bat still raised in the finished swing, pointing it like a wand at the ball as it climbs out above the bull pens.

Buckner's turn. If he concentrates, a good big-league hitter can make perfect contact with batting practice pitches almost indefinitely. He can hit a long ball or a line drive with every swing. Buckner does so now and comes out with a slanty grin lifting his shaggy mustache.

"That was a *real* good fuckin' round," he tells the world.

Steve Crawford, who is pitching tonight, takes a turn. Thanks to the designated-hitter rule, American League pitchers have become comic with the bat. Crawford, who has a big, slow body, takes lunging swings and bloops midget pop-ups around the infield. Rice arrives with his bat on his shoulder. He watches Crawford. Crawford swats at a high pitch, gets it flush, and knocks it high in the air to left field. The ball carries, drifts, falls beyond the fence. Rice doubles over, cackling. I notice Crawford isn't laughing. He lunges and hangs another short pop-up above third base.

"Out front, Shag," Hriniak tells him. "Get it out front."

Rice spills another laugh. "Out front, *shit,*" he says. "Out front'll get you a routine fly ball, that's what out front'll get you."

Crawford ignores this, and so does Hriniak. Crawford takes a final swipe and bleeds a slow ground ball toward shortstop. He comes out frowning, and Glenn Hoffman darts in.

"Come on, Hoffy, come on, Hoffy," urges Rice, the voice taut, yappy.

Hoffman pumps one in the air to medium center field.

"One out," says Rice. "Get someone on, Hoffy."

Hoffman pulls a fly ball gently down the left-field line.

"Two out," observes Rice.

Hoffman swings hard and pops the ball straight up into the netting, which bends with it, holding the ball and then dropping it at his feet.

"God*damn*," Hoffman hisses.

A writer slides sideways around the cage till he is beside Rice. "Uh, Jim?" he says.

Rice sends him a flinty glance and resumes watching Hoffman. Rice's thighs are like boulders.

"How's the elbow?" the reporter asks.

"All right," Rice mutters. He watches Hoffman.

"When will you play?"

"I'll *play*," Rice says, "when the doctor says I can play."

The reporter drifts back.

Evans looms beside me, waiting with his bat on his shoulder to hit again. Our shoulders nearly touch; here's my chance. The trepidation that seizes me, a form of terror, is what I felt as a schoolboy the first few times I called up a girl. I used to stare at the telephone, working up courage.

"Uh, Dwight?"

Evans turns, looks at me neutrally. His face has a chiseled beauty.

"Was it hard coming down here?" I ask.

"No," he says, "the weather's terrible at home."

The voice is deep, with a twangy melody.

"It was hard for *me*," I say.

"Well," he says, "I thought about it some before I went to sleep last night."

"I don't blame you," I say.

"We had it won," he says. "We just couldn't put 'em away."

He smiles and walks off. Not much of an interview, but a

decent beginning, a deep fly ball in my first at-bat. Wait'll I tell my wife I talked to Dwight Evans. And my brother-in-law.

A heavy hand whacks my back. A friendly hand. Gary Carter, with his head of golden curls and his million-dollar smile. My friend Gary Carter, who helped wreck us in the Series with his home runs and exuberant work behind the plate.

"*There* you are," I say. I've been wondering when he'd come out.

"And here *you* are," he says. "Your dream come true."

"It'll take some getting used to," I say.

"You'll get used to it," he says. "Have you talked to anyone yet?"

"To Dwight Evans. Sort of."

"Some'll talk to you, some won't," he says. "It's like that on every ball club."

If this man played for the Sox, I'd have it made.

"Look," he says, nodding toward the dugout. Mookie Wilson is sitting on the bench with a crowd of writers gathered round. "I imagine there's some material there," Gary says.

Rule number one: Follow the beat writers. I thank Gary.

"Good luck with the book," he says.

Mookie is sitting back with his glove on, slapping a ball into the pocket, peeling it out and slapping it in again, as he talks.

"Can't *help* but think about it," Mookie is saying. "No *way* I won't be thinkin' about it. Especially if Buckner's playin' first."

Mookie Wilson looks a thousand years old, wizened, crinkled, wise as old Methuselah. His voice is soft and dances up and down.

"Y'all got to understand somethin'," he says. "I didn't *do* anything. I hit a ground ball, is all. I wasn't tryin' to hit no ground ball. I was *tryin'* to hit the ball out of the yard, man."

The writers all laugh.

"I did think I was gonna beat it out," Mookie resumes. "I will say that. I thought I had the base."

He stops, reflects, laughs. An old, wise laugh.

"I didn't *do* anything," Mookie says again. "I didn't do a thing, but I'm gonna be remembered for it. I *ought* to be remembered for the things I do that's special. Goin' from first to home on a single, remember me for that. How many ground balls have gone through a man's legs? Must be two thousand of 'em."

Buckner's error occurred on a Saturday night—a Sunday morning, actually—sometime around twelve-thirty. My wife and I had gone out to dinner, but only because the hostess had assured us that all who wished could adjourn to the living room in time for the first pitch of game six. Everyone did wish, as it turned out, except our hostess, who puttered in the kitchen, listening to our yells and groans, and finally slipped away to bed. The rest of us stuck it out in front of the big color screen, four men, three women. Our host was Don Carrick, nonpareil illustrator and portrait and landscape artist. Don, artist to the marrow, appreciates the aesthetics of baseball without caring to follow the game day by day. Certainly, he condoned my passionate involvement, and that of the two other men in the room, as a kind of endearing and worthwhile madness. The women were along for the ride. It wasn't going to ruin their winter if the Sox lost, but they knew drama when they saw it.

The game zigzagged along, looking good, looking bad, looking good again. The Mets stayed close, but as the innings went by I began to feel in my bones that the Sox were going to win. It began as a hunch, and grew and hardened to certainty. The game had that look about it. We'd all done some drinking. The bourbon had made me very wise. It made perfect sense that in my fortieth year the Sox were going to win the Series. This was my reward.

The Mets tied it in the eighth, 3–3.

No one could score in the ninth.

And so to the tenth. Henderson hit his home run and went cavorting, leaping and twirling, around the bases. A fierce joy yanked me to my feet. My wife smiled: she'd taken to Hendu, with his gapped, boyish grin. Tess clapped her hands.

"It isn't enough," Kib said.

"Oh, yes it is," I said.

Then Boggs slashed a double, and the reliable Barrett chased him home with a single. The famine was ending. The curse was being lifted.

In the bottom of the inning Wally Backman hit an easy fly ball to Rice. Keith Hernandez drove one to center, an easy catch for Hendu. The announcers began talking about how long it had been, 1918, since the Sox had won the Series. They announced that Bruce Hurst had been judged Most Valuable Player of the Series.

"Do you realize," I said, as much to myself as to the others, "that we're about to see the Red Sox win the World Series?" The world would never be quite the same.

Gary Carter was at the plate. Here I made a fatal mistake.

"Don't make the last out, Gary," I said.

"Are you *crazy?*" Kib said.

"He's a nice guy," I said. "Let him get a single."

Gary looked almost frightened up there, the edges of his mouth pulled back, forehead rumpled. He got his single, cracking Calvin Schiraldi's fastball into left field. Nice going, Gary. The hit will console you through the winter. Now let's finish them off.

With two strikes, the pinch hitter, Mitchell, pushed a ground ball up the middle that crawled somehow between Barrett and Spike Owen. Suddenly, the tying runs were on base. The room got quiet.

With two strikes, Ray Knight punched a floater over Barrett's head, dumping the ball out there with the handle of his bat. Carter scored, Mitchell circled to third, the tying run. We were now in deep, deep trouble. This wasn't going to be as simple as I thought. The hitter was Mookie Wilson, and John McNamara, the Sox' manager, walked out to the mound and called in the overweight righty, Bob Stanley.

"Oh, *Jesus!*" I yelled. "Not Stanley, oh my god."

"Isn't he any good?" Tess inquired innocently.

"He's a *bum!*" I yelled.

The truth is, I've always considered Stanley a decent pitcher, a view not held by most Red Sox lovers. My despairing yell was to propitiate whatever gods were throwing this scare into us. The scare was a lesson: don't get complacent. *All right,* my soul cried. *Now give us our victory.*

Historians have forgotten, if they ever noticed, that Stanley pitched well that night. He threw two strikes past Mookie, and when Mookie kept nicking foul balls, Stanley never gave him anything good to hit. The wild pitch wasn't Stanley's fault: Gedman should have caught the ball. Gary Carter, who likes Gedman personally, was clear about this. Mookie jackknifed out of the way, the ball grazed Gedman's mitt and was gone. Mitchell danced home, and the game was even.

Kib yelled, I remember, "*Oh, no, oh, Jesus!*" A *crie-de-coeur,* stricken and angry both. Kib, too, is an artist, and I value that yell of his. It made us kin forever.

And so the tea leaves had lied to me. My heart cooled and hardened. I was sick to death of rooting for the Boston Red Sox. I sank back in the sofa wondering bitterly how the gods would contrive to allow Ray Knight to score from second.

Having taken the rap for Gedman, Stanley battled on. As Mookie would point out, rolling the ball to the first baseman wasn't what he had in mind. He didn't even pull it hard; if he had, Evans in right might have reached it in time to hold Knight at third or gun him down at the plate. Through Buckner's legs it went, and Knight frolicked home. The Mets swarmed out to celebrate, and Bill Buckner limped off the field a legend.

We left quickly, saying leaden good-byes. The autumn stars winked across the blue-black dome of the sky. Up and down the street the houses all slept. Some were summer houses, asleep till May or June, when this World Series would be history.

In the car my wife said, "Maybe they'll win tomorrow."

"No," I said. "They won't win tomorrow."

"You'll feel different tomorrow," she said, and she was right. Hurst was pitching, and I woke up thinking we could still win the thing.

In the third inning of the exhibition game at Shea, I discover that the skinny newcomer to the Red Sox is Tom Bolton, a lefty pitcher who arrived yesterday from the Sox' triple-A team in Pawtucket, Rhode Island. Bolton replaces Crawford. The kid yields a run in the fourth, but shuts the Mets out the rest of the way.

The game rushes along. The hitters on both sides are swinging without conviction. The game might be fun if it weren't for last October. As it is, the Mets have nothing to prove, and a win by the Sox would only underline their failure to do it here when it counted. The Mets fans are aware of their no-lose situation. Instead of rooting, they celebrate, punching beach balls around the grandstands and sailing paper gliders from the upper decks. In the fifth they stand again and rain applause down on Buckner. Buckner, maybe in a hurry to get back to the dugout, slaps the first pitch back on one hop to the pitcher. During the seventh-inning stretch, the Diamond Vision screen shows Jesse Orosco fanning Barrett to finish the Series, and the pileup on the mound, the Mets converging and hurling themselves on top of each other till they were stacked four or five deep. The crowd pours a long cheer that extends, seamless, to welcome Mookie Wilson to the plate. Mookie hits a fly ball to Evans, and they cheer that, too. Why not?

The Sox go down in order in the ninth, and the crowd winds up the celebration with one more blast of noise. It's over, thank god. I follow the pack of reporters to their elevator. No one talks on the slow ride down.

A rich smell of food fills the Red Sox clubhouse. That, and silence. No one is speaking. The food, lasagne and warm bread, is set out in aluminum pans. The players sit in front of their cubicles, hunched over paper plates laden and soaked with food. Jim Rice is nowhere to be seen. Nor is Evans, Buckner, Gedman, or Barrett.

A television reporter stands in the middle of the room, hesitating there as he sizes things up. His gaze snags on Owen. Little Spike had a good World Series, but this spring his bat has gone dead and he's been sitting on the bench. The reporter summons a smile and goes to Owen.

"Spike, could I have a word with you while you're gulping it down?"

Owen flashes a nervous smile. More a grimace. "On camera?"

"Sure."

"Naw, man. I ain't done nothin' in two weeks."

"Just one question," the reporter pleads.

"Naw," Spike says, smiling that smile.

I don't blame you, Spike. I take one last look around. Mustard-brown walls, rotten-apple-brown. Smell of lasagne, of chewing tobacco. What a place to have to come back to after blowing the World Series.

It seems now as if Buddy and I were best friends for a decade or more, but I can count only four World Series in the paneled den in the big house down the road: '55, '56, '57, '58. I remember best the '57 Series, when Warren Spahn's Braves beat the Yankees. The final out of the Series—I can still see the black-and-white screen, a big one for those days, baseball in dusky shadows and milky grays—was a hot ground ball to third. Eddie Mathews, who was known for his slugging, gloved the tough short hop and threw across the diamond in time. It was over. A tyranny had been overthrown, an oppressive law of nature thwarted. It was hard to believe. I let go a yell and went careening out into the cool fall afternoon. Buddy followed me, yelping like an Apache. The day was overcast, but the sky had glassy brightness. The neighborhood was silent. I ran up the driveway with Buddy trailing faithfully, turned on the empty street, and kept running. At the end of the Burroughs' apple orchard I staggered out of breath and fell in the long, matted grass. A moment later Buddy landed beside me. His skin, his yellow-brown hair, had a thick sweet smell, like vanilla. The Yankees had lost, and we lay in the dark green grass, impossibly happy, gazing at the wide mother-of-pearl sky.

When I think about Buddy, I can't get away from how I bossed him around and generally lorded it over him. He brought out a big-brother sanctimoniousness in me, something priggish. I nagged him about being messy, about being overweight. He used to fight with a kid at the bus stop—the kid was a roughneck, but younger than Buddy—and get beaten every time. I raged at Buddy for losing, for giving up, for having no more stomach for it. I hated seeing him lose. I could make him cry with my harangues. But there were good times, too. I didn't let any big guys pick on him. I taught him how to play ball.

In time, we went our separate ways. He had his friends; I had mine. Sometimes I would be outside when he came shambling past the house on his way from town. He would wave and grin. I wondered what the grin was for. What was he thinking? I wondered what he'd been up to, and had to remind myself it was none of my business now.

Once in a while on summer evenings Buddy would call and ask me if I wanted to come over and play some catch. A simple game of catch on the back lawn, the grass fine as silk from being watered and weeded by the Burroughs' gardener. It was good to throw the ball with Buddy, like old times. He crouched for me like a catcher, and I burned them in there, pounding bruises in his hand. He didn't complain. He never had. The sun would go down behind the trees and our game would lag, like a conversation that had run its course. We both knew it was time to quit.

The last time I ever saw him he was standing by the bar in a noisy local joint with his fist wrapped around a bottle of beer. The place was dark and crowded. It hung out over a harbor. Buddy was now taller than I, a smiling bear of a man in old jeans and an untucked flannel shirt. His voice took me by surprise: deep and pleasing, like cello music. His old smile had turned wry and amused, as if he'd grown wise and could see how droll life was. It was August, and the windows were open above the harbor, pulling in the strong smells of kelp and wharf tar. Buddy was twenty-one and had finished a third year of college. And although his father had been a Navy flier in World War II, Buddy had decided to leave the country or go to prison rather than fight in Vietnam. Listening to this, I remembered berating Buddy because he didn't want to go back and fight again at the bus stop, a gnawing memory I hadn't shaken and never will. I wondered if he forgave me for that, and for everything else. He was killed on an icy road in the Berkshires that winter, so I'll never know. I thought of bringing it up in the bar that night, but couldn't see how to begin. I knew there'd be other times.

Two

Fenway Revisited

THREE HOURS BEFORE GAME TIME YOU CAN USUALLY FIND A
parking space on Van Ness Street, a block over from Fenway
Park. Van Ness brushes Fenway, crosses little Yawkey Way,
and wanders on between two parking lots and past a parking
garage and some brick factory buildings, old things painted white
with blackened windows. Van Ness is a side street, informal.
It has a quiet, backwater feel, though Boylston Street, one of
the city's busy spokes, is a short block away. Weeds have
punched through the asphalt along the chain fences guarding
the parking lots, and on one side, where the lot is sunk below
street level, locust trees shade the sidewalk. At three o'clock
the shifts change over in the factories, and soon the workers
begin to appear on Van Ness, scattering to their cars. Now you
can park.

Once, when I was about ten, I saw a drunk staggering
down the middle of Van Ness away from the ball park. A smile

was scrawled across his reddened face. I was going to the game with my parents. Seeing the three of us coming toward him, the drunk stopped, swiveled around, and gazed at the light towers of Fenway. "*Whoops,*" he blurted, and then confided to my parents, "I was goin' the wrong way." My mother and father thought this was very funny, but the drunk's mistake said something about Fenway Park. Jim Lonborg, who pitched the Sox to an unexpected pennant in 1967, says he walked right past Fenway the first time he looked for it. Gentleman Jim exaggerates, but not a whole lot. The old brick ballpark is tucked away among buildings just as tall, and of the same vintage. The streets around it are all narrow; you can't stand back and see it whole. The only giveaway is the light towers.

There was a time when I wanted to be a sportswriter—a baseball writer, that is, covering the Red Sox. I used to stare at the press gate on Yawkey Way and imagine my way inside. I pictured a private passageway snaking to the clubhouse. Actually, the press gate is just another way into the ballpark. It merely dumps you into the great concourse beneath the grandstand. There's no cop at the press gate, just a slender young high-school art teacher named Mike Smith. Mike wears a short beard and a smile that is at once cordial and appraising. If he knows you, he will whip your pass out of his shirt pocket before you reach the turnstile. He'll talk a little baseball, even baseball literature, if you care to linger. Welcome to the ballpark, is Mike's attitude.

There is no cop at the green door that leads to the Red Sox clubhouse. When you knock, the door is opened by a husky young man in a white shirt—a sort of high-class bouncer—who checks your pass if he doesn't remember your face. If you're entitled, he lets you in with a brief, unsmiling nod. Now you are in a sort of anteroom. To your right, a narrow corridor leads to the manager's office. Ahead, a short flight of stairs descends to the tunnel to the dugout. There's a phone on the wall, and often a player is talking, dropping his voice and tucking his face toward the wall for privacy.

A second door, unguarded, admits you to the clubhouse. The clubhouse is spacious, barnlike. The brick walls are painted brown. The rug is brown. Brown steel girders cross overhead like rafters in a barn, and above them pipes run this way and that. Dressing cubicles run all the way around the walls, each with its canvas chair. A couple of wide brick pillars break the room up.

To get to the field the players pass through the anteroom with the wall phone and the bouncer minding, descend the stairs, and go down a tunnel. The tunnel to the dugout is, roughly, the distance between bases. It is a true tunnel: narrow and low. The cement floor gets wet and is covered with sheets of plywood laid across temporary joists. The plywood shakes and clanks underfoot. A urinal and drinking fountain lurk just inside the entrance up to the dugout.

They all came down this tunnel. Tris Speaker, Smoky Joe Wood, Babe Ruth, Joe Cronin, Ellis Kinder, Bobby Doerr. Williams and Yaz. Jimmy Piersall, Mel Parnell, Jackie Jensen, Frank Malzone. Monster Radatz and Gentleman Jim Lonborg. Tony C. In this dank tunnel you can imagine them more vividly, even, than on the field. Here they all walked, clattering out to play ball. You can imagine the wisecracks, laughter, obscenities, and the bitter quiet after losing.

The dugout is as simple as can be. You step up to the bench. Now and then a mouse can be seen tightroping on one of the electric wires draped along the back wall. The fearless mice of Fenway Park. The floor of the dugout is littered with dried gobs of chewing tobacco.

There are no secrets, really, under the grandstand of Fenway. The clubhouse is old-fashioned, prosaic, easily imagined. When the bouncer opens the door to let in a reporter, fans milling by might glimpse a ballplayer talking on the wall phone.

Everything is right here. It isn't such an enormous leap, getting through the green door, into the clubhouse, the tunnel, the dugout.

I was nine the first time I saw big-league baseball and Fenway Park. My parents had decided the time had come and, early in the summer, had purchased three tickets by mail for a September game with the Yankees. The Yankees! Mickey Mantle and Yogi Berra. Gordie Miller, who lived down the street and who had already been several times to Fenway, asked me what section our seats were in. I quoted him a number and Gordie looked disgusted and said, "Those seats are no good." He seemed to know what he was talking about. A shadow fell on the great day ahead, until my father fixed things. Where, I asked him, trying to sound casual, will we be sitting? Right field, he said. And then: "You'll be so close to Jackie Jensen you could spit on him." I imagined Jackie Jensen a few feet from me, leaning with his hands on his knees, eyes peeled from under the brim of his cap. Keen, noble, blue eyes. I couldn't wait. And who played right field for the Yankees? Hank Bauer did. I'd be so close to Hank Bauer I could spit on him.

On the great day, a Saturday, I woke to the sound of rain slapping shingles. I got up and looked. Dark skies, steady rain. Rain smearing my bedroom window. Son of a bitch. We made the trip, anyway. You never knew about the weather. It was a long drive in those days, on what are now back roads. My father kept me hoping. "It looks brighter up ahead," he'd say, peering north over the steering wheel. "It's letting up," he'd say. It wasn't, though. It was raining just as hard. There was no point in going to the ballpark, so we drove to Cambridge, where my aunt and uncle lived, and my two little girl cousins.

The apartment was spacious and dumpy, a great treat in ordinary times. But not on this blighted day. The grownups broke out the whiskey. I wandered off to play with the girls. After a while, though, I was summoned back to the living room. The grownups sat around with their whiskey glasses in their hands, watching me in an appraising sort of way. Something was up.

"Here's the deal," my father said. The game had been postponed, he said, and they were going to play a double-header tomorrow. He and my mother had to leave in the morning, but if I was willing to ride the train home by myself tomorrow night, my Aunt Belle would take me to the double-header.

World's greatest aunt, my Aunt Belle. A Hall of Fame aunt. When my mother brought me here to go to the eye doctor, Aunt Belle would take me to the Peabody Museum to see the whale skeletons and stuffed snakes and sharks and giant squid. She took me fishing. She threw a baseball with me. She was my mother's sister, a graceful beauty with cheekbones like the two curves of a heart and a comely upward slant to her eyes. A Hall of Famer, all the way around.

Riding the train with a parent was fun, but the prospect of going it alone struck dread in my heart. Chronic terrors woke in my imagination: sadistic teenagers, men with knives in their pockets. What if I got off at the wrong station? I saw myself on a deserted platform with a gang of teenagers closing in. Leather jackets, greased hair. The grownups eyed me, waiting for an answer. My aunt's smile was hopeful. She'd never been to a game and knew nothing about baseball. Let's give it a shot, said her smile. I agreed. I might be killed on the way home, but in the meantime I would see baseball in Fenway Park. I said I'd take the train.

My aunt's two most vivid memories of that long afternoon are her hangover and a woman with a beard who kept touring the grandstands, flaunting herself in front of the sellout crowd. I was too young to recognize a hangover. I do remember the bearded woman. The beard was thick and black. The woman was stocky, and definitely a woman. She kept reappearing, walking the aisles, swaying along in a loose-fitting dress, eyes lowered, as if she had no idea she was being stared at.

I also remember a fistfight in one of the ticket lines under the archways on Yawkey Way, which was Jersey Street then. My aunt had to cash in the rain checks from yesterday. While we were waiting, a man in the next line suddenly whirled and stuck out his chest.

"What are you, a wise guy?" he said.

"Yeah," said the other, "I'm a wise guy."

It was an eye-opener, grownups talking like that. Next thing I knew, the first man threw a punch, which smacked flesh somewhere, perhaps the neck. People shot away in all directions. Almost instantly, a squad of ushers swooped in and pulled the fighters apart. It was over in nothing flat. My aunt, though, had had a scare. I could see it in her face, a difference, as if a layer of skin had been stripped away. Later she said she had considered taking me straight home.

We found our seats, which were in right field to be sure, but a long way from spitting range of Jensen and Bauer. The hitters seemed a mile away. The pitcher threw an invisible baseball that would materialize only when hit, appearing finally against the blue sky or white as an egg on the grass. My aunt and I studied the scoreboard on the left-field wall, like a slate blackboard with its neat rows of numbers, and prettified by the red and green lights, which reminded me of Christmas. I couldn't spit on the right fielders but could see them pretty well, Jensen and Bauer in the first game, Karl Olsen in the second, and a rookie named Elston Howard. The Yankees, of course, swept the doubleheader.

As we were leaving, moving with the crowd through the concourse under the grandstand, with its smell of beer and cigars and peanuts, all new to me then, my aunt stopped by a vendor's cart. The man was selling souvenirs; caps and pennants and junky trinkets.

"You may pick something," said my aunt.

We stood just out of the way of the moving river of the crowd, and I studied things over. There was a propped-up piece of cardboard with cloth over it, and stuck up and down it were round pins with pictures of ballplayers on them. Attached to each pin was a blue ribbon, and clipped across each ribbon was a brass bat. I looked no further. I chose Ted Williams, wondering why they even bothered to print up anyone else. My aunt fastened the pin to my shirt and drove me to South Station.

The silver Budd car waited, belly leaking steam. My aunt explained the situation to the conductor, a nice man who inspected my pin and said he wished he had one. My aunt knelt and wrapped me in a hug. She was still out there when I settled into the fuzzy blue seat. The train was half empty. The only teenagers were a noisy group of girls in pleated skirts and baggy sweaters. Grownups smiled at my Ted Williams pin. This wasn't going to be so hard, after all. The train jerked and began to crawl. My aunt waved and slid out of sight. We glided out of the station and rolled south with the sun painting the train windows. The colors of the field and uniforms jingled inside me, and I still heard the sea-roar of the crowd. My father was waiting on the platform of our little station. I came down out of the train with a grownup-sized leap, anxious for him to notice Ted Williams. He did, right away.

On May 12 the American League Champions are in fourth place, seven games behind the division leader. They've won fourteen, lost seventeen. They are being asked about this, naturally. Almost all have the same answer: Losing Clemens and Gedman, they say, shaking their heads as if not just Clemens and Gedman, but the entire team, had been betrayed by the owners. Their tone becomes philosophical when they cite Oil Can Boyd's arm trouble. Injuries are part of the game. Injuries, you can accept. But not betrayal.

Roger Clemens, winner of the Cy Young and Most Valuable Player awards in the pennant year, walked out of spring training and didn't come back till a couple of days before the season opened. Clemens's contract had expired. He'd asked for a million dollars; the front office had replied with an offer of less than half that. The team had Roger over a barrel. He hadn't logged enough seasons to become a free agent and had no choice, theoretically, but to play for the Sox on their terms. Clemens, though, created an option of his own: he went home to Katy, Texas. The owners reacted mildly, as if Roger were a naughty child. Blandly, they announced that he was being fined a thousand dollars for every day he stayed AWOL.

In the midst of all this my father asked me to write him an editorial on Clemens's celebrated holdout. Here it is, from the March 25 Falmouth *Enterprise*:

> The Boston Red Sox owe it not only to themselves but to all of New England to pay Roger Clemens what he is asking to throw his nonpareil fastball this summer. The obstinacy of the owners is a disgrace. "New England's team," the Red Sox style themselves. New England's team is insulting us all.
>
> The owners of big-league baseball are trying to bring down the enormous and absurd salaries they have been paying their ballplayers. No one can blame them, although it was they who established the salary scale. But overpaying ballplayers is one thing; underpaying them is another.
>
> New England's team won the pennant last year against the odds. Without Roger Clemens they wouldn't have come close. Every time the team

stumbled into a losing streak—every time—Clemens stopped it with a win. He was the heart of this team. On the mound he was poised, collected, relentless. As well as his unequaled fastball, he possesses what Hemingway called "grace under pressure."

The owners can afford the million dollars Clemens is asking. Thousands flock to Fenway Park just to watch him pitch. Without him, the Sox have no chance of bringing home another pennant. The owners are like the trustees of a museum who have been paying ridiculous prices for pop art and suddenly have a chance to buy a Rembrandt for the reasonable, going rate. Instead of grabbing the masterpiece, they offer less than half what it's worth and far less than they've been paying for the junk. They explain their parsimony with sanctimonious talk about how times have changed.

New Englanders understand thrift. They also know that some things don't change with the times. The value of a Rembrandt, say. Or the value of the world's best pitcher.

A player of Clemens's stature graces all of baseball, and just before Opening Day the commissioner, Peter Ueberroth, intervened. Ueberroth got everyone together and suggested a formula in which Clemens would get his million in deferred payments, with some juicy incentives thrown in. Clemens was satisfied, and the owners, feeling perhaps that they'd made their point, accepted the commissioner's solution.

But in mid-May, the damage is still evident. Clemens hasn't regained his form. His teammates have taken the owners' treatment of Clemens personally. The veteran Evans speaks darkly of the owners' intransigence, and is willing to be quoted. Another veteran, relief pitcher Joe Sambito, spouts off uninhibitedly. The Clemens affair has soured the air.

On the evening of May 12 Harold Reynolds, who plays second base for the Seattle Mariners, is draped against the batting cage watching Boggs hit. Along comes Rich Gedman, stocky and stone-faced.

"Hey, Geddy," Reynolds greets him.

"Hey, Harold," replies Gedman.

"How's your back?"

"Great," Gedman says gloomily.

"No, really," Reynolds says. "How is it *really?*"

"Fuckin' super," Gedman says, and turns his back on Reynolds.

Gedman has been suffering back spasms, the latest in a series of misfortunes that have been buffeting him nonstop since March, when he took it into his head to become a free agent. Gedman's contract had expired, and like Clemens, he asked for a million. The Sox offered him eight hundred thousand. I was with the owners in this one. Gedman had helped win the pennant, but his batting average had fallen from .295 all the way down to .258. He'd driven in fifteen fewer runs. And they *were* offering him a raise. He became a free agent and was surprised to discover that no one wanted him, at least not for a million a year. On Opening Day he was at home in Worcester, Massachusetts, where he stayed until May 1, when he rejoined the Sox for what they'd offered, minus pay for the month he'd been absent.

He has one hit, a single, in twenty-one at-bats, and he looks bad behind the plate. Pitches escape him, runners steal on him. He won't talk to reporters.

Clemens, Gedman, Boyd. The volatile Can hasn't pitched since March, and on this May evening he is fidgeting around the clubhouse like a restless kid with nothing to do, slapping a ball in his glove and frowning fiercely. He is bare above the waist; an ice pack is wrapped against his right shoulder. The Can is small, skinny, all legs. Spidery. A pair of writers interrupts his pacing.

"Uh, Dennis?"

Dennis smacks the ball in there one more time and jerks to a stop, snapping his body like a whip. No one pays any attention when I join the group with my notebook.

"How's the shoulder, Dennis?" asks a writer.

The Can hoists a dolorous sigh.

"Well," he says, "I throwed today. Right now I got good stuff, I got a lot *on* the ball, but it's all *over* the place." He's wild, Can means. The voice jumps, skids, floats, drops. Erratic. "It'd be a good positive sign if I could just come back tomorrow and throw like I throwed today."

"What's the problem, exactly?"

Can tilts his head like a bird and thinks for a moment. "It's been mysterious," he says. "Been *spooky*. It's tendinitis, but what's tendinitis? It comes and goes. Right now I'm able to throw real fluid. Five days, four even, and I'll be convinced it's gone completely. The guys wonder, you know, what's goin' on. If they don't see you cut up, if they don't see you *bandaged* up, they think you must be okay."

The Can pauses. He rubs his worried brow with the back of his hand, and suddenly a twinkle appears, and then a smile. Can's smile runs out of room at the edges of his skinny face.

"I can *sleep* on my bad arm," he says. "My right arm goes to sleep just like my left arm."

The two writers smile. "Thank you, Dennis," they both say, and the Can puts the frown back on and resumes pacing.

A few minutes later I find Buckner alone in the dugout, his cap pushed back on his shaggy head, his gaze fixed thoughtfully on the ball field. The grandstands are still empty, and the crack of a bat rings out. You can hear the slap of balls in gloves. The sun rinses the outfield, the pea-green left-field wall, and the facade below the bleachers, which meet in deep center at a random-seeming angle. In the distance the pitchers are running, exploding back and forth in short bursts. Buckner sits with his cap pushed back, his face slack, alone with his thoughts.

I sit down nearby, but not close enough to crowd him.

"What do you know?" he says.

Amazing.

"Hello, Bill," I say. The guy is one of my favorites. Legging it around the bases in the Series, playing crippled.

He watches the field.

"Is your ankle okay now?" I ask.

"Oh, yeah," he says.

"Are you playing in any pain?"

"Naw. I don't even think about it. I can run okay."

"It was your Achilles tendon, right?"

"Yeah. I had the operation. I got rid of all doubts. Physical doubts, anyway."

"As oppposed to . . . ?"

"It's been a mediocre season for me so far," he says. "One hit here, one hit there. They moved me from third to seventh in the order." Boggs, who batted leadoff last year, has been installed in the prestigious number-three spot. Buckner squints out; his mouth skews up sideways, lifting his mustache. "Third to seventh's kind of a drastic move, if you ask me," he says.

"It is," I agree.

"Well, take it easy," Buckner says, and grabs his mitt. He climbs the dugout steps and goes to first base, walking with his shoulders thrown back. Swaggering.

Rice is in the cage, taking batting practice with the substitutes. He, too, has been hurt, something with his elbow.

He's missed ten games and is hitting .205. I watch him from behind the cage. His swing is compact, short, no more than a swat; as if hitting, for this man, were a matter of controlling all that raw strength, of reining it in. You have the feeling that if Rice were to let go from the heels like Mantle or Mays, he would squash a baseball like a grape.

He is driving Bill Fischer's pitches to all fields. The drives flare, arcing low into the alleys and against the left-field wall. At this quiet hour you can hear the ball hit the wall. It drops against the wall and pops back, and only then do you hear the clunk, nearly a second later. Rice concludes this round with a long ball off the wall in center and strides out of the cage. Time in the cage is precious, but Rice doesn't hurry. Henderson goes in, glancing at Rice as they pass each other.

"Shit, you ready to play," Hendu says.

Rice says nothing.

Play ball.

After three innings the Sox lead the Mariners, 3–1. In the home fourth, one out, Buckner walks and goes to third on a single up the middle by Eddie Romero. To the plate comes Marc Sullivan, Gedman's understudy, who has troubles of another sort. The ball yard is inundated with boos as Marc is announced over the PA system.

Marc's problem is that he is the son of Haywood Sullivan, a former Red Sox catcher himself and now one of the owners of the team. I say "problem," but it depends on how you look at it; the fans are asserting with their boos that if it weren't for his old man, Marc would be hacking at minor-league pitching into the indefinite future. As Gedman's backup last year he hit .193. He is laboring this spring at .160. Marc does look like a catcher: a strapping kid, broad-shouldered and flat-hipped.

The booing spends itself for the time being, and Sullivan takes a moment to watch the third-base coach, Joe Morgan.

Morgan fidgets busily, touches his cap, his elbow, his nose, the letters on his chest. Marc has the sign, or thinks he does, and prepares to hit. The pitcher throws, Sullivan steps around to bunt, Buckner comes home. Sullivan watches the pitch sail by, high. Buckner, halfway down the line, slams on the brakes, stranded. The catcher chases him toward third, lets him get close, and pegs the ball to the third baseman, nailing Buckner easily.

Booing erupts again, thicker, angrier, than before. They blame Sullivan, naturally, though it might have been Buckner who misread the sign. Sullivan might have had no reason to think he had to put his bat on the ball. The boos roll down, and Marc takes a big, redemptive swing at the next pitch and pops it straight up. The pitcher makes the play on the mound, and the booing continues, chasing Sullivan into the dugout. He buckles on his pads and charges back out, and the noise begins all over again, a weight on his back, I imagine, as he crouches behind the plate.

He hits again in the seventh. They boo his name on the PA. He takes a strike on the outside corner; more boos. He watches strike two zip by, same spot; more boos. He cracks the third pitch into right field, a waist-high drive that the right fielder gets to, sprinting hard, nice catch on the gallop. Sullivan put good wood on the ball, but the booing hounds him to the dugout.

The Sox win it, 3–2. The game nearly gets away at the last minute, and ends with a scare. Wes Gardner, the Sox' third pitcher, gives up a single to Mike Kingery with one out in the ninth. Gardner whips three strikes in a row past Rey Quinones, and the game seems won. It seems to be over when Reynolds lifts a short, lazy fly ball to left field. Rookie Mike Greenwell, out there in Rice's place, lopes in. The shortstop, Romero, zooms out, unaware of the near proximity of Greenwell. The ball lands in Greenwell's glove in the same split second that

Romero hits him, spilling him to the ground and knocking the ball away. Kingery, who was off with the crack of the bat, spikes third and keeps coming. Greenwell scrambles up, finds the ball, and throws home. The throw reaches Sullivan on one neat hop. Kingery tries to slide around the tag, but Sullivan takes the ball to him, whirling with it in both his hands. Out. Nice work by Sullivan.

The clubhouse afterward reeks of greasy food. I have heard of these postgame buffets. "Lavish" is the reporters' favorite modifier. *Lethal* would be my word. The lasagne feast at Shea Stadium was an abbreviated version. Here the long, varnished table is crowded with aluminum tins of sausages, French fries, breaded veal cutlets, and pasta shells with meat sauce. There is enough oil here, enough animal fat, to clog the Callahan Tunnel. A bowl of salad, enough perhaps for two men with good appetites, goes uneaten.

The reporters, after a visit with the manager, surround Sullivan. Marc sits in his canvas chair with the white television lights burning down on him. Microphones are poked in his face as he thoughtfully answers questions. On his lap is a paper plate heaped with pasta shells. He has sandy hair and wholesome, straightforward good looks. I'm at the back of the pack and can't hear what he's saying, but I can see that this is no spoiled kid. His broad face, laved now in sweat, has a quiet air, a decency. I feel bad about the booing.

When the reporters have finished with him, Sullivan gets up, bringing his food, and finds Greenwell on his way into the shower with a towel wrapping his waist.

"Beautiful throw, Greenie," Sullivan says.

"I knew he was comin'," Greenwell says, animated and smiling. "I didn't even look."

"Oh, he had to come," Sullivan says.

"Absolutely," says Greenwell.

"Beautiful throw," Sullivan says again. Classy kid.

Meanwhile young Wes Gardner, who had good stuff to-night, is answering questions. Gardner's face is radiant. He speaks over the blare of a radio and the yells and laughter in the shower, the noise of winners.

"I'll tell you what," Gardner is saying, "we won a lot of games like this last year. It tells you somethin', winning this kind of game."

He means luck swinging their way—Greenwell finding the ball in time to nail Kingery, the ball rolling right. Maybe Kingery loafed until he saw Greenwell lose the ball. You can't win a pennant without some luck.

"This team," Gardner continues, "has a lot of character. It's got *enthusiasm*. I think we got a heck of a shot to win. A *heck* of a shot."

The next evening Wade Boggs is sitting on a little folding chair in the tunnel near the dugout end, bouncing a ball off the wall. Boggs zips the ball low against the concrete wall; it shoots down and kicks up off the plywood into Boggs's glove. You can hear it from the dugout, *ka-bump*, *whap* . . . *ka-bump*, *whap*. It is three quarters of an hour till game time; time to go up and eat the free meal in the employees' and press lounge. I find Boggs in the tunnel, *ka-bump*, *whap*, sitting hunched on the little chair.

"Excuse me," I say.

He holds the ball, eyes me as I go by.

"Yup," he says.

He almost smiles: at my courtesy, perhaps, which may be unnecessary here. The face is ascetic, what you'd expect in the world's best hitter; startling in its intensity and dispassion.

Flushed with victory, young Wes Gardner says that the Sox have *enthusiasm*, but as we have seen, Evans and Sambito have been grousing about the owners' treatment of Clemens and Gedman; Gedman is ailing and depressed; Henderson is slumping; Boyd is perplexed by his injury; and Rice is hurt, though perhaps no more morose than usual. Enthusiasm is in short supply, and tonight, May 13, they take a 4−2 lead into the ninth and blow the game.

Stanley enters in the seventh with two out and the tying runs on base; Steamer, as they call him, retires Reynolds on a ground ball. He holds the Mariners easily in the eighth, and gets the first man in the ninth. People begin to sift out of the ballpark. A mistake.

Jim Presley pulls a ground ball into left field. Alvin Davis whacks one up the middle, a base hit. John McNamara climbs the dugout steps and trudges out with his hands stuffed in his hip pockets. It is a cool night, and McNamara wears his blue windbreaker and blue gloves, his costume on the cold nights of the World Series. The manager looks out to the bull pen and taps his left elbow, meaning he wants the lefty, Sambito. Sambito opens the gate and jogs smartly in across the floodlit lawn of right field.

Sambito was once a premier relief pitcher over in the National League. In 1982 he burned out his elbow and could no longer throw the hard fastball. The Houston Astros released him; the Mets tried him and let him go. The Sox looked at him in spring training a year ago and signed him up. They thought he'd be useful at certain moments pitching to left-handed hitters. A "situation pitcher," they call it. The hunch panned out in '86, more or less. Sambito won two and saved twelve, though his earned-run average, 4.84, was awful.

McNamara summons him now because Kingery, a left-hander, is up. And yet McNamara is figuring—let's hope so, anyway—that Dick Williams, the Mariners' manager, will send a righty to hit for Kingery, and thus regain the advantage, lefty against righty. One supposes that McNamara prefers to see

Kingery out of there. Williams chooses John Christensen to pinch-hit, a young outfielder.

Sambito falls behind, two balls and a strike. Christensen can now assume Sambito will lay the ball over the plate, which Joe does. Christensen is ready and clocks one to deep left center, a parabola that beats the outfielders to the wall, bouncing once on the way. One run, two runs, and Christensen slides into third with a triple.

So much for Sambito. McNamara returns to the mound and touches his right elbow, Gardner. Wes prances in, still pumped up, maybe, from last night. Sambito gets booed as he leaves. So does McNamara. McNamara was Manager of the Year in '86, but his pilotage during the Series left a bad taste in the mouths of Red Sox lovers. No one in New England blames Buckner for his sixth-game error—the man could barely walk. But why, fans wonder, was he out there with a two-run lead in the tenth?

Wes Gardner pitches to Rey Quinones with the tie-breaking run on third. Quinones raps one on the ground to Boggs, who snatches it, looks and sees that Christensen is staying put, and throws Quinones out. We're almost out of the woods. But Reynolds, a switch-hitter batting left, punches a line drive past Boggs, base hit. Kingery scores, and the Mariners have the lead. The Sox die quietly in the bottom of the ninth.

The reporters all leave the press box in a hurry as soon as the final out is made. A single small elevator serves the rooftop region of the ballpark; the reporters don't wait for it, but go down the cement steps that are used also by paying customers who sit in roof box seats. The steps double back over themselves and are built up the outside of the ballpark. They drop you at the press gate. In we go, fighting the crowd boiling through the concourse, slithering against the flow to the green door. There's a short wait here, till the bouncer opens the door. He admits us one by one, scanning faces and passes, steering each of us through with a hand on the shoulder. We pile in, turn right, and bunch up in the narrow corridor outside Mc-Namara's office. Presently the manager opens his door.

He sends a melancholy glance down the corridor, as if he had sort of hoped to find it empty. His eyes are bright blue, his face rubicund and Irish-craggy. He has thick, silver-gray hair, a fine head of hair artfully trimmed and shaped. He's holding a can of Bud Light. He circles around behind his desk and sits down.

The room is bare, Spartan. Yellow brick walls. A refrigerator, a little bathroom. The walls are undecorated, the desk empty. An audience of vinyl chairs is gathered around the desk.

We crowd in. The chairs fill up; the rest of us jam in as best we can. McNamara's lucent gaze travels the room. Silence. The manager brings up a sigh, loud as steam. He pulls at his beer, sets the can down, and begins unbuttoning his shirt.

"What'll you have?" he says.

No one seems to want to begin.

"Ask," McNamara insists. The voice is soft. Mournful.

"A bitter loss," someone says helpfully.

"Well, we were leadin', 4–2, goin' into the ninth. You expect to win that kind of ball game."

"What's your pitching rotation look like for the weekend?"

"Look, we just had a tough ball game," McNamara says, voice rising. "If there are any changes, I'll tell you tomorrow."

Silence. McNamara leans forward and peels back his shirt, unwrapping a heavy belly in the tight-fitting baseball jersey. He tosses the shirt, number one, into the corner.

"How's Rice?" someone tries.

"Rice is better." McNamara tilts forward. He is noticing a message tucked under his telephone. "He's still got some pain in his elbow, but we think he'll be back soon. Right now he's day-to-day."

He looks up, surveys us with what I would call a distinct lack of enthusiasm.

"Anything else?" he says.

Silence.

"If not," he says, "I have a phone call to make."

At that, the reporters begin to funnel out of the room through a second door leading to the clubhouse.

"Thank you, John," says one.

"Thanks," says another.

"Thanks, John."

"Shut the door, will you?" McNamara says.

The game has been over nearly an hour by the time I leave the ballpark, but a little crowd still waits in the dark on Van Ness Street at the entrance to the players' parking lot. I see fathers and their sons; I see teenage girls. The parking lot itself is hidden by a wooden fence painted pea-green, but when I was a kid the fence was wire mesh, and after a game people would gather against it, craning and jostling for a view of the players coming out to their cars.

Recollecting this I think of my mother, who after a game always wanted to linger by the fence. I did, too, of course. My father, whose mind was on the long drive home, would give us a few minutes then drag us away. We never saw any star players; just pitchers who had been knocked out early.

My mother loved baseball in her own way. She loved its rituals, and she loved its clarity. She had a special feeling for the lonesome burden of the man on the spot—the pitcher, the hitter at a big moment, the outfielder with the ball flying his way.

Almost a year to the day after my aunt brought me to my first game, I came back to Fenway with my parents. Again the

Sox were playing the Yankees, and this time we had proper seats, a commanding view from above the Yankee dugout. I could see everything. No rain, either, but a bright September afternoon. The year was 1956, and the Yankee pitcher was Don Larsen, who in a couple of weeks would throw a perfect game in the World Series and win immortality.

Larsen was still on the mound in the ninth with the Yanks leading by a couple of runs. Shadows had advanced to the edge of the outfield grass. With two out, Larsen gave up a couple of singles.

The batter was Ted Williams.

A hungry roar went up, and old Casey Stengel, shriveled and gimpy even then, called time and went shuffling out in the blue-gray shade to remove Larsen. He'd pitched a fine game but had run out of gas. Besides, Casey wanted a lefty, Tommy Byrne, to pitch to Williams.

Byrne opened the bull-pen gate and began the long, solitary walk to the mound, stately with his jacket slung over his shoulder. Williams stood near the on-deck circle watching Byrne. Now and then Ted would take a couple of practice cuts, then go back to watching Byrne. Larsen departed. The crowd applauded his job well done; Larsen lifted his cap as he walked. Stengel limped in behind him.

Byrne kicked dirt around, raked it with his cleats, and commenced his warm-ups. It seemed, to me, to be taking forever. Williams had gone closer to the plate and was swinging at Byrne's warm-up pitches. I can still see him there, long-legged and ungainly, yet so smooth when he swung, gliding into the pitch and lashing the bat like a feather. The noise began again, encircling him as Yogi threw the last one back to Byrne. Williams gave his belt a hitch and walked with long strides to the plate.

Byrne rubbed the baseball. He picked up the rosin bag, jiggled pine dust out of it, drying his left hand. Williams dug in, swishing the bat back and forth. Byrne leaned down and looked in for Yogi's sign. Williams's bat stuck up vertical; his fists were low, tucked down under his ribs. The greatest hitter of all time. Byrne threw.

Williams swung. No long fly ball, no drive into a gap; nothing but a bouncing ball right to the second baseman. After all that. The second baseman—it may have been Gil Mc-Dougald—gloved the ball at belt level and tossed Williams out at first. It was over. Such was life.

On the way home we stopped at a log cabin bar called the Cedar Lodge on the old road. The Cedar Lodge was about halfway, and stopping there was to become a ritual of our trips home from Fenway. It was a roadhouse, dark inside, with a pool table and booths. It would have been no place for the three of us later on, but at this hour it was nearly empty. I loved it because of the Anheuser-Busch oil painting of Custer's Last Stand, which in my memory covers an entire wall. The bartender was a chunky man with sharp eyes and a poker face, but after he got to know us he would chat with my father, lingering after he'd set down the cheap beers and Coke in a glass. My father would buy me all the Cokes I wanted. After the first one he'd send me to the bar alone to buy my own. When I'd had enough I'd go and study the painting. Looking back, I doubt it was legal for me to be in there at all.

That first evening in our booth in the Cedar Lodge we talked about the ball game. My father appreciated baseball in a different way from my mother. He liked its nuances, its subtleties. He would notice, for instance, how far from the bag a quick first baseman could dare to play. He noticed a hitter griping at an umpire without looking at him, jawing as he stepped out of the box and kicked dirt around.

Tonight it was my mother who said, "I love watching the relief pitchers come in." She sat erect in the old booth. Her mother had taught her to sit like that, shoulders back, and she taught my sisters. "He walks in so *dramatically*. You notice how slowly he walks? Taking his time. Everyone waiting for him to come in and fix things."

They jog in these days. Young Wes Gardner prances like a Kentucky thoroughbred. It has become the style. Even so, I think of my mother when I see a relief pitcher coming into a tight game. Everyone waiting for him to come in and fix things.

Three

Those Were the Days

OLD-TIMERS DAY!

Forget the present, forget that we are next to last in the division. Forget even that the Yankees are in first place, eight and a half games ahead of us. Forget all that. It is time to go back, get sentimental, have some fun. We have to play the White Sox later, but never mind. Enjoy this. Let your memory go, let it run wild.

It is eleven-thirty on a cool, breezy morning in late May. A damp day with a nip; not a nice day. But the streets around Fenway are filled with people streaming in to watch old men play three innings of baseball. Look at the faces: everyone smiling. And look: there are as many young people as in any baseball crowd, people who weren't alive in '67, let alone '46. Cars jam both sides of Van Ness Street. I have to park in the lot, eight bucks, and I thought I'd come early. Yawkey Way is clogged. A car creeps through the crowd, rolling an inch at a time.

At the press gate Mike Smith finds my pass in his shirt pocket and gives me a cheery hello. Mike is grinning; the gaiety is in everyone's blood. People are milling through the concourse, smiling. They are piling around the concession stands. I knock on the green door. The bouncer opens it, wordless as ever. It's hard to make *him* smile. The clubhouse door is shut, but through it swells a commotion of voices—big voices, deep and booming. It sounds like a party.

I walk in and find that something wonderful is happening. Magic winds itself around me, something in the air of the big brown room. The clubhouse has been taken over by old fat men and old skinny ones. They talk, they shout, they bellow laughter. Some are undressing, jerking neckties loose and stepping out of trousers. Some just stand around yakking and laughing. The magic flows from their joviality, which seems somehow bighearted, and from the familiarity of their faces, larger in aging, as if hacked out of weathered stone.

Strips of adhesive tape have been stuck along the tops of the cubicles, covering the owners' names, dispossessing today's stars in favor of these old men, who have come back all these years later to play ball again. Their names are inked in assertive block letters on the strips of tape. MALZONE. LONBORG. DOERR. TIANT. PIERSALL. PARNELL. WILLIAMS.

Williams! There he is, sitting in Rice's or Baylor's canvas chair—not theirs now; his—loudly talking hitting. What else would he be talking? In his old age Ted has gone heavy. The lank chest, the belly hollow as a wolf's, have taken on bulk, spreading enormous down to his belt. The weight makes Ted look as if he'd been a big man, a Willie Stargell, a Boog Powell even, but Ted wasn't. He was spare, flat-chested. They called him "the Splendid Splinter." His power was in the technique, not in raw strength.

His hair is still thick and wavy, though iron-gray. The face is the same, the square jowls, the jug-handle ears. He is wearing a safari jacket and khaki pants. He sits there gripping a bat and talking hitting to Dwight Evans. Evans, the only youngster in the clubhouse, stands while Ted sits. Evans is drinking in every word.

"*Now*," Ted is saying, "how do you hold your bat?"

Evans accepts the skinny-handled bat, grips it at the very end, his left hand snug against the knob.

"Naw," Williams says. "Look. Up *here*."

He retrieves the bat, holds it with his lower hand perhaps an inch from the knob.

Evans, in uniform, stands graceful as always, one knee canted. "What's that, about an inch?"

"Inch and a half," Ted says.

"Huh," grunts Evans, thoughtful but not committing himself.

"Almost all my home runs I hit holdin' the bat like that," Ted tells him.

"Maybe," Evans speculates, "you get more control that way."

"That's right," Ted says. "That's absolutely right."

"Well, it's been real nice talkin' to you, Ted," Evans says, but does not go anywhere.

"You need a haircut, Dewey," Ted tells him.

Here comes big George Scott, crossing the room in a swaggering prowl, fat as can be. The Boomer. He isn't that old; he was with the Sox as late as '78, when we lost the play-off game to the Yankees. The Boomer was at first base in that game. Here he comes, immense and round in a cashmere sweater that is white with pink stripes. A candycane mountain.

"You ol' son of a bitch," he greets Williams, yelling it, the voice shrill and hoarse both, made of sparkling ground glass. Boomer leans down and enfolds Ted in a hug.

"Hey, Boomer," Ted says. "You gonna hit one out to-day?"

"Hey, I'm swingin' the *bat* today," Boomer says. "I ain't bull-shittin' around, Ted. I come to get my *rips*."

Evans is gone. Where *is* everybody, where's the team? It is as if they've vanished into thin air, as if these old guys, who are looking less old and more like themselves by the minute, have sprung to life from the pages of yellowing newspapers. Magic.

"Anyone who can swing the bat," Ted Williams is saying, "can hit the inside fastball. I don't care who it is. If you can swing the bat, you can hit the inside fastball."

I see Jim Lonborg, still slender, still debonair, smiling as he begins slowly to undress—slowly, as if he is savoring pulling clothes off in this room. Gentleman Jim looks the same, just gray is all. In this ballpark Gentleman Jim beat the Twins on the last day of the '67 season, and delirium swept the city. An hour or so later word came: the Tigers had lost, and so the Sox had won the pennant. That fall, of all places, I was in Europe. But I do have this memory: a Florentine morning the color of yellow wine; a villa, yellow stucco, on a big shadeless square where children played. I was going to school in the villa, and on this wine-yellow morning I climbed the stone steps and went into the oak hallway, where we had cubbyholes for our mail. Waiting for me was a telegram. It had been sent by my aunt and uncle—the aunt who brought me to Fenway when I was nine—and it said, RED SOX WIN PENNANT.

Who else is here? Well, there's Frank Malzone, who goes way back, late fifties, early sixties. Malzone still works for the Sox, does some scouting. He's often around, shooting the breeze in the clubhouse or in the lounge up top, where he'll belly up to the bar and drink a martini. For a while, he was the best third baseman in the game. He walks bandy-legged with his shoulders thrown back; I remember that. Olive skin, big hooking schnozz, toothy smile. And fat: his gut sags down, belt holding onto it like a sling.

The Monster is here, Dick Radatz, the giant relief pitcher of the early sixties. Huge man. Used to shoot both arms into the air after he'd finished them off to end a game, his victory gesture. He was called Monster for his size and not his personality. His hair is still brown, the skin of his face still pink and smooth, but he's added a ton of weight. He looks bloated; face, stomach, ass. He's *huge.*

"Hi, Monster." It's Johnny Pesky bustling by. Pesky's playing today.

"Needle." Radatz grins. He sticks out a loaf of a hand and they shake. "Nice to see ya, Needle."

"How you feelin'?" Pesky asks.

"I been takin' Motrin for the last week," says the Monster. "Four times a day, eight hundred milligrams."

"Jesus Christ," says Pesky.

The Boomer booms, "The ball's juiced up this year. You can't *tell* me the ball ain't juiced up, way folks hittin'."

And here is Luis Tiant, chomping a fat cigar and a toothpick, too, grinning mischievously, twinkling, the face wise and humorous and anything but sinister with its Fu Manchu mustache. El Tiante. What spells he used to cast from the pitcher's mound, mesmerizing hitters with his tricks. He always carried a fair-sized belly, but he was as weightless on the mound as a ballerina. He would pause on one leg, his left leg hooked in the air, and glance back over his shoulder, or in front of him somewhere, third-base seats, or out toward left. It was as if time had stopped in the middle of his delivery. They used to say that if you were in the ballpark, sooner or later he'd look right at you.

Gentleman Jim, who still looks elegant in a baseball uniform, grabs his glove and heads for the door. Russ Gibson, who caught him in '67, socks his fist in his mitt and follows Lonborg. Gibson has taken on weight; he plods out, walking with his feet splayed, like a duck.

Before I go out, I have something to tell Piersall. I've been watching him, waiting for my chance. I didn't want to intrude when he was talking with his old buddies, and then a reporter tied him up in an interview. He is getting into his uniform, number thirty-seven. He has grown a little heavy; not too, but his hair is thin and mousy, he peers through glasses, and he looks withered, not hale like Ted Williams.

"Mr. Piersall."

"How ya doin'?" He snaps it, not unfriendly but nervous.

"When I was a little boy . . . "

"Where?"

"Where?" I say.

"Where'd you grow up?"

"Cape Cod."

"Tough life you had."

"Yeah." I smile. "Anyway . . . "

"When you were a little boy . . . "

Piersall's legs are thin and gray. The veins look broken.

I say, "You wrote the book *Fear Strikes Out.*" About his breakdown. Always nervous, even zany, Piersall had cracked up and after treatment had come back and starred for the Sox. "A friend of my mother's," I say, "worked at the company that published the book. She got me your autograph. You wrote, 'To Johnny, Your pal, Jimmy Piersall.' "

"Yeah, I used to do it that way," Piersall says.

"Well," I tell him, "I remember riding home on my bike with that thing. I thought I'd died and gone to heaven."

Speeding home in near-darkness, fat Schwinn tires rolling on air, it seemed, carrying me home with a piece of paper written on by Jimmy Piersall. I was smiling. I remember smiling.

Piersall says, "That wasn't a bad book. Did you read it?"

"Of course I read it. I still have it."

Piersall belts his pants. "You know what I like?" he says.
"What?"

"I don't have to win today." He smiles, lips parting over
his gums, which I also remember, a photogenic smile but too
gummy. "I don't have to fuckin' win," he says. "I dressed in
here a million times, and I always had to win."

"Does it look the same?" I ask.

"Naw, it's all changed. It's more comfortable now. They
used to have these fuckin' tin lockers." He claps on his cap.
He takes his glove off the shelf of his cubicle. "It's still a shitty
clubhouse," he says.

He is on his way, and I follow him. Out the door, down
the steps to the tunnel. The plywood grumbles and clanks under Piersall, under me. He was zany, but he could play ball.
He made a throw from center field once—I was here with my
parents—that stretched taut as a high wire from center field to
first base, no bounce. The batter had singled, and Piersall had
thrown behind him, not ahead of him, thinking to nab him
making a wide turn. Damn near did nab him. The throw was
so perfect, so beautiful, a glistening wire stretching over yards
and yards of green, that the crowd had let out an awed sound,
something between a sigh and a gasp, instead of cheering.
They'd been too surprised, too moved, to cheer.

It drizzled this morning; the tarp blankets the infield. I
stick with Piersall. Lonborg is standing under the lid of the
dugout with his hands on his hips, looking out at the ball field,
smiling.

"What time do we hit?" he says to no one in particular.
He means batting practice.

"You don't hit," Piersall tells him. "You're a pitcher, for
Christ sake."

Lonborg puts on a hurt look. He hasn't stopped smiling,
though. "I hit one over that wall one time," he tells Piersall.

The Boomer is pacing up and down, restless as a bull in a

chute. "Take the tarp off the field, man!" he yells out of the dugout to the empty green yard.

Tiant emerges, the uniform snug over his midriff. He stands perfectly still, gazing out over the field. He is smiling faintly, amused by something he has just seen or thought, or perhaps by the whole business.

And here again is Evans, evidently enjoying rubbing up against the ancients. He grins at Scott, who continues to prowl up and down, acting ferocious. Ken Coleman, the Sox radio announcer, has materialized.

"Dwight," he says, "could I get you to sign this?"

He presents a baseball and a pen.

"That's an old-timers ball," Evans says. "Am I in that group?"

"You be there soon, man," says Tiant, twinkling.

The PA blurts music, "Turn, Turn, Turn" by the Byrds, which rolls down sounding as fresh on this gray morning as the day it was made. Piersall has tossed his glove on the bench and now he shoves a leg up onto the steps, resting his heel there and bending over his knee, stretching his hamstring. The steps are a dull sand color and very beaten up by cleated shoes. Piersall's heel rests on the second step from the top. He flashes the gummy smile.

"I used to reach that son of a bitch up there," he says, pointing to the top step.

The Boomer prowls past. He is carrying his bat, shaking it like a weapon he is itching to use on somebody.

"I don't mind this overcast," Piersall remarks, suddenly all business.

"I don't like this wind, man," says the Boomer. The flag in center is curling in, but lazily. It isn't much of a wind.

Piersall finishes stretching. He gives me a vexed squinching look. "See, this is why I don't go to the ballpark anymore."

"Why not?"

"I don't like that fuckin' music," he says.

"It depends what they play," I say.

"I don't like any of the fuckin' stuff," he says. And, veering, "Who's pitchin' against us, anyway?"

"I heard Bob Gibson was," I tell him.

"Oh, shit," Piersall says, but with a chuckle. "When I got traded to the Mets"—he'd played for Cleveland, Washington, the Mets, the Los Angeles Angels after the Sox, a whole second career—"they threw me right in the lineup, batting lead-off. Guess who's pitchin' against us? Bob Gibson. Holy shit, what a way to start in the National League. My first two times up, he strikes me out. I didn't touch the fuckin' ball. Third time, he hangs a slider and I get the sucker, send it right back over Gibson's shoulder. Almost nail the son of a bitch. Next time up, he drills me. Almost breaks my fuckin' ribs. I didn't go to the mound, either. I just let it be." He flashes his smile. "I used to go after the skinny guys, like Jim Bunning."

Lonborg has sat down with a young reporter. Gentleman Jim sits with both arms stretched along the back of the bench. His legs are crossed. The writer asks him about being traded away to the Brewers, which happened to him in 1972.

Lonborg stares out awhile. He answers softly. "It broke my heart to leave here. It took me three or four years to recover."

Ralph Houk, who will be the manager for this little game, comes out with his lineup card. He tapes the card to the dugout wall and settles down on the bench. He sits shapeless as a sack of flour, thin legs crossed. A chaw pushes out his cheek. Houk managed the Yankees for many years. He managed the Tigers, too—and the Sox before McNamara.

The Boomer stalks over and peers at the lineup card.

"Who made that lineup?" he hollers, baleful gaze jerking this way and that. "Shit!" snorts the Boomer. Houk sits there grinning.

"He wants to bat cleanup," explains Pesky.

"Gah-*damn*," says Scott as a smile seeps through, turning him jolly.

To Piersall I say, "Do you remember your last game here?"

He looks at me quickly, startled by the question. He thinks a moment. "No," he says finally, as if surprised that he cannot remember. "No," he says again and shakes his head.

Here is Mel Parnell, the greatest southpaw the Sox ever had. In '56 Parnell threw a no-hitter here. In the lounge upstairs there is a photograph taken afterward in the clubhouse, Parnell with one arm draped around the shoulders of his catcher, Sammy White, the other arm around Mike Higgins, the manager. Parnell has large soft eyes, very dark above the flash of his smile. The three faces shine with sweat. I remember the headline in the *Boston Herald*: " 'I WAS JUST LUCKY'— MEL."

He comes out of the tunnel and stands with his arms folded. He has been altered almost beyond recognizing. He is small, as if the years had whittled him down to half-size. He is little and thin and quite old in his white baseball uniform. Ralph Houk gets up, stands beside him.

"Mel," he says, "I thought I'd have you pitch to one man in the third inning. We're only playin' three." Houk's voice is slow and kind.

Parnell looks at him. "I can't throw," he says.

"No?" says Houk.

"I tried a few years ago," Parnell says. "It didn't work out at all." He looks away, toward the ball field.

"Well," Houk says, "there's no need to, Mel. There's no need to, at all."

Ken Coleman stands at a microphone at home plate and introduces the members of both teams, reading florid little summaries of their careers and summoning them from the dugouts to stand along the base lines. The visitors come out first and line up on the third-base side. They are a random-seeming agglomeration, though all were stars. Enos Slaughter is the oldest. Slaughter played in the '46 Series against Pesky, Doerr, and Williams. In the late fifties, still useful, he was sold to the Yankees. The youngest old-timer is Mark Fidrych, the gawky pitcher, yellow curls and a freckled face like Huck Finn, who would still be throwing in the big leagues if his arm hadn't quit on him. The home crowd cheers them all. Many of them I saw play here. Bobby Richardson. Jim Gentile. Jackie Brandt, who was almost as wacky as Piersall. Hell, I even saw Slaughter.

Of course, the Sox get bigger cheers. The biggest by far is for Williams, whom Coleman brings out last of all. "*The greatest Red Sox player ever*," intones Coleman, and the crowd comes to its feet, springing up to fill the place with noise. "*The greatest hitter of all time . . .*" Each word, amplified, hangs a moment, quivering. The ovation roars on. "*The last .400 hitter . . .*" Williams now has climbed the dugout steps. He pauses; the din swells, thunderous. Coleman says no more. Not even the name Ted Williams. Coleman just waits, and Ted jogs out, head slightly tilted, as he used to hold it circling the bases after a home run. There was always something boyish, aw shucks, in that tilt of the head.

In the press box two old men are sitting together. Ex-writers, perhaps, or friends of somebody connected with the team, guests for this game. As each old-timer comes out they nod, they smile. They beam when Williams comes out. Ted trots to the first-base line, stops, turns, lifts his cap. The crowd roars on. It seems endless. The two old men in the press box look again at each other, and one, suddenly, has tears in his eyes.

The visitors win, 6 – 1. No one cares, not the players, not the fans. For the visitors, Ritchie Allen, who has not been out of the game very long, launches a home run over the old green wall, over the screen atop the wall, a king-sized home run, a young home run. He is only forty-five, after all. I can remember seeing Allen play in Connie Mack Stadium in Philadelphia. He looks the same, lean down below and powerful up top, coltish. He gets another turn at the plate and whacks one effortlessly off the wall, a double.

Piersall gets a walk against the great Bob Feller, who looks creaky out there. Jimmy motors to second on a feeble ground ball by Pesky, and up comes Williams. Another huge ovation. For old times' sake, for fun, the infielders all shift toward the right side of the infield, which is the way many teams played Williams, because he hit the ball so hard that way. Allen, the third baseman, abandons the bag, whereupon Piersall steals it, scooting over with a grin, the bad boy always. There is supposed to be no stealing, but instinct and mischief take over. Williams, who used to have epic confrontations with the great Feller, is his old self swinging in slow motion. Feller throws stiffly, sails one over Ted's head, wild pitch, and Piersall scuttles home, still grinning. Ted then pops one foul to the first baseman. Another standing ovation. They don't care; they love him. In the final inning he faces Jack Fisher, against whom, in his final at-bat in the major leagues, right here, he hit a home run. They don't announce this. No one in the press box mentions it. Has everyone forgotten? Ted takes that swing and bounces one back to Fisher, who easily tosses him out. And the Boomer? Scott gets one turn, and for all his talk of getting his rips, he only lifts a high, high foul ball to the first baseman.

It is time to play for real, and to make a long story short, the Sox lose, 9–1. None of the pitchers—Nipper, Bolton, Sellers, Gardner—can stop the White Sox, who rain hits all over Fenway. Their pitcher, Floyd Bannister, doesn't give up a hit until Gedman pulls a line drive over the right fielder's head with two out in the sixth, the ball grazing Gary Redus's glove and escaping for a double. After that, nothing, until Ellis

Burks puts one in the screen, home run, in the ninth. By then, half the big crowd has melted away. The weather has not improved. The lights have come on, glittering pale as strings of tiny moons in this gray daylight.

Cliff Keane is in the press box today. This is appropriate: Keane is an old-timer himself, a retired sportswriter who followed the team for the *Boston Globe*. He is a squatty bulldog of a man, jowly, florid, with a far-carrying salty voice.

"This team," he tells me, "will never win a game they shouldn't win." He's talking about luck, the final ingredient for winning pennants. He's saying that you make your own luck, you alchemize it: "They'll win only when they ought to."

He doesn't talk about Clemens and Gedman. He has another explanation for the team's stumbling beginning: "They miss Rice. He's a ballplayer, I don't care what you think of him personally. He produces. You may not like him, but he produces."

After the slaughter, McNamara receives the writers on his feet, bent down forward with his arms laid across the back of his chair. We gather round his desk. Someone coughs. McNamara passes a hand over his silver hair.

A reporter prods him gently: "Comments, John?"

McNamara sighs. "We haven't hit. When you don't hit, it's contagious."

He begins to undress. We leave. He shuts the door. Gloom muffles sound in the clubhouse. The showers fizz, but no one is talking in there.

A radio reporter asks Nipper to say something, but Nip circles away as if the man had flashed a knife. "What do you want to know?" Nip snaps, still backtracking. "I gave up three runs and I didn't pitch very well."

The reporter tries Stanley, who is pitching tomorrow. "I don't want to talk about it," Stanley grumps. "My luck hasn't been too good lately."

Barrett refuses, courteously, to speak on camera.

Only Hurst is in any mood to talk. He's an attractive man, Hurst; tall, with a natural elegance, a grace and dignity he was born with. He dresses stylishly but never loudly. He can be insouciant, bouncing around the clubhouse, kidding the guys, clowning it up, but he never sheds that easy dignity. If Clemens is the lion of this team, Hurst is its prince. The writers need somebody to talk—anybody—so they go to Hurst, even though he took no part in today's walloping.

"You just can't keep good teams down," Hurst insists. The smile is cordial, good-natured. "We're going to play up to our potential. We're going to hit a streak, reel off six, seven in a row. Now, if we're playing the right teams when we hit the streak, we'll be fine. You guys'll see," he finishes brightly.

Many years ago, fifteen, seventeen, I was working in Boston for a hundred dollars a week for a little organization called the Massachusetts Correctional Association. Our mission was to make prisons more humane and more efficient, aims that we believed were synonymous. We worked out of an old brick row house on Beacon Hill, in the shadow of the State House. Our building was tall and venerable but shabby inside, the walls flaking yellow paint, the stairs squeaking, the air musty but charged with optimism, even fun. I was on first-name terms with state legislators, convicted murderers, county sheriffs, newspaper reporters, Quaker agitators, aides to the governor, and Cambridge revolutionaries, and was having the time of my life. One of my assignments was to attend the weekly meeting of the Lifers Group at Walpole Prison. The group was a kind of club, social but interested, too, in influencing the outside world to pay some attention to their plight. They were an amazingly congenial bunch, always anxious to have guests at the meetings. Politicians and reporters—anybody who might make a difference—were the most desired, but beggars can't be choosy, and the lifers welcomed anybody who would drive out there on a Tuesday night. Anything to break the tedium. I was always trying to think of people to invite, and it hit me one day to try the Red Sox.

I wasn't naïve; I knew that many men doing life at Walpole were disciples of Karl Marx and George Jackson, and that these men would as happily torch Fenway Park as they would the State House and Walpole itself. But revolutionaries seldom came to the meetings, anyway. Why not call the Red Sox? And so I did. The man in the PR office thought for about five seconds and then told me crisply and in a businesslike manner that he would send Gary Wagner and Johnny Pesky.

Gary Wagner. A pitcher. I'd seen him, too, in old Connie Mack Stadium, pitching for the Phillies. Yes: the night Warren Spahn had thrown so beautifully, the night I'd skipped studying for my Latin final. Wagner was a tall right-hander who came over from the Phillies to the Red Sox in '69 and pitched through the 1970 season. Pesky, at that time, was on the Sox' broadcasting team. I was hoping the PR guy would let me drive them to Walpole, but he said no, just give him directions and name the time.

Pesky looked about the same as he does now, except that the hair was a shiny, shoe-polish black. A little guy, nicely built, weathered good looks, a canny squint. Wagner was a lean giant, at ease in the prison, with its metal doors banging shut behind you, sealing you in wherever you went. It was December, very cold. With us was the outsider who had helped set up this Lifers Group some years back, a passionate and intelligent man named Lou Brin, who was an editor at the *Jewish Advocate* in Boston. Lou was no baseball fan and had his doubts as to the usefulness of tonight's meeting. But he was my friend; he went along with it.

Picture it, this piece of work of mine, Johnny Pesky and Gary Wagner standing in front of seventy or so sad, bitter men in prison blues sipping coffee lightened with Pet evaporated milk and talking baseball. *Baseball*. Maybe I was naïve, at that. Wagner was kind of hip, which helped. Pesky was smart—shortstops have to be, they have to smell things, size things up—which helped even more. The lighting in that concrete room was harsh, unpleasant. There was an ugly, sweetish whiff of disinfectant, a prison smell. The prisoners' names were inked in block letters on the fronts and backs of their blue workshirts; some shirts bore crossed-out names with the new names beneath. Recycled. The men wore jeans that didn't fit any of them, always too baggy.

They talked baseball, though. They threw questions up at Pesky and Wagner. "Mr. Pesky" and "Mr. Wagner," they said. Wagner talked tough and hip, and of course he had that physical presence, the shoulders and big strong hands, so the cons could take him seriously. Pesky was quick-thinking and smooth, always smooth. They talked baseball, give-and-take, some laughs. The cons' faces had a lucent pallor, an unhealthy pearl sheen, and a prisoner's face—one serving big time, that is—is careful, secretive, the gaze flat. Still, the conversation that night might have been with any group of fans—a Rotary Club, a bunch of guys from an Army base or a factory.

It went along fine until one of the lifers, a man I recognized but had never spoken with, raised a hand to ask a question. The chairs were all taken and he'd had to stand. He was at the side, and he hung his long pale hand out sideways like a semaphore. He was an odd one, I knew that. He never spoke at the meetings, never said a word, just took it all in with dark, deep eyes. He had a thick walrus mustache, and the sad, avid eyes missed nothing. He seemed haunted. Had he committed some atrocity? Dismembered somebody? He hung out his hand, and Pesky, still grinning from the last exchange, pointed and said, "*Yes*, sir?"

The room got quiet. The lifers all turned, watched the man with neutral gazes, flat prison gazes that committed them to nothing. He was obviously a special case.

"Tell me, Mr. Pesky." The voice was slow, slurred, dark. "What's your opinion on capital punishment?"

Silence. Seventy flat gazes swung back to Johnny Pesky, one of the Sox' best shortstops ever, a .307 lifetime hitter. Silence. Lou Brin, who had daydreamed his way through the hour or so we'd been here, suddenly woke up. The prisoner waited. The room waited. None of these guys was under the death sentence, but almost all could have been. At least one had a brother over on Death Row. The difference usually was a plea bargain. Cop a plea, and you'd get life instead of the chair. Every lifer wants to know where the outsider stands on capital punishment. If you're for it, you're the enemy, you don't understand a thing.

The room waited.

Pesky cleared his throat and looked up into the air somewhere. "You know," he said, "it's something I haven't thought about much." Smooth, but not overly genteel. He looked down, frowned. Then he met their gazes, looked them all in the face as he shaped an answer.

"I've been here over an hour," he said. "We've talked, and I've enjoyed it. To me you're just a bunch of guys, you're people, and if capital punishment means taking your lives, then I'd have to say I'm against it." He paused, and though the silence held, you could see he'd come through in the clutch. The cons still watched him closely, but the faces had relaxed, there were no burning eyes, there was no danger out there. Pesky added the finishing touch: "So I guess I got something out of this visit. I know where I stand on capital punishment."

"Right on," someone said.

"Let's talk baseball!" hollered another, and we were off and running again. But the mood had brightened, the talk was less correct, more candid, dirtier. The man who had asked the question had shown no emotion as Pesky had answered. His long face had remained stony and unblinking, but now he was forgotten. His question had served its purpose, and no one cared anymore what he thought. Ten o'clock came too quickly, and after good-byes we were led out through the slamming metal doors, a series of them, and finally out into the winter night. Pesky and Wagner went straight to their car, and the night was a memory. Wagner didn't make the team that spring.

Seventeen years later Johnny Pesky, assistant to the general manager, is sitting in uniform in the Red Sox dugout watching the Sox take batting practice. His legs are crossed. His cap is perched forward. He is chewing tobacco, a sizable chaw that he shifts from place to place with his tongue: right cheek, left cheek, inside the lower lip, squeezing it and pushing it and spitting frequently on the dugout floor. Pesky in his uniform looks tougher, more leathery, than I remember him that night at Walpole. Pesky's title, Assistant to the General Manager, is intentionally nebulous; he does a little of everything. He is a scout, a coach, a public speaker. He hits fungos in pregame practice, then retires to the press box to study the game from above. In the early sixties he managed the Sox, and for years he coached first base.

I sit down beside him. He gives me a friendly nod. I introduce myself and tell him I was the one who arranged a visit he made to Walpole Prison fifteen, seventeen years ago, to talk to the Lifers Group. With Gary Wagner.

Pesky cranes out, shoots a molasses ribbon of tobacco spittle to the floor. "Yeah, matter of fact I *do* remember that. Me and Wagner, that's right. Yeah, Jesus, that was the night . . ." He pauses, busy with his chaw. You can see it's all coming back to him. ". . . this guy, strange-lookin' bastard, asked me about the death penalty."

"I'll never forget it," I say.

Pesky looks at me. Smart, lively eyes. "Jesus Christ," he says, "I didn't know *what* the fuck to say. I 'bout shit my pants."

"You did great," I tell him.

He looks at me. "Yeah?"

"You were terrific."

He considers the compliment, watching the ball field. "Well, I didn't want to say, 'You dumb bastard, you committed a murder, what do you expect?' On the other hand . . ." He thinks some more, squinting, working the chaw. "I'm not sure I don't believe in justifiable homicide. I couldn't say *that*, Jesus, they'd put *me* in there."

"You did just right," I tell him.

He considers for another moment, then sums up: "I didn't know what the fuck to say."

"You did good," I repeat.

He draws back, looks at me with interest.

"What'd you say your name was?" he asks.

I tell him.

"Well, it's good to see you again, John," he says, and sticks out his right hand. His handshake is hard and friendly.

You can't win without pitching, and the Sox' pitching is in tatters. On May 28, Oil Can is still hurt and hasn't pitched a single inning. Hurst is pitching okay and so is Clemens, though the Rocket Man has already lost as many games—four—as he lost all last season. Schiraldi, the bull-pen ace of '86, is carrying an earned-run average of 6.88. Nipper has won four, lost four, and has an ERA of 4.34. Young Bolton hasn't won a game. Stanley is two and six. The team needs Oil Can, and the good news tonight is that the Can has decided to go to the mound and air it out this evening before the game with the Indians. His arm feels that much better. He's going to let loose.

The Sox are in sixth place, nine games down, but Johnny Pesky isn't worried. He sits in the dugout, hands resting on the knob of his fungo bat, waiting for Oil Can to take the mound. Everyone is waiting. "You like to get out of the gate quick, but we'll be okay. You win seven or eight in a row, and you're right back in it."

Seven or eight in a row. Hurst was saying the same thing a week ago. That streak, seven or eight wins in a row, is the Holy Grail of the Sox' '87 season. It is the answer to everything, and it is sure to come, sooner or later. Ask anyone on the team.

Can is warming up in the bull pen. The guys are taking batting practice meanwhile. Hendu swings a bat behind the cage, grinning, showing that front gap. Hendu, no longer the starting center fielder, is hitting .242 and has six home runs.

"Got a birthday comin' soon," he is saying. "Be twenty-nine in July." He pronounces it *Ju*-ly.

"I'll be twenty-nine before you," Barrett says.

"Be twenty-nine," Hendu says, "but I *feel* young. I feel good."

"I feel like horseshit," growls Buckner, who is thirty-seven.

Oil Can is coming. He and Fischer, who has been catching him in the bull pen. The Can frisks in, a spider dancing across a lawn. Fish trudges in with his catcher's mitt, mean-looking. The Can is coming, and everything stops. They all wait: the pitchers and outfielders in the distance, the guys around the cage, the reporters scattered everywhere, Pesky in the dugout.

Hriniak, who was a catcher in the big leagues, comes huffing out in catcher's gear, shin guards clacking as he runs. Hriniak is always hustling. His yellow hair is sweat-plastered to the sides of his head. His face is very pink. He clamps the mitt and mask under his arm and jams a new chaw into his mouth, shoving it in deep with two fingers. Then he enters the cage.

The Can is on the mound, pawing dirt, darting baleful looks around the ballpark, slapping the ball into his glove. Nervous, kinetic. The Can acts impatient with all this attention, but I believe he loves every minute of it. It's just that it bewilders him sometimes, doesn't let him think straight. He's just a strutting kid, an innocent, trying to live up to the expectations. He goes to the pitching rubber. Frowns. He is ready.

McNamara has come out in his blue windbreaker to watch from behind the cage. Fischer stands with him. McNamara squints, worried. This is a big moment. People are talking about juiced-up baseballs flying out of ballparks, but what is happening in 1987 is an epidemic pitching slump.

Ed Romero, the backup infielder, takes his bat into the cage.

"Better get a helmet, Eddie," McNamara says through the netting.

Romero gives a quick look back, very serious, but says nothing.

"He hasn't pitched since March 28," says McNamara.

Romero bolts wordlessly out of the cage and grabs a helmet. He comes in again jiggling the helmet down over his dark curls. The Can places his right foot on the rubber and hunches way down, peering in at his catcher. Hriniak hunkers down. He isn't built like a catcher. He looks like a high-school kid in all that gear. Romero taps the plate with his bat. Is ready.

Can winds up slowly. As he does, quivers, like electrical impulses, ripple all through his wiry body. You can see that from here. I've never been this close to big-league pitching: right behind the cage, a few feet from Hriniak and Romero. Can pivots, hooks his left leg daintily in the air, and throws, grunting with the effort.

The ball comes in an instant. Snap your fingers: it takes that amount of time for the ball to travel from out where Oil Can is to here. In that snap-of-the-fingers instant the ball climbs and swells, enormous under your eyes, a great big lethal medicine ball, a comet, blazing too fast to dodge or duck. I flinch back; the ball is going to hit the net and hit me, it's going to crack my skull.

Romero swings and fouls it straight up.

I read once that the rising fastball is a myth, an illusion; that a thrown ball cannot rise, it can only drop, and that when a pitch comes in level instead of tapering down, we *think* it is rising. We think so because the eye is trained to expect a ball to sink. Well, Oil Can Boyd's fastball is rising. They can't hit what they can't see, we used to tell our pitchers, talking it up around the infield. But seeing the Can's stuff isn't the problem. The ball comes up huge and murderous. I can see the red seams.

Hriniak flicks it back to Can, who hunches down, winds, lets her go again. Romero cuts and misses. I hear this one, slicing air, sibilant; it pounds into Hriniak's mitt with a hollow pop, like a big but wet firecracker. McNamara looks at Fischer.

"How'd he throw in the bull pen?" asks McNamara.

"Just like this," says Fish.

"Jesus," McNamara says.

Romero fouls another one straight up. The ball drops at his feet. He punches a gentle ground ball to the right side and scuttles out of the cage. Marc Sullivan strides in.

Can is sweating, and the comic balefulness has been wiped from his face. His mind is all on throwing. He knows he's throwing hard and is energized by the discovery.

Windup, pitch, *"Git down,"* he tells the ball. *"Git down."*

Sullivan takes that big stiff swing, a lumberjack with his ax, and jerks foul balls into the netting above, bounces them in the dirt. Oil Can begins throwing curveballs. "Curve," he tells Hriniak and Sullivan as he winds up. "Fastball."

Sullivan can't hit anything and Greenwell comes in.

"Curve." The ball spins down hard, changing its mind in midflight and diving for Greenwell's kneecap. Mike fights it off, foul tip, the ball whizzing into the netting above our heads. "Fastball." This time Greenwell feathers a soft base hit into left field, the first one. Can doesn't even look, just goes to the drum-shaped box of baseballs and snatches out another. The three hitters take another round, Romero, Sullivan, and Greenwell. They can do almost nothing, even knowing what kind of pitch is coming. Romero strokes some grounders. Sullivan lofts some high, shallow fly balls. I'm no longer flinching. It has sunk in that there is a strong rope net between us. The Can keeps throwing. Between pitches Hriniak lifts the mask and spits tobacco. Can sweats and pitches on. That thin, light little body sending the ball with such speed, such power. Fifteen minutes, twenty, and the Can has had enough. He throws the fastball and whirls off the mound.

"That's it," he says.

He circles behind the mound, walking fast and jerky, strutting. He finds his windbreaker, scoops it, and breaks into a prancing trot toward center field.

Buckner has been watching from the dugout. This is his time to sit, to enjoy the evening sunshine and the sounds ringing out in the encircling quiet of the empty grandstands. I sit down beside him, careful to leave some space between us; Buckner gives me a cordial nod.

"Can was throwin' pretty good, huh?" he says.

"I'll say," I agree.

"That'd be a shot in the arm, wouldn't it?" The face is tough and wry. Droopy Civil War mustache. Buckner snorts a laugh. "Fuckin' Can," he says. "One day they're gonna operate on his arm, next night he's out there throwin' bullets."

Can is in the outfield, frisking up and down, tiny against the left-field wall. He lifts his knees high, dancing.

McNamara comes to the bench, strolling deliberately with his hands pocketed in his blue jacket. The reporters home in on him, they come slanting in from all directions. McNamara descends into the shade of the dugout and sits down. Immediately he is surrounded.

Silence.

"The Can looked pretty good," someone says.

"He was throwing the ball," McNamara says, "about as well as anyone can throw a baseball." I'm trying to think what it is about the man's voice, an elusive dissonant quality, something in his tone that makes my stomach clench up. The Sox' manager makes me nervous. The voice is clear but soft, even gentle. And yet . . . *sour*. He speaks as if a chunk of lemon, not sweet tobacco, were emitting its juices on his tongue.

"He seemed very hyper," says the man from the *Globe*, Larry Whiteside.

McNamara makes a face, squinching up. "He *what?*"

"He seemed hyper," says Whiteside.

"You been around here longer than I have," McNamara says. "If he seemed hyper to you, fine."

He leans forward and squirts what looks like a giant brown amoeba against the dugout floor. *Splat*.

"As I was saying," he says, "Oil Can had outstanding velocity. His control's not there yet, obviously, but the velocity is as good as ever."

Everyone scribbles. It will be in all the papers tomorrow; to read it, you would think this had been the most pleasant, friendly of conversations. The give-and-take continues, more or less civilly. I've stopped writing and am studying McNamara. He is, it hits me, a handsome man. He has a fine, sad face, and the squint now seems knowing and weary, not crabbed. I should tell him I'm writing a book. I've told Evans, who has forgotten. I've told Buckner, who asked me a few days later what paper I wrote for. So I stopped telling people. Ballplayers, anyway. I've told Pesky. I should tell the manager. It's only fair.

The press conference breaks up. The reporters wander away, to the field, the clubhouse. McNamara sits alone, a leg crossed over, his cap pushed forward. The older guys all chew tobacco and shove their hats down forward when they sit on the bench. Pesky, Fischer, McNamara. I ease down beside the manager. He sends me a quick sideways glance and looks away.

"John," I say, "I think I should tell you what I'm doing here." I sound ridiculous to myself, perhaps because I know he couldn't care less what I'm doing here. Still, I owe it to him. "I just wanted to let you know that I'm writing a book about the team and about being a Red Sox fan."

At the word *book* he turns and fixes me with those brilliant eyes. Globes of blue ice, bright with frigid light. His thin mouth stretches sideways, disgusted. He stares at me, holding me in the chilling light of those eyes. I return the stare as directly as I can. McNamara says nothing. He just stares. At last he turns, twists down away, and drops another viscous gob *ker-splat* on the dugout floor. He watches the field.

"Encouraging, the way Oil Can was throwing," I say.

"Yes, it was," he agrees.

"Why," I ask, "is it so hard for teams to repeat?"

"Well, in our case, you had the Clemens and Gedman holdouts, and Oil Can's injury. It's tough."

"Yeah," I say.

"You get all those things at once, it's pretty damn tough."

"Do teams play harder against you when you're the champions?"

"No," he says quickly. "Who won it last year, uh . . . ?"

"Kansas City," I say.

"Yeah, Kansas City. We didn't change when we played them. You always try to win."

"Of course," I agree.

"Excuse me," he says, and gets up. He climbs the dugout steps, trudging up as if weary.

Oil Can, meanwhile, has finished his sprints. He takes his time coming in, pausing to chat with teammates who stand around in twos and threes, gabbing while they wait for the hitter to send one their way. The Can talks animatedly. He laughs, tossing back his head. Some of the guys slap him five. The reporters, always alert, see Can come in, and he goes clanking up the tunnel with a procession strung out behind him. He knows we're there but ignores us until we converge at his stall by the door, mobbing around so thick the players must squeeze by. They don't like this. When reporters cluster around somebody at his cubicle after a game, the owner of the adjacent stall can get testy, depending on who he is. "Hey, pal, do you *mind*?" Clemens will say, and walk right over you if you don't make way. No one dares inconvenience Rice or Baylor, which is tricky because Boggs dresses right next door.

Oil Can, naturally, is in his talkative frame of mind, almost glad to see us. "Control is not the issue right now, I'm not concernin' myself with no control, just with *throwin'*." The voice whizzes, falls, shoots up. "I was throwin' with everything I got, can't *throw* no harder than what I was. If there was pain, I wanted to make it happen. I said, 'Come on, pain, come on if you're there.' But she wasn't. Wasn't nothin' in this arm but mustard."

The fastball.

You can either hit it—*get around on it* is the expression— or you can't. Mostly, I couldn't. I thought too hard, and you can't think your way through hitting the fastball. Finally, your mind has to shut off and let your body do the thinking; split-second thinking, solving the thorniest of problems in hand-and-eye coordination. I would try to think my way through it, would go to the plate with instructions to myself tumbling round and round in my head. The ball would be by me, swung at and missed, before I could put what I knew to use.

In Little League I was tormented by a lefty pitcher named Stanley Rabesa, who blew them by me game after game, year after year. Stanley played for the Cubs, who came from a rural section of town. The main road out there twisted along past cranberry bogs, junkyards, and vegetable stands. The Cubs' home field was beside a brick elementary school with tall windows and a mustard-yellow cupola. The ball field was dry and dusty, the grass yellow-green, half-dead, far too sparse and shriveled to slow a ground ball or kill a high bounce in the outfield. There were no dirt infields in our Little League in those days, just bald, teardrop-shaped patches worn around the bases and pitching rubber. The Cubs were all Portuguese or black Cape Verdeans, and they could play ball. Stanley Rabesa lived on the main road across the street from the school, and he and his father, Joe, would walk over for the games.

Stanley was happy-go-lucky, always smiling. A nice smile, tugging his eyes down at the corners, but when I was eleven and saw Stanley coming across the street with his old man, bringing that smile, I felt dread in my gut and pangs of envy. I'd have been nervous all day, quiet, preparing myself for that night. And here would come Stanley Rabesa, bopping along, grinning, not a care in the world. He would shut us out that night. He would strike me out three times.

He had a wedge of dark hair spilling on his forehead. Always, a touch of the smile. He would rear back, hesitate like a spear thrower, then cut loose. Fastball. There were no curveballers in Little League—not in my day—so it was only a matter of getting around on the fastball. Stanley's was the best. "*They can't hit what they can't see, Stanley*," his coach would bellow, providing unnecessary encouragement, but I did see Stanley's fastball. I can still see it, I can see the red seams. He kept it low. It didn't rise; it sank, if anything. But it was large in front of me, *suddenly* large, under my eyes too quickly to comprehend, whacking the catcher's mitt as I stood there trying to process the miracle. *Steerahhk*! bawled the umpire, Mr. Sample, who worked for the electric company. Coaches become enraged at kids who watch strikes go by, so I swung at the fat comet that was Stanley's fastball, and never got it. In three years I never got a base hit against him.

We were teammates in high school, but by then the lightning had gone out of Stanley's left arm. He was a good pitcher, but not the prodigy he'd been in Little League. I was pretty much the same throughout my career, always striving to hit the fastball. I barely hit .200 my senior year in high school. We had a terrible team. We did win our last game, which was against our archrival. Stanley pitched, and in center field I made one of my hottest catches to end the game, circling back to intercept a low line drive that had double written all over it, getting to it somehow before it sheered down, dropping gradually, like a bullet; getting to it impossibly, letting my feet go out from under me, falling, sliding as I snagged the ball backhanded. The game was saved.

Stanley Rabesa came jogging out to meet me, smiling the old squinty smile, and shook my hand. Coach Allietta grabbed my hand, too. "Best catch you ever made," he said, which he could not have known. The June afternoon was gray and still. Everywhere hung the sweetness of mown grass.

I saw Stanley Rabesa a couple of years ago at our twentieth class reunion. He was standing at the bar holding a drink. He hadn't changed. He was smiling.

"Remember how you used to strike me out in Little League?" I asked him.

"I was *bad* in Little League," Stanley said, quite loudly. He'd had a few. Everyone had.

"You threw hard," I said, and again I saw him rearing back, watching me over his shoulder as he paused with his right foot in the air, then throwing. Fastball. *Git down*. Huge and scary, gone as I hacked at it.

For once Stanley's smile faded; he stared past my shoulder. "Those were the days," he said.

Four

A Three-Day War

IT'S FRIDAY NIGHT, AND THE YANKEES ARE IN TOWN FOR THE weekend. It is late spring or early summer; you could call it either. Hot. I get to the ballpark early, park on Van Ness Street. There are more people about than usual at this hour. Lots more. A crowd has gathered on either side of the entrance to the players' parking lot. The players' cars slide swiftly in from Yawkey Way and turn fast into the lot, windows sealed. The players don't return the doting stares. On Yawkey Way the carryout place is doing good business: fried clams, French fries, and the ubiquitous sausages. Early-comers wait for the ballpark to open, and passersby slow down or stop, arrested by the excitement brewing here. Faces shine, expectant, eager for the show to begin. Red Sox and Yankees.

Like all blood feuds, this one has its comprehensible origins; and like all blood feuds, it has acquired a life of its own, a sustaining passion that has rendered those origins irrelevant.

75

Who cares that Harry Frazee sold half the team, including Babe Ruth, to the Yankees sixty-some years ago? So what? When fights break out in the grandstand during Red Sox-Yankees games—bloody fights, face-smashing fights—the combatants are not thinking about Babe Ruth and Harry Frazee. The American League simply isn't big enough to accommodate both the Red Sox and the Yankees.

Is it my imagination, or are people edgy tonight? I sit awhile, as I often do, on the cement steps under one of the archways on Yawkey Way. The man in cowboy clothes is perched here as usual, hands clasped between his knees, smoking his pipe and watching the heavyset black man at the old red pushcart stuff peanuts into tiny paper bags. The cowboy, who owns the pushcart, has a well-groomed, iron-gray beard under bronzed cheekbones. He wears a straw cowboy hat, flannel shirt, even in this heat, jeans, and cowboy boots. He watches the black man closely.

The old cowboy takes the pipe out of his mouth. "Don't fill 'em too full," he grouches. "Don't put too much in 'em."

"I won't," says the black man.

"What were you doin' in the bar?" demands the cowboy.

The black man takes his time answering. "Went to get me a cold beer," he says quietly.

"Cold *beer*?" Cowboy sounds scornful.

"Got thirsty."

"Thirsty, huh?" Cowboy shakes his head as if it were unlikely, if not preposterous. He sticks his pipe back in. He's usually pretty pleasant. In fact, he often pulls a carton of peanuts over to the steps and helps fill the paper bags himself.

In front of us a big man, a redhead wearing a business suit and carrying a briefcase, bolts suddenly out into Yawkey Way, springing at a lean white kid in baggy bib overalls, who cannot react in time to duck or dodge, and is caught. A strong hand clamps onto his bony shoulder. The kid's long face goes sullen, but shows no fear. The big man hauls him to the sidewalk. With his other hand he feels the kid's trouser pockets, slapping and plucking. He doesn't find anything, apparently. He lets the kid go.

"I arrested your buddy, you know," he tells the kid.

"So?" the kid says.

"So I catch you with tickets, you're goin', too."

Scalpers. The cop was checking the kid's pockets for tickets.

"Now, beat it," the cop says. "I don't want to see you around here anymore."

The kid departs, walking fast on long, rubbery legs. The cop watches him to the corner then turns and walks the other way, a businessman again with his briefcase. Two minutes later the kid is back, loping effortlessly in those baggy pants. He stops where a small, plump woman sits on the steps, glances up and down the street: no cop.

"Can you believe it?" he says to the woman. "I thought he was a lawyer or somethin'. What next?"

"You be careful," the woman says.

"Fuck 'em," the kid says.

"Here," she says, digging into her pocketbook. She has a pursy little mouth, like a hen's beak, bright red in lipstick. She brings out an envelope and hands it up to the kid. He stabs the envelope into a deep pocket and looks up and down Yawkey Way.

"I was you, I'd just leave," the woman says.

"I know what I'm doin'," the kid says. "See ya." He slinks away, glancing this way and that.

The woman turns to me and says conversationally, "I hope he don't get in trouble."

"Are you related to him?" I ask.

"No," she says, "he lives downstairs from me."

"Ah," I say.

"Them cops really get me," she says. "Talk about stealin'. No one steals more than cops." She sighs. "What's he gonna make, anyway? Fifteen bucks? Big deal."

"Is that all?" I say. "Fifteen bucks?"

"Maybe more for Yankee tickets. People'll pay anything for Yankee tickets."

A few minutes after five, McNamara is lounging behind his desk chatting rather graciously with any writers who care to wander in. He is working on a big chaw, has a wastebasket beside him that he spits into. Emboldened by his good mood, the writers ask about the chemistry on the team this year as opposed to last. Something has changed. Feeling. Passion. Something.

McNamara won't grant this. "The attitude on this ball club is no different from last year," he insists. "We've had things go wrong from day one. Clemens and Gedman. That killed us. Oil Can's injury. By the way"—he bends down and squirts, *pang*, into the wastebasket—"we just put Buckner on the DL. And Gedman's got a groin pull."

"It's hard to repeat," someone says helpfully.

"Listen," McNamara says, "these guys are tryin'. They're playin' *hard*, they're *workin'* hard. And I'll tell you somethin': it's not out of reach. What are we, eleven and a half out? There's time. We have to put a streak together, that's all."

He shoves the wastebasket back and stands. He is wearing his under-jersey, gray with dark blue sleeves. It hugs his gut. Why do so many old ballplayers let themselves go? It is as if they swore off exercise the day they hung up their cleats. I know guys older than McNamara, never the athlete he was, who run marathons.

"If you fellas will excuse me," he says, "I got to go to batting practice."

We rise and file out.

"Thank you, John."

"Thank you."

"Thanks, John."

McNamara does not go to batting practice quite yet, but instead summons Buckner. Buckner is hobbling around naked with an Ace bandage wound around his middle, strapping an ice pack to his hip. Down in Baltimore Jimmy Dwyer of the Orioles ran into Buckner at first, resulting in a debilitating bone bruise to the hip. Dwyer was racing out a bunt. Buckner thinks Dwyer hit him unnecessarily. He also thinks he can play and wants no part of the disabled list. He crosses the room stiffly. The ice pack bulges like some tragic excrescence, some disease of the Middle Ages. Buckner's dark eyes are melancholy. He looks depressed. His naked back is a triangle, the muscle layered so thick across his shoulders that it heaves when he moves, bunching and sliding as if there were too much of it to fit easily. There have been murmurings in the papers about his future. Is he worth keeping, at his age? McNamara ushers him in and shuts the door.

The reporters are everywhere tonight. New York reporters, Boston reporters. A broadcast crew from NBC television is here studying up for tomorrow, when they will send the game out nationwide, "Game of the Week." I see Bob Costas, I see Tony Kubek. Costas is a little man with a big, deep voice. Kubek, once a top-of-the-line shortstop, is one old ballplayer who has not let himself go. Tony looks ready to play. He is tall, broad-shouldered, with long, athletic hands. His shirt is open at his sunned, muscular neck. His skin is tawny. Young skin.

I remember Kubek, of course. Played for the Yankees. Rookie of the Year in '57. His most famous moment in baseball was a bad one, though not his fault. There is a photograph from the final game of the 1960 World Series: Kubek sitting on the ground looking glassy-eyed, drowsy, bewildered, his hand raised gingerly to his Adam's apple, where the ground ball had just drilled him, a sure double-play ball that took a crazy hop off a pebble or something and shot against Tony's windpipe, base hit, rally, turn of the tide. The Pirates had then taken the lead—the double play would have just about finished them—and, with the magic running their way, had won it in the ninth on Bill Mazeroski's home run.

I heard the whole thing on the radio, listening by myself in our old house with its low-built rooms holding the peaceful smell of mildew. I'd skipped freshman football practice so I could hear the game. Mazeroski hit his home run leading off the ninth. Staticky cheering poured from the radio. I turned it off, I don't know why, and went out into the stillness of the dying afternoon. It was nice that the Yankees had lost, but a peculiar sadness had come over me. I was regretting cutting practice, but this sadness was more than that, bigger than any one thing.

And still, when I think of Kubek sitting on the ground with his hand at his Adam's apple, when I remember or see the picture, sadness touches me. I remember the empty house and the dying light outside. I imagine the long shadows of an autumn afternoon; imagine them touching me and reaching right on inside. I couldn't rejoice in Tony Kubek's bad luck, even though he played for our ancient enemy.

This first Red Sox-Yankees game of 1987 is one of those prolonged, seesaw battles that seem to break all of baseball's natural laws. Surprise succeeds surprise, until nothing surprises. Given the choice, I would ask to see a pitching duel every time, but a game like this is also baseball at its best.

The game begins as a pitching duel. Hurst is on the mound for us, Ron Guidry for the Yanks. Guidry is the wiry lefty who, not so long ago, was one of the game's premier pitchers. A strikeout pitcher with a wicked slider. This year, like Gedman, he tried free agency, went unhired, and rejoined his team on May 1. He has won none, lost two. Hurst is seven and five, his ERA 3.07. Solid.

Old pro Willie Randolph taps a single up the middle to open game, and a generous cheer rises from the packed crowd. Yankee fans. Henry Cotto whiffs on three pitches. Gary Ward takes a third strike and grumps at the umpire. Up comes Dave Winfield, the giant right fielder and cleanup hitter.

A bat looks like a toy in Winfield's hands. The field now seems as small as a backyard, Winfield a kid trying to slap the ball onto a garage roof. Hurst teases him with slow stuff, bending the ball away from him. Winfield attacks, lunging, swatting too soon at Hurst's shy curveball. He strikes out, a victory in itself, and the crowd lets go a roar that has an edge to it, a cutting shrillness.

The Sox push Guidry around in the first but, with the bases loaded, cannot score. Hurst holds them in the next inning, and in our half Owen singles and steals second. Sullivan, now hitting .167, strikes out, swinging mightily but stiffly, trying so hard. They boo him. Two down, Owen still waiting at second.

Burks.

I like Ellis Burks. Back home I go around telling people what a good ballplayer he is, asserting it in a knowing way, as if it were inside information that hadn't gotten out yet. I tell my brother-in-law, whose passion for the Red Sox has become a kind of tragic yearning. Patrick clutches at any hope, and so I give him Burks, young and cunning, speedy but able to hit the long ball. Last year—think of it—he was playing double-A ball in New Britain, Connecticut. Now this. He stole thirty-one bases last year. Not since Piersall have we had such a runner, such a combination of speed and power.

Ellis is built like a greyhound, elongate, no waist, no belly, broadening only slightly across his sinewy shoulders. He has a small head, huge serious eyes; an intelligent, careful face, the face of a wise man biding his time. This is one smart ball-player.

With Owen at second and two out, Burks rams a ground ball over third base. The ball runs away into the left-field corner, behind that wedge of the grandstand, an easy double. The Sox have the lead.

It stays there, 1–0, till the sixth. The Sox' only hit since the second is by Henderson, who is in right field tonight. Evans has taken Buckner's place at first. Evans at first? I miss seeing him play right field, which he does with so much flair and self-confidence. Why not play Romero at first?

Hurst walks Randolph to begin the sixth. Cotto puts down a bunt in the direction of Boggs. Boggs charges the ball, digs it up, and throws to Evans, who seems to have lost the bag, is behind it in foul territory, where he takes Boggs's throw too late. They give Cotto a single, but if there'd been a real first baseman down there, the throw would likely have nipped him. Ward bunts, but clips it in the air straight back at Hurst. One out. Winfield is the hitter. Hurst puts him in a hole, two strikes, and then tries to pick Cotto off first. The throw is fine, belt-high, but Evans doesn't see it coming, and the ball grazes his glove and thumps off his chest into foul territory. The runners take off and easily gain second and third. All Winfield has to do is knock the ball in play on the ground, which he does, to Owen, who has to throw to first and let the run score. Ron Kittle pokes a single into right, and the Yanks lead, 2–1. Kittle doesn't hit it hard, just arches it out there.

Boggs stings a single to center to begin our half of the sixth, and Lou Piniella, the Yankee manager, comes out and lifts Guidry. He calls in the big lumbering right-hander, Tim Stoddard, to pitch to the Sox' righty power-hitters. Rice bangs a single to right, but Stoddard gets Baylor on a pop fly and strikes out Evans with a teasing change-up, Dwight swinging early, primed for the fastball. McNamara sends a lefty, Greenwell, to bat for Hendu; Piniella answers by bringing in a lefty pitcher, Pat Clements. Greenwell grounds out.

The Yanks go down without scoring in the seventh.

Piniella brings on another pitcher, Rich Bordi, a right-hander, to pitch the bottom of the seventh. The Sox score, anyway. With Owen at third, Burks delivers a clean single to left. Sox 2, Yanks 2.

Top of the eighth. Ward, who has done nothing, launches a majestic fly ball into the center-field bleachers, a monster home run. Hurst walks Winfield, and McNamara strolls mournfully out and points to the bull pen. The request is for Schiraldi. Hurst walks off to a handsome ovation.

Piniella sends in a lefty, Mike Easler, to hit for Kittle. Easler walks, and we are in big trouble. Piniella chooses another left-handed hitter on his bench, Mike Pagliarulo, to bat for the righty, Len Sakata. This is the knee-jerk strategy of big-league managers everywhere. Is an Easler, a Kittle, a Sakata, a Pagliarulo that much worse off when the pitcher is throwing from the side he hits on? Pagliarulo, at any rate, fights to a 3−2 count and finally drills one into center, straight to Ellis Burks. Again Piniella plays the strategy, Mark Salas for Rick Cerone. Salas lifts a pop fly to Boggs. The batter is Bobby Meacham, a switch-hitter, who of course bats left against Schiraldi. Meacham strikes out. So Piniella had four left-handed hitters against Schiraldi, and got nothing but a harmless walk.

Leading by a run, Piniella summons Dave Righetti, the star of his bull pen, to pitch the bottom of the eighth. Righetti is a southpaw, but with such enormous ability that no manager is going to concern himself much with who's hitting, righty or lefty. Righetti can mow anybody down.

Usually. Tonight, Boggs hits his first pitch on a mean, low ricochet at Meacham at second; Meacham swipes at the bullet in self-defense and deflects it, base hit. Rice forces Boggs at second, but Baylor flips one into left field, a little Texas-league single, short enough to enable Rice to go to third, the tying run.

Evans. "*Dew-wee . . . Dew-wee . . .*" croons the crowd, saluting Dewey Evans by his nickname. A strike, a ball, and Dewey hits one up the middle, waist-high, perfect, base hit, tie ball game. "*Dew-wee . . . Dew-wee . . .*" The tribute loudens, spliced through deafening cheers. The game seemed lost, but is not, after all. Greenwell forces Dewey at second, but Owen walks. The bases are loaded. Hell, we might win it right here.

Sullivan is due to hit, and McNamara has no choice but to send a pinch hitter to the plate. According to the old strategy, Marc has the advantage over Righetti, but there are other considerations here. Sullivan has whiffed twice tonight; his average has fallen under .167. With two out, we have the potential winning run at third base. We need a base hit. McNamara anoints Romero.

Eddie is on his way to the plate when the first fight of the series breaks out over behind the Yankee dugout. People are rising, waves and waves of them, standing and stretching to see the fight, two men slugging each other, firing punches into each other's face. Righetti looks over there as if mildly curious. Romero pays no attention. Ushers are on the move, scurrying along the aisles, which lead them roundabout, up, over, down, to the fight. Righetti loses interest and picks up the rosin bag. The ushers close in, sliding between seats, clambering over them, the people all squeezing out of their way. Finally they get there, descending from different directions, and haul the fighters apart. From the press box, which is a good distance away, the fighters look unrepentant as they are escorted from the ballpark. They walk with their heads up, swaggering. Their shirts hang open. People are sinking back into their seats as Righetti slips a strike past Romero.

Romero studies the next pitch, ball one. I don't think anyone expects much. Eddie is actually hitting .284, but Owen has taken shortstop away from him. He has driven in exactly three runs. The fans are suspicious of him. We cross our fingers. Righetti throws, and Romero whacks it into left field, base hit. From third Baylor jogs home; from second Greenwell scores. Two runs! The crowd stands, is celebrating while little Spike turns too far beyond second, is spotted by Pagliarulo at third, who pegs it to the shortstop as Spike goes sliding back in too late—out. The cheering dies momentarily then rises again. After all, we scored three runs. We lead by two. *"Ed-dee . . . Ed-dee . . ."* The new chant makes the air shudder. We go to the ninth.

Wayne Tolleson, a good-field, no-hit shortstop, is Schiraldi's first task. Tolleson is a switch-hitter, which gives him the advantage every time, according to the old rule. Tonight he is nothing for three. He now flies out gently to Burks. Cheers, relaxed and happy. The Yanks need two to tie.

Randolph, such a canny veteran, gives Schiraldi a battle. Willie won't swing at a bad pitch. Not ever. The count goes the limit, three and two. With every pitch the crowd sends down a new wave of noise. Schiraldi throws a strike and Randolph gets hold of it, sending a flattened arc to the left-field wall, the ball hitting low and scooting away from Rice, a double. Worrisome, but the Yanks need two to tie it, so you can forget Randolph and give entire attention to the hitters.

Henry Cotto. Now, you'd think that your number-two hitter would be a good bet against anybody, but Piniella must tamper in the usual way. Cotto sits down and Dan Pasqua gets a bat, a stocky lefty who is hitting a crummy .203, seventeen points less than Cotto. The question, I suppose, is what is Cotto hitting against right-handers? Less than .203? Maybe he hasn't faced any.

For the past two seasons Pasqua has been dividing his time between the Yankees and their triple-A team in Columbus, Ohio.

He is very strong but has trouble hitting the curve. Schiraldi hardly ever throws the curve—cannot rely on it, apparently. In the sixth and seventh games of the Series, he kept trying to pump the fastball by them, and the Mets were ready for it. Perhaps Piniella is thinking about this when he dispatches Pasqua to hit, perhaps it is more than the knee-jerk response in the big late-inning at bat.

Schiraldi misses the strike zone with a couple of breaking balls. Pasqua swings and misses twice, looking terrible. Schiraldi, unfortunately, throws ball three. Now Pasqua can expect the fastball. He is comfortable, he is waiting for it. Schiraldi pours it in there; Pasqua detonates on the ball, which is on the outside half of the plate, and lifts it, uppercutting, sending it to dead center, deepest part of the ballpark, the ball climbing, burying itself at last in the packed bleachers. Tie ball game.

Up here, one of the radio guys, very young, writhes and bounces in his chair, hollering. "*A dinger!*" he yells. "*A dinger! Jesus Christ, a dinger, I don't believe it!*" He is laughing, shouting, and sounds almost hysterical.

Pasqua romps around the bases, a young bull, as the Yankee fans whoop it up. Their cheers sound gloating. There's the same shrillness, the same edge, as when Hurst struck out Winfield. The home fans just sit there.

Schiraldi strikes out Ward, and with two out, nobody on, Winfield tries something interesting and lovely that fails by the thinnest sliver of a second. He has bounced one into center field, is halfway to first, when he decides to go for the double. You can see it; he stops watching the ball, tucks his head down, surges. Burks is playing him deep, of course. Winfield rounds first, eating distance in no time with long, galloping strides, giant's strides that pull him to second base with incredible suddenness. Ellis Burks, though, isn't asleep out there. Ellis races in to meet the ball, scoops, comes up throwing. Barrett covers second. The throw is low, good; Winfield dives for the bag, raising dust, as Marty brings the ball to him in time. Winfield springs up, barks briefly at the ump, then walks away shaking his head. There are players who are, alone, worth a trip to the ballpark. Piersall in his prime, Williams always, Boggs. Add Winfield to the list.

Last of the ninth: a run, and the game is ours. Righetti pitches on. Burks leads off, pulls a ground ball to the shortstop, deep to his right; Tolleson gets to it, but Ellis has the infield single. Barrett dumps a bunt toward first, sacrifice, Burks gaining second. That's the winning run out there. They walk Boggs on four pitches—not an out-and-out intentional walk, but amounting to the same thing, keeping the ball well away from him. Wade throws the bat away and trots to first.

Rice and Baylor, both right-handed sluggers. All we need's a single. Rice lifts a fly ball to center field, not deep. Burks tags up and speeds to third, anyway. Baylor chops a ground ball to third, easy out. We begin extra innings.

McNamara summons Sambito, a lefty, to pitch the tenth. Piniella has, all in a row, the three lefties who pinch-hit in the eighth. He has about emptied his bench and can only let them hit against Sambito. Sambito puts them down in order.

Righetti does the same in the bottom of the inning.

In the eleventh Sambito strikes out Meacham, gets Tolleson on a ground ball. Randolph singles. Sambito strikes out Pasqua on a three-two pitch. With Sambito on the mound Pasqua cannot assume the fastball. Sambito looks terrific.

Righetti has thrown his quota of innings, so Piniella calls Charles Hudson from the bull pen. Not "Charlie," *Charles*. Charles started the season like a house on fire and then began to stagger. In fact, the plan is to send him to triple A tomorrow to straighten him out. However, he gets Romero, Burks, and Barrett. The crowd begins to melt down the ramps. It is after midnight. We go to the twelfth.

Ward strikes out for the fourth time, missing the curve on

a three-two count. Sambito strikes Winfield out with slow stuff. Easler cannot hit the slop, either. He waves and misses badly, and with two strikes manages to put the bat gently on the curve, serving it to Owen, who gloves it easy as playing catch.

In the bottom of the twelfth, Hudson gets Boggs and Rice. Baylor pulls another single to left. Evans fans. We go to the thirteenth.

Sambito, it turns out, hasn't pitched more than three innings since he joined this team. McNamara has no more lefties in the pen except Bolton, and I guess he doesn't want to use the kid under pressure against the Yankees. Pagliarulo is up first, and Pags creams the first pitch, yanks it low down the right-field line, a shot into the crowd, inches fair. Applause sputters, weary-sounding. We have been here so long. Salas, another lefty, hits a deep fly ball to right, almost a home run. Meacham singles hard to left.

With Tolleson hitting, Sambito sails a wild pitch past Gedman. Tolleson is nothing for five, but Sambito walks him. Ball four shoots off Gedman's mitt, a passed ball. Meacham scoots to third. McNamara hauls himself up the dugout steps and comes slowly out across the chalk line, melancholy as an undertaker. He accepts the ball from Sambito and waits for young Gardner. Sambito jogs in to a shower of applause, as much as the tired, thinned-out crowd can manage. The thinking is, Sambito is paid to pitch one, two, maybe three innings at a time. He has done his job; it isn't his fault he got shelled here in the thirteenth. This is a rather charitable view of things. They'd be booing the hell out of Stanley.

The game is far from lost. The Yanks have only a run so far. McNamara has asked for Gardner, a righty, to pitch to the righty Randolph. Pitcher's advantage, but Randolph walks. Bases loaded. Out trudges McNamara to summon Bolton, finally, to throw to the lefty Pasqua. Pitcher's advantage, but Pasqua pounds the ball into the alley in right center, a double—two more runs. The Yankees are blowing the game to pieces. McNamara, no doubt figuring the game is gone, leaves Bolton in there to cope. Ward drives a hit into center field, bringing Pasqua home with the fifth run of the inning. The crowd is dribbling away. Bolton walks Winfield, but fans Easler. Pagliarulo, who began the conflagration with his home run, hits the change-up into center field: a single, reloading the bases. This could go on forever. But we have come again to the dregs of the lineup. Salas, who entered the game in the eighth inning and has already batted three times, pops a fly ball to right field. It is over. Salas is nothing for four.

There is no magic left in the ballpark, only a deadening fatigue, which can be felt, breathed, like heavy humidity. The crowd dwindles and dwindles, and now the cavern of the grandstand gives back echoes. The last of the thirteenth goes quickly. Gedman hits an easy fly ball. Owen hits a pop fly. Romero adds a lazy fly ball. Yanks 10, Sox 5. It is after one in the morning. In nine hours we will all be back—all except Charles Hudson, who won this game with clutch pitching, and who nevertheless will pack his suitcase in the morning and fly to Columbus, Ohio. That's the Yankees for you.

Johnny Pesky succeeded the great Joe Cronin as the Red Sox' shortstop in 1942. He hit .331 that year and led the league in hits. He then went into the Navy and didn't play in the big leagues again until 1946. Ted Williams also spent those three years in the service, and nearly two more during the Korean War. Williams never complained—he wanted it that way—but it depresses me to think of the game's best and purest hitter dropping out of baseball for nearly five years. It cost him, by my calculations, about eight hundred base hits. Pesky was no Ted Williams, but his three years in the Navy may have cost him a place in the Hall of Fame. In '46 he picked up where he'd left off, batting .335 and again leading the league in hits.

In 1952 the Sox traded Pesky to Detroit. His average took a dire plunge that year, but in '53 he hit .292. The following year the Tigers traded him to the Washington Senators. That year, '54, was his last. He was a lifetime .307 hitter.

Pesky, like Bill Buckner, is a good ballplayer doomed to be remembered above all for a single unhappy moment. Already friends have been urging me to ask Pesky about the '46 Series. They don't remember the Series, weren't even born then, but they know about the day Johnny Pesky held the ball. It is baseball lore, like Fred Merkle's failure to touch second base. In the final game of the '46 Series, Sox and Cardinals, Enos Slaughter was at first base with the score tied in the bottom of the eighth. With two out, Harry Walker singled. The relay throw from the outfield came to Pesky, who, legend goes, held the ball while Slaughter came all the way around to score. The Sox couldn't score in the ninth, and the Series belonged to the Cardinals.

I once saw the play on film, and I remember wondering what all the fuss was about. If Pesky held the ball, he didn't hold it long. He was a smart, aggressive shortstop; he knew what to do with the ball.

The morning after the epic battle with the Yankees, Pesky is sitting in the dugout with his fungo between his knees, squinting out at the empty, sun-drenched ball field. The day is hot and moist. Sticky. The Sox aren't taking batting practice because of last night's long ordeal.

"This race isn't over," Pesky says. "We'll get back into it." He leans forward, pulls his package of tobacco off his hip. Beech Nut, wintergreen flavor. He already has an ample chaw, but he digs out a stringy wad on two fingers, tilts his head over, and sticks the tobacco in deep.

I asked him if he chewed tobacco when he played.

"I didn't chew anything," he says. "You're not careful, you'll swallow the son of a bitch."

He shoves the package of Beech Nut down into his hip pocket. "I remember '48," he says, "the year we finished the season in that tie with Cleveland. We had a great team, but we couldn't win shit at first. Then we took off. I mean, we got *hot*."

That '48 Red Sox team won ninety-six games. They did not win the pennant; Cleveland beat them in the single-game showdown for all the marbles, played right here. Pesky was twenty-eight that year. He played third base and batted .281. Williams batted .369. Dom DiMaggio played center field. Mel Parnell won fifteen games.

Pesky says, "In '48, '49, and '50 we had about as good a team as you can put on the field. How we could have failed to win a pennant, I'll never know. It baffles me to this day."

The hearts they must have broken. Listen to this: In '49 they went to New York to play the final two games of the season, leading the Yankees by a game. They needed only one of those two games. The Yanks swept them. That year Pesky batted .306. Williams batted .343, hit 43 home runs, and drove in 159. Dom DiMaggio batted .307. Parnell won twenty-five games, Ellis Kinder won twenty-three.

In 1950 they finished third. The Yankees of course took the pennant and the Series. Pesky hit .312. It was Piersall's rookie year.

I say, "My father tells me you were one of the great short-stops in the game."

"Well . . ." He juices up, spits. "That's very nice of your dad, but he don't know what the fuck he's talkin' about, either."

I laugh. "Sure, he does."

"I played for some good teams," Pesky says, as if that were enough.

There is a scrabble and thud on the dugout roof, and a kid sticks his head down, little moon-face eyeing us upside down.

"How 'bout an autograph?" he says.

"There's nobody here, kid," says Pesky.

"*You're* here," the kid points out.

"Yeah, but I'm nobody," Pesky says. The face doesn't budge. Pesky turns to me, says, "A kid fell in one time. Almost broke his fuckin' coconut. I laughed like hell, too."

The face disappears. Footsteps clank in the tunnel and Pesky's buddy Joe Morgan comes out. Morgan is the third-base coach. He was a journeyman big-league infielder in the early sixties, and from '74 to '82 managed the Sox' triple-A team in Pawtucket. He grew up in Walpole, which is about a half-hour drive from Fenway Park, and speaks with the local accent, the broad, elastic vowels. There's a serenity about Morgan, an easygoing, quiet way. He's a dry, intelligent man who keeps his emotions to himself. He looks more like a biology teacher or high-school principal than an old ballplayer; musty, somehow. He's the only elder on the team who doesn't chew tobacco.

He comes down the bench, sinks down beside Pesky.

"Lemme see that," he says, lifting Pesky's fungo.

"It's got life in it yet," Pesky says.

More thudding on the roof, more kids.

"Why do you tape them?" I ask. I've never seen this, adhesive tape wrapping the meat end of a bat. We used to tape the handles. We would wrap them with adhesive tape or with electrician's tape, which blackened our hands and made them sticky. You could save a cracked bat—for a while—by taping, but certainly a lot of the life went out of a broken bat. Eventually the fracture would lengthen until you could bust the bat in two over your knee. The death of a bat was one of the rituals of sandlot ball. We would break the bat in half and bury the two pieces, using a good bat to pound them deep into the ground. Today a house sits smack in the middle of our sandlot field. The front door opens onto second base. The people don't know it, but they live on an Adirondack and Louisville Slugger graveyard.

Morgan gets up, goes to the bat rack by the entrance into the tunnel. He pulls a fungo. Brings it.

"Feel that," he says, offering me the taped barrel. "You can feel the bruises." Beneath the tape, the wood is dented, softened. "They get dangerous," Morgan says. "Shit, I've hit a fly ball with these things, seen 'em knuckle, damn near conk somebody."

Pesky says, "Get rid of that fuckin' bat, Joe. It's no damn good anymore."

Morgan holds it up, inspects it. "You're right," he says. He mounts the first two steps, peers up over the lid of the dugout. "Hey kid," he says. "Want a bat?"

"*Yeah!!!*" A shrill, silvery blast.

Morgan tosses the bat; it clunks on the roof above our heads. I think, *Why couldn't something like this have happened to me?*

Above us another voice, maybe fifteen feet down, asks, "Who was it?"

No answer.

"Look it up in your fuckin' program," Morgan says. His voice is surprisingly soft, but he talks like a ballplayer.

Mike Greenwell comes out of the tunnel. He stands very still, forehead knitted, studying the empty, sunny field. Greenwell, like Burks, appears to be very serious.

" 'Lo, Greenie," Pesky says.

Greenwell turns as if he hadn't noticed us till now. "Hi, Johnny." I like Greenwell. Him and Burks.

A nosegay of kids' heads appears at the end of the dugout beyond Greenwell. The kids are leaning out across the barrier and peering sideways into the dugout. They let go a chorus of squeals.

"Mike! Mike! Mike! Mike can I have your autograph? Please

Mike. Mike you're my favorite. You're awesome Mike. Please Mike. Please Mike pleeeeeze . . ."

Greenwell, who is twenty-four, remains still as a statue, mouth drawn tight under his little split mustache.

"Pleeeeze . . ."

Greenwell whips around, goes quickly to the end, to the cluster of heads, the hands waving scorebooks, pictures, baseballs. Greenwell clamps his glove under his arm and begins signing autographs.

"Attaboy, Greenie," Pesky calls down.

"Fuckin' kids," says Morgan.

The two men sit, thinking their thoughts. Pesky spits.

After a while Morgan says, "Charlie Wilson."

Pesky looks down between his feet. "Uhhh . . . an infielder. Played for the Cardinals."

"Keep goin'," Morgan says.

"Must have been right-handed."

"Switch-hitter," Morgan says.

"Shit," Pesky says.

"How 'bout *Eddie* Wilson?" says Morgan.

"Dodgers."

"And?"

"Outfielder. Left-handed."

"Fuckin'-A right," says Morgan.

"I got a Wilson for you," says Pesky.

"Let's hear it."

"Grady."

"Grady Wilson?"

"Yup."

"Shit," says Morgan.

"You give up, Joe?"

"Yeah."

"He come up with Pittsburgh in the late forties. An infielder."

"Huh," grunts Morgan.

"I got one," I say.

"It better be good," Pesky says.

"No one I've asked has ever gotten it," I say.

"We'll get it," Pesky says.

"If he ever gets around to askin' it, we will," says Morgan.

"Who," I say, "is the only guy who's played two big-league sports in the same place?"

"Gene Conley," Pesky says.

"The same *place*," I say, "not the same city. The same field, same arena, whatever."

"Well, shit," Pesky says, thinking.

"No one's ever gotten it," I say.

"It's a trick question," Pesky accuses me.

"No, it isn't."

"Danny Ainge," Morgan says.

I'm amazed.

"Am I right?" asks Morgan.

"You're right," I tell him.

"We don't fuck around, do we, Joe?" Pesky says.

"Damn right, we don't," says Morgan.

That afternoon we flatten them, 9–4.

Nipper pitches, and in the first inning the Yanks hit him hard, as if the fire that erupted in the thirteenth inning early this morning were flaring up again. Nipper is a righty, so Piniella has loaded his lineup with left-handed swingers. The leadoff hitter today is the veteran outfielder, Claudell Washington, whose apparel off the field is as stylish as his name. Nipper walks Claudell.

Willie Randolph—steady, disciplined, intelligent—hits one off the left-field wall, a double. Claudell stops at third. Easler pushes a ground ball to Owen; Spike gets the out at first as Claudell scores. Nipper walks Winfield on four pitches. He walks Pasqua on four pitches. It looks like a long afternoon. Ward pops a little fly ball into center; Burks slips and cannot make the easy catch. The ball drops in, a Texas-league single, and Randolph comes home. Up comes Pagliarulo. Nipper is laboring. The count goes to three and two, and Pags blasts one into the valley of center field, a long sprint for Burks, who pulls the ball out of the air on the run, a beautiful catch. Winfield tags up and walks home. Salas, another of Piniella's lefties, pops out. Three runs.

The Yanks' pitcher is the miracle southpaw, Tommy John, who has been in the big leagues since 1963, when I was a junior in high school and John Kennedy was President. I suppose John threw hard once upon a time, but now he gets by on control and a screwball that rolls underneath the swipe of the bat, causing ground balls, whole bushels of them, when John is on his game. He has an easy, unembellished delivery, a quick windup, hardly any kick, and an effortless follow-through that scarcely bends his back. He looks as if he were tossing darts at a board.

He hasn't got much today. Evans singles home a run in the second. Boggs singles home a run in the third. John gets Owen and Sullivan to begin the home fifth, then Burks, Barrett, Boggs, Rice, and Baylor rain base hits all over the outfield; and with four runs in, Piniella comes out and yanks John. Rich Bordi puts out the fire, but we score another in the sixth on hits by Burks and Barrett. And in the seventh, with Baylor at first, Evans launches one of his rockets into the screen, and it's 9–3.

Nipper meanwhile is stopping them cold. Winfield flicks one off the wall in the third, a double, but dies out there. Other than that, nothing is happening. Nipper is changing speeds, pushing the knuckleball at them, now and then slipping in the fastball. He strikes out Claudell, Randolph, Pasqua, Ward, and Salas. In the ninth, Pagliarulo dumps a home run into the Yankee bull pen, but the bases are empty, the run harmless. Nipper finishes the game.

Afterward, McNamara is almost genial. Sunlight pours down through the dirty little windows. McNamara pulls at his Bud Light and tells us that Nipper put his knuckleball to good use and changed speeds beautifully. "It was," the manager summarizes, "a very gutty performance." Gutty. It is Nipper's fate, perhaps because he doesn't throw hard, to be praised for his grit rather than for his skill, as if courage were his major asset.

"This is what we've been waiting for," McNamara says. "This is how it's *supposed* to work: the guys at the top of the order get on base, the guys in the middle of the order hit." He takes a slug of beer. "We didn't do much wrong today," he says.

The reporters funnel out and congeal around Nipper, who is usually courteous and giving. The talk is of the knuckler, a recent addition to Nip's arsenal. He says he threw forty-five knuckleballs at the Yanks this afternoon. He is dark, high-boned. He looks Incan.

"I wish I didn't have to worry about the knuckleball," he says. "I wish I didn't have to throw it at all. I wish I could throw as hard as Roger Clemens." He lifts and quickly drops his shoulders, a habit of Nipper's when he is talking; a melancholy shrug, as if he wished he had more answers. "I can't throw like Roger," he continues. "I wish I could." He shrugs again, as if the knuckleball were the pitch of last resort.

Nip brightens a bit. "We'll still be there," he says. "The way Hurstie's been throwin' . . . We'll get Oil Can back. If Oil Can throws like he's capable, we can win two out of any three games we play."

Optimism. It is running loose in the clubhouse, the heady tonic of victory over the Yankees.

Rosy-cheeked little Spike, who has been hitting, stands with a towel wrapped around his middle, pausing on the way to the shower to gobble a wedge of pizza. "Oh, yeah," he says, eating, "we're gonna get it goin'." The voice, Texas-twangy, is small and light, like Spike. "You know," he says, "sometimes you can try too hard. You can try to do too much. You got to relax in this game."

And Evans, who cracked the home run that put the game away, tells the reporters, "This could be the start of something, right here."

On Sunday afternoon Clemens pitches against an obscure righty named Bob Tewksbury, who yesterday arrived from Columbus, trading places with Charles Hudson, who beat the Sox Friday night. Tewksbury has done a lot of traveling the past couple of years between New York and Columbus.

Clemens puts down the first seven men he pitches to. He fans Ward, a big and baleful-looking man who seems always good for a strikeout or two, and Pagliarulo, one of Piniella's crew of lefties. Finally Henry Cotto—he bats right-handed, by the way—singles in the third.

In the fourth, Clemens walks Ward. Winfield knocks one high off the left-field wall, a double that brings Ward in with the first run. There is still nobody out, and a posse of lefties coming to bat. The first one, Easler, strikes out on a three-two pitch, a change-up that seems to dangle in front of him as he swings viciously, primed for the fastball. Next comes Pagliarulo, who pulls a ground ball to Evans at first. Two down. Pasqua floats one to Burks in center field, and the inning is over.

Tewksbury, meanwhile, is shutting us out. After six innings the Yanks lead, 1–0. Nice game.

The Yanks scratch another run in the seventh. Clemens walks Pasqua and Cotto, and with two out Piniella sends Claudell Washington up to hit for the shortstop, Bobby Meacham. Claudell comes through with a line drive over second base, a clean single, and Cotto comes home.

The Sox tie it in the bottom of the seventh. Boggs singles. Tewksbury gets Rice and Baylor, but then throws two balls to Evans. Two balls, no strikes, man on first, late in a close game: nobody exploits this situation more efficiently than Dewey Evans. Evans coils, weight on his back foot, awaiting the fastball. Tewksbury, anxious not to throw ball three, obliges. He pours it in there, maybe adding a prayer that Evans won't get all of it. But Evans does. This is Dewey's specialty. He hits it on the nose, blasts it sky-high, an Everest of a home run that clears not only the left-field wall but the screen above it, arching majestically down into Lansdowne Street. It is becoming apparent that Evans, who is thirty-five and has been a member of this team longer than anyone else, is having his year of years. The roar of the crowd is deafening, pounding surf and wind groaning, "*Dew-wee . . . Dew-wee . . .*" Dewey trots the bases with his head lowered. Williams did it like that. On the whole the Sox stay away from displays of emotion on the field, the joyous leaps, the raised fists, which have become common in baseball. Evans cruises the bases all business. Joe Morgan grabs his hand as Dewey spikes third base. "*Dew-wee . . . Dew-wee . . .*" The crowd stands, roars on, asking Evans now to come back out of the dugout. They cheer him, they croon his nickname, but Evans stays where he is. The din subsides. Yanks 2, Sox 2. A brand-new ball game.

Gary Ward helps us by striking out again in the eighth. Winfield grounds out, Owen to Evans. Easler then belts an outside pitch off the wall in left, a double, you would think, except that Easler hesitates after rounding first, unsure whether to try for two. He pays dearly for his indecision. He goes, Rice gets off a good throw, and Easler is out by a mile, sliding on his belly. This must drive Piniella crazy. Easler rises slowly to his knees and bows his head. He stays that way as the Sox come off the field, on his knees at second base with his head bowed in mourning.

When Buckner went on the disabled list, Todd Benzinger, a twenty-four-year-old outfielder, was summoned from Pawtucket to take his place on the roster. Benzinger arrived

Friday night. He has been in the minors since 1981, advancing steadily year by year. He looks like a high-school boy, blond and fair-skinned, a look of wonder brightening his face. A switch-hitter.

In the bottom of the eighth, McNamara sends him into the game to bat for Marc Sullivan. Over the press box loud-speaker Dick Bresciani, the public relations director, reminds us that this is Benzinger's first major-league game.

Benzinger presses a helmet down over his stiff blond curls. He pulls his bat from the rack and climbs the dugout steps. He walks with a bounce, as if impatient to get going, carrying the bat upright. He's big and strong, but just a boy. A boy who can get around on the fastball. Thirty-three thousand people are watching, the game is tied, the opponent is the Yankees. Todd Benzinger's blood is surely racing, but whatever terrors the moment holds, Todd knows in his heart that he has a fighting chance. He knows he can get around on the fastball.

He has faced Tewksbury in the International League this spring, which makes this easier. He has seen Tewksbury's fastball. He knows his tricks. McNamara, of course, had this in mind when he chose Benzinger. Really, it isn't at all a bad moment for the kid's baptism.

Tewksbury throws the fastball outside, ball one. Benzinger is batting left-handed against the righty. Ball two, outside. Ball three. Benzinger won't bite, though he must be anxious to take his first cut. Tewksbury throws another fastball outside, ball four. Benzinger tosses away the bat as if he'd been playing here for years, and frisks to first. The Fenway crowd applauds warmly. The kid has come through in a quiet, smart way.

Burks, who hasn't had a hit today, takes ball one, Tewksbury's fifth straight errant pitch. Tewksbury now is in big trouble. He's got to find the strike zone. Ellis Burks is sitting in the catbird seat, as Evans was an inning ago. Pitchers are always talking about staying ahead of the hitters, and this is why.

Burks has a body like a whippet's, but he can hit the long ball. Tewksbury guides the ball over the plate, and Ellis wallops it straight into the screen above the wall, a home run. It takes the ball about three seconds to get there. The Sox have the lead, 4–2.

Clemens mows them down in the ninth. We have won the weekend war, three games to two.

"Roger's going *after* people now," McNamara says in his office afterward. "He's not tentative the way he was. His problem was, he was throwin' too many off-speed pitches, too many changes and slow curves. He wasn't usin' his fastball and slider."

He takes a long pull at his beer. The dour face is almost happy. "He doesn't realize how good his fastball is," continues McNamara, talking without being prodded. "Christ, they can be layin' for it, and he can *still* throw it by 'em."

"Burks came through," a reporter suggests.

McNamara takes another swig. "Now *there's* a guy . . . I believed in him from the start. I believed in him two years ago. He has the intangibles. He's smart. He has a good head on his shoulders."

While this is going on I find myself actually considering asking a question of my own. The Sox took the weekend series, McNamara's in a good mood; why not?

I'm remembering the top of the seventh, when Clemens walked Pasqua, and McNamara went to the mound. It might appear that the manager was out there to talk to Clemens; in fact, McNamara's mission was to give the home-plate umpire a piece of his mind. The rule book prohibits arguing balls and strikes from the dugout, and the umps are pretty strict about it. So when a manager has something to say on the subject, he will visit his pitcher, stay until the ump walks out to break up the meeting, and then give the ump hell. Clemens didn't need advice in the seventh, and anyway McNamara always sends

Fischer for preliminary conferences. I knew what McNamara was doing and watched closely enough to see him jawing at the home-plate umpire, Terry Cooney, when Cooney came to the mound. McNamara kept barking at Cooney as he walked back to the dugout. If you were looking for it, it was obvious.

The reporters are leaving. McNamara comes around from behind his desk. At the door I say, "John, you had a few words for Cooney when you went out to the mound in the seventh."

McNamara looks at me with a sudden cold brilliance in those wonderful eyes. "No," he snaps.

Uh-oh.

"Who told you that?" he demands, and stalks out into the clubhouse without waiting for an answer, leaving me standing there in his office

"Sorry," I call after him, but he keeps walking.

The reporters engulf Benzinger, whose locker is adjacent to Oil Can Boyd's, just inside the clubhouse door. After Benzinger comes Burks, then Greenwell, and then Pesky and the coaches. The youngsters look as supple and tawny as deer beside the older men.

Benzinger tells the reporters that his father is a retired schoolteacher who works part-time at a racetrack in Cincinnati. Todd calls his father every night. Yes, he was nervous out there today. Yes, he's aware of the rivalry between these two teams; it seeps down, the guys feel it when Pawtucket plays Columbus.

Benzinger tells us that when he drove out of the players' parking lot yesterday afternoon, the crowd at the gate stared at him blankly. "Someone yells, 'Who's that?' And somebody says, 'That's nobody.' 'Yes, it is,' yells another guy. 'It's the bat-boy.' "

Boggs, meanwhile, is standing with his arms folded over his bare chest, staring over heads as he speaks. Wade had three hits today. He's hitting .375.

"We might as well stop playing," he is saying, a bit impatiently, "if everyone thinks the race is over." The Sox are in fifth place, ten and a half games out. "I got news," says Boggs. "It's not over, folks. The '78 Yankees came back from fourteen games out in the middle of July and won the whole thing. Miracles do happen."

It surprises me, for some reason, that I never pinch-hit in all my years trying to play this game. Not in Little League, not in Babe Ruth, not in high school. You'd think that I'd have been called upon just once to swing for somebody.

I was once led to believe I was *going* to pinch-hit and the memory of that afternoon couldn't be more powerful if I *had* pinch-hit in the last inning with two out and the bases loaded. The guys who do a lot of pinch-hitting have my admiration— just the idea of it is scary.

I was thirteen, a seventh-grader and borderline member of the junior high team. There was a limited number of uniforms, and the coach, Mr. Kalperis, would vary his squad from game to game, depending on the opposition. When we played the strong teams, he naturally dressed his best players. When we played the little schools from towns half our size, Mr. Kalperis gave his big guns the day off and fielded a team of his most promising seventh-graders.

As a seventh-grader I wasn't good enough to merit a uniform for the big games, but I came close enough, and yearned so deeply to take part that Mr. Kalperis thought up a way to include me. He dug up a shirt somewhere, maybe an extra from the jayvee team, and let me sit on the bench in half-uniform. They weren't strict about uniforms, and I would have been allowed into a game if it had come to that. I always cherished the possibility. I would bring my glove, put on my spikes, and loosen up my arm before the game began. Then I would sit on the bench in my uniform shirt and blue jeans, hoping I'd get into the game somehow, and hoping I wouldn't. These guys were good. The pitchers threw hard.

It was a cold, gray day in April, and we were trailing by a run or two against a fine pitcher. The game was flowing along, well played and tense. Mr. Kalperis, a large, nervous man who taught science, paced up and down the bench in an army-brown rubber jacket. In about the fifth inning he stopped in front of me, placed his chin in his hand, which was his way in the classroom, and measured me gravely. He had olive skin, very Greek, and beautiful big teeth.

"Hough," he said sharply.

I perked up, stiffened.

"If I sent you up to pinch-hit," he said, "you think you could hit this guy?"

My mouth went dry as flannel. Hit *this* guy? He had a big-league fastball.

"Yeah," I said, "I think so."

"Good," snapped Mr. Kalperis, as if it were settled. He turned and resumed pacing.

Well, I was in a state. My heart was pounding, my mouth was full of ashes. I turned all my attention to the opposing pitcher, which did nothing to ease my terror. He threw smoothly, without much leg action. He took a long waltz step and sailed it in there, hard.

I got up, went to the end of the bench, where the bats lay in the dust. *Never cross them; crossed bats are bad luck.* I chose a bat, got clear of the bench, and took some practice cuts. I kept my eye on Mr. Kalperis, but he wasn't paying any attention to me. I laid the bat back down and returned to my seat. Who would I hit for? Fredericks, the pitcher, that's who. Fredericks was an oddity, a junkball pitcher in junior high school. An eighth-grade Eddie Lopat. He couldn't run, couldn't hit.

The game flowed on. I got up again and took some more practice swings. I went to the old drinking fountain behind the backstop and took a drink. We were in the last inning, the seventh. Somebody reached base, and I saw Fredericks hoist himself up off the bench and go to get his bat. He kept his windbreaker on, like a big-league pitcher. Mr. Kalperis stood in front of the bench, hand to his chin, deep in the game. I looked from him to Fredericks and back again at the coach. I wanted it decided, one way or the other. Fredericks was trudging to the plate. He stopped halfway, took off his jacket, and threw it in the direction of the bench.

Mr. Kalperis cupped his hands around his mouth and shouted at Fredericks. "Come on, Freddie, base hit now, base *hit*."

My heart slowed, I was myself again. I wondered why Mr. Kalperis had mentioned pinch-hitting in the first place if he wasn't going to use me. I knew I should be angry at him, and disappointed that I hadn't gotten into the game. And I was, in a way. But I was more relieved than anything. I knew, deep down, that I'd been spared something.

How different life would have been if I could have hit the fastball.

Five

Why Wade Boggs Is the
Best Hitter in Baseball

IT'S FOUR-TEN. THE FIELD WAITS EMPTY, GILDED BY THE SUN hanging over the roof beyond third base. We have reached the end of June; the days are shortening, squeezing themselves imperceptibly, hardly anything yet. The field waits, prettied up by the grounds crew. The dirt has been combed, the grass freshened with sprinkled water. The grandstand is empty all the way around. A bowl of silence. Out beyond, traffic sighs and grumbles.

Footsteps, spikes, clank in the tunnel. Joe Morgan comes out with his glove and fungo. Wade Boggs is right behind him, hatless, socking his fist in his glove as he walks. In the dugout Morgan searches around, finds the drum-shaped box of baseballs. He digs one out. The two men climb the scarred wooden steps into the sunshine. They begin to play catch.

Easily at first. Gingerly. They are maybe forty feet from each other. They throw lazily, gently stretching their arms. Any

106

kid who plays ball knows the ritual. Start slow. Step by step Boggs and Morgan retreat from each other. They throw a little harder. A little harder. The whap of the ball in their gloves carries across the stillness.

Boggs turns playful. He throws Morgan some curveballs. The ball twirls as it flies, breaks sideways, bending wide, easy to catch. A playground curveball. Morgan gloves it without comment. Wade bunches up his fingers, gets a claw-hold on the ball, and sails a knuckler at Morgan. The ball bloops in without spinning or rolling, traveling frozen; it collapses suddenly toward Morgan's waist. Joe snares it almost without looking.

"Phil Niekro," Boggs says.

"Yeah," Morgan says.

"He dropped one of those on me one time," Boggs says.

"You drive it?"

"I got a hit on it," Boggs admits. He glances to right field, to the digital clock at the back of the empty, sun-washed bleachers. Four-seventeen.

"You ready, Joe?"

"Yup."

Boggs turns smartly and heads for third at a jog. There's a smartness in all his movements, a succinct elegance. Morgan gets his fungo. He ambles to the plate. He checks Boggs, who leans forward on the balls of his feet, ready. Morgan hangs the ball in the air with a little toss and hits it on the ground to Boggs. Wade scrabbles in, gloves it, pegs it gently in on a bounce. Morgan hits him another. And another.

Sid Monge, the batting practice pitcher, comes bustling out. Monge was a pretty good relief pitcher back in the seventies. He bounces up the steps and, without a word, hustles out to second base. Boggs grabs the next ground ball and snaps it hard to Monge at second. Monge lobs it in to Morgan.

Morgan is hitting them harder now. He is hitting them to the side of Boggs, right and left. Wade glides to the ball, pulls it smoothly up in his glove, and snaps the hard throw to second. Over and over. He has taken some fifty ground balls by now. With a jerk of his head he orders Monge to first. Monge runs over there and turns just in time to snag Wade's next throw. Morgan keeps hitting them. Boggs is sweating hard. Charge, glove, throw. Charge, glove, throw. Practice makes perfect. Boggs takes a hundred ground balls a day. A hundred *extra* ground balls. Later there is the pregame infield drill.

It is after four-thirty. Boggs dismisses Monge with a wave but isn't quite done, himself. Morgan hits the next one on a line at Wade's feet, just too short to be caught in the air. Boggs hunches down, locks his eyes on it, gloves the short hop. Almost every kid in the world, almost every adult, will avert his head, twisting instinctively away from the short hop. A big-leaguer keeps his face right down there and his eyes on the ball, a matador getting eye to eye with a bull. Morgan keeps drilling the ball into the dirt. Then he lines it wide; Boggs dives, flattens out, snares the hop. Again. Again. Again.

Boggs picks himself up one last time and says, "That's it, Joe." He jogs in, sweat-soaked, dirt-smeared, breathing hard. He clatters down the steps, goes clanking up the tunnel, lathered and blowing like a racehorse.

Walter Hriniak is the Red Sox hitting instructor. Hriniak has definite ideas, a gospel on the art of hitting that some embrace and some do not. Wade Boggs hits Hriniak's way. If the Hriniak gospel has been vindicated by any one man, the man is Boggs.

Hriniak himself could barely hit his weight. He did bat .346 in nine games with the Atlanta Braves in '68, but in seven games the next spring he hit .143. The Braves traded him to the San Diego Padres after this meager beginning. For the Padres in the rest of '69, Walter hit .227 in thirty-one games. And so baseball's most inspired hitting teacher lasted two years in the majors and batted .253.

But nobody ever said you have to be a great hitter to be a great hitting teacher. When Hriniak was playing for the Braves, one of the coaches was Charlie Lau, who spent many years wandering the big leagues as a .250 hitter and borderline catcher. All this time, apparently, Lau was developing a theory as to the best way to hit a baseball. He became a coach, wrote a book on hitting, and in the late seventies won fame as a hitting instructor with the Kansas City Royals. Lau died of cancer several years ago. Hriniak, who had absorbed all of Lau's ideas when they were together on the Braves, was already preaching Lau's gospel. And so Walter Hriniak is the heir to Charlie Lau. He has written a book of his own.

Every day after batting practice Hriniak leads three or four of his disciples out to the wall below the center-field bleachers. A garage-sized door leads underneath. In this big room under the bleachers is a long net cage and a pitching machine. Here work resumes; hitting, hitting, hitting. The kids—Greenwell, Burks, Benzinger—accompany Hriniak eagerly. Evans walks grandly out, carrying his bat like a swagger stick under his arm. Dewey is one of Hriniak's most devoted adherents.

I approach Hriniak with even more than the usual timidity, warned back by his rough, tobacco-chomping manner. I go to him one night after a game. He is sitting in front of his cubicle, naked above the waist. His pale body is lumpy with muscle. He keeps himself in pretty good shape. He listens to my request for an interview, nods a couple of times, and tells me to speak to him tomorrow. His voice is thick; each word sounds blunt, heavy. He talks tough, looks tough, but there is more to Hriniak: a penetrating intelligence in the large blue eyes, and a sadness, perhaps from long ago, as distinct in his rugged face as burn marks.

Next evening after batting practice I remind him of our appointment.

"Yuh," he grunts. "After I'm done in the cage. Be about forty minutes. I'll meet you on the bench."

I thank him and sit down with Pesky and Morgan.

"Did you have a batting coach, John?" I ask.

"Nah." He puckers, bends forward, lets it go. *Ker-splat.*

"I guess things were simpler then," I say.

"These guys today," says Pesky, "they're too fuckin' *mechanized.*" He leans over. *Ker-splat.* "You keep your eye on the ball, you hit the son of a bitch. That's *my* theory of hitting."

"Maybe you didn't need a teacher."

"Don't get me wrong," he says. "I have a lot of respect for Walter. He works hard."

"Very hard," Morgan agrees.

"The question," Pesky says, "is whether you can tell everybody to hit the same way. Different guys have different styles. *Natural* styles. You gonna take a Ted Williams and change his style?"

"I guess not."

"Shit, no. But I respect Walter. You have to respect the guy."

Forty minutes later Hriniak and his pupils come spilling out from under the bleachers. They loiter in, pausing to chat with members of the opposing team—it is the Orioles tonight—who are strewn in twos and threes over the outfield. Hriniak emerges last, identifiable in the distance by his straw-bright hair. He walks in with Greenwell, talking all the way, lecturing, hacking the air with knobby, reddened hands. Greenwell keeps nodding. Hriniak gives him a slap on the rump and comes down the dugout steps. He jerks his head toward the far corner and I follow him there. He is flushed and pouring sweat. He is almost always sweating.

I ask him about Charlie Lau.

"Okay," Hriniak says. "The things I teach, the things I believe in, ninety percent of 'em I learned from Charlie. Charlie was my friend and my teacher. It was a terrible loss when Charlie passed on."

I have heard that Lau taught his students to swing down. It looked that way: the great George Brett would attack the ball with a short hack, parrying and driving the pitch. Evans and Gedman have evolved an eye-catching follow-through— flourishing the bat high with one hand, a kind of signature. They appear to be swinging down, then pulling the bat up and away, like a backhand swipe in tennis.

"Do you teach them to swing down?" I ask.

"No," Hriniak says, "absolutely not. Charlie didn't teach 'em to swing down, and I don't teach 'em to. That's a misconception. I believe a good swing starts low and finishes high. This way the bat has a shorter distance to travel. I can prove it to you. Short, quick swing: start low, finish high."

Start low, finish high?

"Here," he says, and gets up. He orders me to my feet with a jerk of his head. "You're the hitter," he says. I spread my legs, grip an imaginary bat. Hriniak grabs my left wrist, the front one, and pushes away my right wrist, pawing it away impatiently. We don't need the right hand for this. He guides my left wrist through a slow-motion swing—a straight chopping motion, like a sharp whack with a hatchet.

"You don't want to loop your swing," he says. "For obvious reasons. A loop is longer than a straight line."

It seems to me I'm swinging down, but I don't say anything. If I don't get it, I figure it's my fault, not his. He returns my wrist ungently to the hitting position and pulls it through another slow swing.

"Start low, finish high—see? You got it?"

"Yeah," I lie. We sit down again. "What about the one-handed follow-through?"

"Believe it or not, what your body does *after* you hit the ball affects what it does *before* you hit the ball."

"Hmmm," I say.

"A good follow-through is of the utmost importance. I just want 'em to finish smooth. They don't all let go of the bat."

"No," I say. Rice doesn't. Baylor doesn't. Boggs doesn't, as a matter of fact.

"What about stance?"

"Your stance has to be comfortable. I like the feet about shoulder width apart. I want the weight on the balls of your feet. And above all, you got to relax up there."

"Now that's something I know about. I could never relax at the plate. That was my biggest problem."

He slips me a smile. Rueful. "I couldn't, either," he says.

The confession surprises me. I feel honored. He is, I think, wired too tight to relax at the plate. He eyes me now, and smiles. The smile is amused, as if he saw I didn't quite get it all. There's a lot to get, the smile says.

"The most important thing in hitting—" He stops. "I'm not gonna tell you. I want you to watch Boggs tonight. I want you to watch his head. He's the best hitter in baseball, and the reason is what he does with his head."

"Give me a hint," I say.

"I just *gave* you a hint—the head. Come tell me after the game."

"All right."

I figure if I'm stuck, I can get the answer from Pesky.

Boggs, who is hitting .384 at the outset, goes three for three tonight and walks twice. The third hit is a home run. The game is a hitters' binge. Batting practice. Anarchy. No lead is safe. The Sox finally win it, 13–9.

The Orioles have fallen on hard times. Tonight's release points out that they have lost twenty-five of their last thirty games. They have no pitching, a team that produced harvests of superb young pitchers all through the sixties and seventies. Mark Williamson starts tonight, a kid I've never heard of. The Sox shell him out of the game in the fourth. The relief pitcher is Dave Schmidt, and I can't say I recognize his name, either.

The Sox bomb Schmidt out of the game in the sixth. Enter John Habyan, another stranger. Habyan, too, takes an early shower, and Tony Arnold finishes up. Tony Arnold?

Forget the cliché: Boggs doesn't make it look easy. How can hitting big-league pitching—even these guys—look easy? Boggs goes to the plate and works. Hriniak evidently doesn't care about the tilt of the bat before a swing; Boggs's bat sticks up vertical, whereas Evans lets the bat dangle down behind his shoulder like a back scratcher. Boggs's bat bristles. As the pitcher winds up, Wade's hands begin to twitch, anxious hands itching to swing the bat.

I watch his head. *Keep your eye on the ball*, the coaches all say. Even Little League coaches know that one. *Keep your eye on the ball*. Well, here is the old dictum put into practice as perhaps never before. Boggs's head is thrust forward and down as he hits; his eyes are right there, he sees his bat lick the baseball. He sees the ball fly off the bat, sees it shoot away toward right field or wherever as he spins out of the batter's box. And when he chooses not to swing, he watches the ball until it is swallowed by the catcher's mitt: his head swings around, he inspects the ball as it goes by. In this manner he watches many strikes zip by—especially on the first pitch—and you don't worry. Wade knows it's a strike—how could he not, eyeing it so carefully?—and simply elects not to hit it. Often he'll let strike two go by; he has his reasons. Once in a blue moon he'll get called out on strikes, and then you have to wonder about the umpire.

In the first inning Williamson bounces a curveball off Benzinger's young back. Todd chucks the bat away and trots to first without rubbing his new bruise, the time-honored nongesture that tells the pitcher and everyone else that it didn't hurt, it wasn't thrown that hard.

Cliff Keane is in the press box tonight, and full of contempt for these fallen Orioles.

"This guy," someone remarks of Williamson, "has pretty good movement."

"Yeah," Keane says, "bowel movement."

Guffaws down the blue counter.

Boggs inspects ball one, then pulls his first hit into right field, smooth step and swing; perfect, perfect line drive.

"He's in his own league," admits Keane. No irreverence for Boggs.

Next time, Williamson pitches warily to the game's best hitter. There's an out and the bases are empty, so he can afford to walk him. He does, on four pitches. Two innings later Williamson can't do this because Barrett is at first. A ripple, like a breeze on water, stirs the crowd. Everyone knows Boggs is red-hot. Wade watches one strike and one ball, then cracks a low pitch into center field, another single.

Schmidt is pitching by the time Boggs hits again. Barrett is at first. Boggs almost always lets the first pitch go, but don't get careless, don't make it too fat. Schmidt puts it in there fat and Boggs takes the crisp Hriniak swing, which now produces the long ball—a low arc into the Red Sox bull pen. *Wade Boggs*, reports the electronic scoreboard, *is now hitting .391*.

Like Evans, like almost everyone on the team, Boggs makes a snappy businesslike tour of the bases. He runs with his head lowered, unsmiling. The crowd bathes him in applause. And when he returns to the plate in the seventh, they stand and pour down an ovation that begins to seem endless. The new pitcher, Habyan, walks him and gets booed.

The reporters flock to Boggs afterward. Wade is always bare-chested by the time we get to him. He assumes his pose, arms folded, head high. Noble.

Is he doing anything different these days?

"No," he says. "I'm just pullin' the trigger, is all. I'm waiting well. I'm waiting on the ball as well as I ever have."

Waiting on the ball. A familiar, painful phrase. How I worked, struggled, prayed for this gift. My high-school coach, who had briefly played triple-A ball, would stand behind me, behind the cage, and yell "Now!" as the batting practice pitch sailed in. I was not to begin, not to move a muscle, until the coach hollered. Then I would swing with everything I had. It seemed to work. But this was batting practice, some sub laying the ball across the plate with no speed to it, no mustard. In a game I would instinctively commit my bat, would begin to stride and turn my shoulders into the pitch before it was anywhere near me, an involuntary reflex trying to preempt the fastball. So when the pitch did arrive, I would be caught, perhaps a quarter of the way into my swing, which did me no good at all. I could only get a muscle-bound three-quarter cut at the ball.

"What about the home run, Wade? What kind of pitch was it?"

"A palm ball." Boggs shrugs as he says this, as if the type of pitch were beside the point. "I got out in front of it and flicked it out," he adds. His gaze roams past us, idly scanning the far side of the room. He waits with his arms folded, his gaze someplace else. The TV lights, white on his face, are extinguished. The reporters have enough.

"Thanks, Wade."

"Thank you."

"Thank you."

Boggs acknowledges the gratitude cascading over him with a curt nod. He unbelts his pants before the reporters can clear out and undresses quickly, as if making up for lost time.

McNamara comes out early the next evening and sits on the bench, the wordless invitation to the writers to gather round. He crosses his legs. His hat is pulled low. The reporters find places on either side of him and facing him on the dugout steps. Low purple clouds begin to shed fat raindrops. The Sox are taking batting practice.

"Shit," McNamara says at the rain, and punctuates it with a squirt of tobacco.

"It's just supposed to shower briefly," someone offers.

McNamara nods slowly at the information, as if to say, Maybe you're right, maybe you're not.

The sky lets go, silver needles over the green ball field.

"Keep hittin'," yells Hriniak from behind the cage.

But the grounds crew, kids, have their orders. They come out in a disciplined rank, trundling the rolled tarp in front of them, spreading it as they go. Barrett is in the batting cage.

"Fuck it," barks Hriniak. "Keep hittin'."

Keep hittin'. Barrett clips a line drive that whizzes a few feet above the head of one of the kids pushing the tarp. The kid looks up and then at Barrett, but what's he going to say? However, someone presses a button somewhere and the batting cage collapses, retracting down like the top of a Cadillac convertible. Barrett shrugs and heads in. Hriniak spins, angry, but comes on in. The players in the outfield are running for cover.

"Shit," McNamara says again.

"It won't last," the reporter promises.

Pesky, sitting nearby with his fungo, says, "You know what they do in Russia when it rains?"

"What?" someone says.

"They let it."

This elicits a smirk from McNamara.

"John," says a writer, "can we talk about Wade Boggs?"

McNamara looks pleasantly surprised. "I would *love* to talk about Wade Boggs," he says.

"Can he hit .400?"

"He's capable of hitting .400, yes."

"Wade won't make that claim."

"Well," McNamara says, "it's very difficult to know what Wade Boggs is thinking, because he doesn't like to talk." He leans and spits. "He reminds me of another person I know." A sly smile.

The reporters chuckle politely.

"Someone you know well?"

McNamara's grin tightens.

"John, could I get a few words about Boggs on tape?" A radio reporter has closed in with his microphone and little leather-encased tape recorder.

McNamara tilts back and stares at the interloper. "Wait," he says slowly, in a lecturing tone, "till I'm through with the gentlemen of the press."

Gentlemen of the press?

"Sorry," says the radio man, backing away and smiling nervously. "I thought there was a pause."

"There's always a pause," McNamara says, still in that patient, didactic voice. "Then they think of something else to ask me."

The reporters cough up some obliging laughter. Is McNamara trying to amuse us or insult us?

"Wade," he continues, "downplays his own skills. Defensively"—*dee*-fensively, they all say—"he's very underrated. He's made himself a good third baseman by working at it. He works and works and works."

Already the rain is stopping. The low sky cracks as if the sun had scorched it open. The sun burns the clouds off, and just like that it is a sunny evening. The wet grass sparkles in this sudden light. The grounds crew hurries out to roll up the tarp. Play ball.

"The Orioles are having even more pitching problems than you are, John," someone observes.

Wrong button. McNamara's eyes turn chilly. "I don't have anything to say to that. I don't talk about their pitching."

Joe Morgan tells a story about Boggs hitting in an exhibition game against the great Nolan Ryan. Boggs was in a hole,

no balls and two strikes, and Ryan threw his lightning bolt fastball. The pitch was low.

Morgan gets up, shows Pesky and me Boggs, striding,
straining, then passing up the pitch. "A wicked heater," says
Morgan, "but it's down here. *Just* low. Anybody else would
have swung at it with two strikes." Ryan fires again, low; Boggs
is tempted, but again restrains himself—ball two. Another fastball, low again, and again Morgan shows us Boggs stepping,
considering, refraining.

"Now it's three and two," says Morgan, "and the son
of a bitch"—this is Ryan—"throws a slow change." By this
time almost any big-league hitter will be so primed for the fastball, so accustomed to it, so worried about how to hit it, that
he will see speed where none exists. But not Boggs. Ryan
floated the change-up, and Morgan shows us Boggs waiting,
striding, meeting the ball perfectly and hammering it back at
Ryan.

Talk about waiting on the ball.

"Almost took Ryan's fuckin' ear off," says Morgan. "Best
piece of hitting I ever saw."

Boggs is standing in the sunlight by the batting cage with
his wood on his shoulder, chewing gum, studying the lefty batting practice pitcher, Sid Monge. Wade has shed his beard. He
has left a mustache, a fox-red crescent.

"Uh, Wade . . . ?"

It isn't easy, walking up to the world's best hitter and
asking a favor. Boggs's gaze swings round, appraises me briefly.
He looks back out at Monge. I stammer my request. Boggs
thinks a moment.

"How much time you need?" he says.

"Fifteen minutes?"

"Break it up," he says.

"Excuse me?"

"Break it up. Fifteen minutes is a long time. We'll do five

minutes here, five there. Patch it together, you know what I mean?"

I'll take what I can get. "When's a good time?"

"I get here at three o'clock every day," he says.

"Tomorrow, then?"

He nods and resumes watching Monge.

"Thanks," I say.

He nods again but doesn't look at me.

It isn't quite true that he gets here at three o'clock every day, because it is three-twenty when he comes gliding into the clubhouse next afternoon. The TV is showing pro wrestling, a favorite of the two clubhouse boys. Boggs scoots past me as if I weren't there. He grabs the mail out of his cubby and carries it to his stall. He drops into his canvas chair, facing in, and begins scanning the envelopes. He is wearing jeans and an untucked white polo shirt. I stay where I am, alone in the middle of the room, until it is clear Boggs has no intention of acknowledging me. Maybe he's forgotten. It's possible. It's up to me, then.

"Uh, Wade . . ."

The pale gaze comes up, flat and careful.

I say, "We were going to talk?"

"Right," he says. "It'll happen at four o'clock. I have a few things to do. I'll meet you on the bench."

"Right," I say. Aye, aye, sir.

I kill half an hour in the dugout watching early batting practice and chatting with Monge, who tells me he's going to try to make a comeback next season. In October he'll be heading for Mexico to pitch winter ball. Monge grew up down there; his English is perfect but accented. He is thirty-six and last pitched in the big leagues in 1981.

At four Boggs comes out singing "My Girl" in falsetto, Frankie Valli style. Like Hriniak, Boggs is charged with nervous electricity. He comes bustling, crackling, down the bench and drops beside me, flopping against the back wall.

"Bang away," he says.

"Well," I say, "the first thing I wanted to ask was about Walt Hriniak's influence on you."

"I really had the philosophy before I came here," Boggs says. "I'd read Charlie Lau's book, which made perfect sense to me. The Lau swing is natural for me, anyway."

He stops, waits for the next question. He is looking out over the empty field, giving me perhaps two-thirds of his attention. His voice is flat, like his gaze. All business.

"Who else influenced you, besides Lau?"

"My dad. My dad's a perfectionist. He taught me that way. He taught me from the time I was little, then coached me in Senior League."

"What's Senior League?"

"Thirteen through sixteen years old."

"Oh, yeah. In our town it was Babe Ruth League."

He says nothing.

"How do you feel about playing in Fenway Park?" I ask.

"Fenway was built for me. My dad told me that when I was twelve years old."

"Do you have any sense of the history of the place? I mean, Babe Ruth played here, right? Ted Williams. Do you think of that? All the tradition and everything?"

"I don't like to live in the past. This is the place where Wade Boggs plays."

He already sounds tired of me. He sounds disappointed, as if he expected better questions.

"Do you have any . . ." I'm groping for a way to put this. "It's so *beautiful*," I blurt. "The old brick, the odd angles . . ."

"I don't really react to it," Boggs says.

"You just play ball," I say.

"I just play ball," he agrees.

We are interrupted by the leader of a film crew, who seems to have made some arrangement with Boggs to shoot him discoursing on the art of hitting. The man only wants to remind

Wade of their appointment, but Boggs looks inquiringly at me, wondering if I might excuse him.

"You want to go," I say.

He shrugs.

"Can we talk again tomorrow?" I say.

"Right."

"Four o'clock?"

"Right," he says, and is gone.

He does come out at four the next afternoon. He glances at me, sitting alone on the bench, and plops down about fifteen feet away. He contemplates the field. He's waiting for me to come to him. *I'm too old for this*, I think, and pick myself up. I go to him and sit.

"Bang away," he says, eyes still front.

"Why do you usually take the first pitch?" I ask. Pleasantries would be a waste of his time.

"I like to see what they're throwin' me. The pitchers are constantly experimenting with me. I never know what I'll see. It can be different every time."

"You obviously take pride in your own performance. Some people say that personal goals have no place in baseball. I happen to disagree. I mean, what's wrong with setting goals for yourself?"

"I don't set goals," he says.

"You don't?"

"I don't want to limit myself."

"How do you mean?"

"A goal is a limitation. Suppose you say, 'I'm gonna hit twenty-five home runs,' and you get there on September 1. Now what? You've reached your goal. You're gonna relax. You're gonna go through the motions."

"Not if the goal is a certain batting average," I point out.

"Batting averages can be misleading," he says. "There are balls you hit hard, but right at somebody."

"Over a season, batting average is pretty telling," I say.

He shrugs. "I don't set personal goals."

Better drop it. Boggs stares out, waiting for the next question.

Last summer his mother was killed in an automobile accident. Boggs left the team for a few days in the midst of the division race; the papers were discreet, but his agony came through, poignant as a silent scream. Six months later, my own mother died of lung cancer. She was sixty-four. Boggs has no idea how much I know about him. A notion comes to me, a fantasy, in which I tell him about my mother, and he looks at me, really, for the first time.

He is fiddling with the lacing of his glove.

"Did you play Little League ball?" I ask.

"Yup."

"You were good," I prompt.

"I hit about .600."

"What'd you hit in high school?"

"Junior year, I hit .425. Senior year, I hit .485."

"When I was a kid," I say, "I wanted to be a big-league ballplayer. When I was, oh, about thirteen or fourteen I realized I never would be. When did you know, when did it come to you beyond a doubt, that you *would* play in the major leagues?"

He doesn't stop to think. "When I was six years old."

"That's when you knew, or when you started dreaming about it?"

"That's when I knew."

"Are you improving?"

"You don't improve at my level."

"By 'level' you mean . . ."

"Batting average. Up in the .360s. You don't improve on that."

I wonder how long we've talked. Five minutes? Ten? Boggs stares out, expressionless, keeping his thoughts to himself.

"Well," I say, "I'll let you go. I really appreciate it."

"Yup," he says, and hops off the bench. He climbs the steps effortlessly two at a time, and shoots out across the infield to take his one hundred ground balls.

He is in the cage one night taking his batting practice cuts against Bill Fischer. He hits batting practice pitching with such ease and perfection you can't help feeling he could do it with a blindfold on. Fischer, heavy in a loose blue windbreaker, sails them in, intent on his work.

"*Hey*! What do you think they got a mat out there for?"

It is Stump Merrill, the Yankees' first-base coach, addressing Fischer from behind the cage. Stump is referring to the strip of canvas laid like a rug down the center of the mound to keep it tidy for the game. Fischer is throwing from the side of the mound, away from the canvas. Merrill is kidding, of course. Fischer doesn't hear him and pitches.

"*Hey*! What the hell you think they got a mat out there for?"

Fish realizes he is being spoken to. He squints in.

"Get on the mat," yells Merrill.

"Hey, Fish," says Boggs, "talk on your own fuckin' time, okay?" Stump Merrill stops smiling, and Fischer pitches.

"This is gonna sound crazy," Hriniak says, "but the only way to wait on the ball is not to wait."

He smiles. Strong teeth, tobacco-stained. He is standing in the dugout, gesturing as he talks. At times he will drop a hand on my shoulder—I can feel the strength in it—and look me in the eye as if I were one of his students.

"Charlie taught me this in '68," Hriniak says. "I didn't believe it. I said, 'Charlie, I don't fuckin' believe it.' But he showed me. He showed me with one of those dual cameras, whatever you call 'em. Shows the hitter in one frame, the pitcher in the other, simultaneous. What you see is, the pitcher's winding up, coming around, and the hitter's already beginning. He's got his bat *here*, and he's startin' his stride. I didn't fuckin' believe it."

Here is where every good hitter begins his swing, the bat cocked at about forty-five degrees, the hands well back. What Hriniak is saying, what he is showing me, is that the hitter can hold his bat any which way—Boggs's bat bristles straight up, Evans's dangles over his shoulder—but as he begins to stride, the bat moves to this universal position, cocked to hit. My old coach was wrong, standing behind the cage yelling *Now!* The only way to wait is not to wait. You can't do it all at once. Boggs is into his stride, the first stage of his lovely crisp swing, before the pitcher lets go of the ball. He will stride into every pitch, but that doesn't mean he will swing. He will wait and see.

"I couldn't wait," says Hriniak. He shows me. His hands rebel, jerk forward. My problem, too. "I couldn't hit the ball hard," he says. "I could slap the ball, but I couldn't hit it hard."

"Could you have been a better hitter if you'd been taught right?"

"Everyone can," he says. "These people who say you can't teach hitting are full of shit. Sure, I could have been better." He smiles a dry, sad smile. Whatever has seared him has not left him angry or bitter. "But," he says, "I wouldn't have been a lot better."

"I know it wasn't for lack of drive," I say.

"I tried," he says softly.

Pesky said it right: You have to respect the guy.

Hriniak says, "I never see what kind of pitch is thrown. Curveball, slider—I never know. I'm watchin' the hitter. That's all I see, is the hitter."

Inevitably, he misses things. If he has questions about what he has just seen, he will, when the inning is over, call for the tape. In the center-field bleachers, in the wedge of the bottom left corner, a camera is taping the Red Sox hitters. There's a videocassette for every player—a tape library of his Fenway at-bats. Hriniak can call for a cassette, and in a little room off the hallway outside the manager's office, Walter will roll the tape till he finds what eluded him as he watched from the first-base coach's box. Then he hustles out to the dugout and administers a quick tutorial.

"It never ends," Hriniak says happily. "You know what the only thing harder than hitting is?"

"What?" I can't imagine anything harder than hitting.

"Teaching hitting. Listen: if you fail seven out of ten times as a hitter, you're not just good, you're a star. Think what this means: there are gonna be times when you go seven, ten times without a hit, it's inevitable. And I don't care who you are, if you go ten times without a hit, you're gonna start doubtin' yourself. The teacher, see, not only has to know when the hitter's still doin' it right, but he has to convince him he is. *You're not doin' a fuckin' thing wrong. Stay with it.*"

Hriniak grins.

"Hitting's a science," he says. "It's . . ." He's looking for the right word. ". . . *fascinating.*"

Without ever taking his eyes off the hitter in the cage, Walter shoves in more tobacco. He tamps it deep with two fingers. It is warm, but he wears his jacket, forcing sweat. The sweat plasters down his yellow hair. He squats on his haunches for a new view. He bobs up again. He circles to the other side of the cage. The glove wadded in his hip pocket is an old one, the leather worn and cracked. A playground glove.

"You got to get *on* the fuckin' ball," he is saying now to Wade Boggs. "If you can't get on the ball, you can't hit. I don't care *who* you are."

Boggs nods.

Hriniak spits.

Barrett comes out of the cage, and Walter snags him by the arm.

"Where was your head on that last one, Marty?"

"It was *good*, wasn't it?"

"*No*, sir."

Barrett looks astonished. "It *wasn't?*"

Hriniak watches Benzinger take his swipes, then drags him aside for a rapid-fire lecture:

"The only difference between hitting the ball to the opposite field and pulling it is, when you hit to the opposite field you meet the ball farther back. *Here* instead of here. When you pull the ball you step out, you step into it. You're *on* it. Some guys want to step down the line to pull, they want to step into the bucket. You'll hit it that way, but you'll hit it foul. Step *to* the ball. Be *on* it."

Boggs is sitting in the tunnel on his folding chair, bouncing a ball against the wall. Keeping those nervous hands busy. He sits hunched, feet apart, and zips the ball against the cement wall with a flick of his wrist. He hears me coming but doesn't look. Perhaps he knows by the sound that I'm not wearing spikes. He is indifferent as to who this might be.

" 'Lo, Wade," I say.

A glance, then back to his game. " 'Lo," he offers.

Wade, I'd like to tell you something. About my mother. The fantasy recurs, the way dreams do.

"Excuse me," I say.

Wade holds the ball as I pass by. Behind me, immediately, the game resumes, whack and thump and plop in the glove, over and over, a sound of monotony and discipline.

Six
Old Photographs

I BECAME A PITCHER BY ACCIDENT ONE SUMMER EVENING WHEN I was eleven. My Little League team was practicing, and I was taking a turn throwing batting practice. The pitcher's mound was nothing but a rubber slab on a teardrop-shaped patch of dirt where the grass had been worn away. There was no infield dirt and no bleachers. Behind the backstop the ground rose, and here the parents would sit in the long, matted grass and watch us play.

After I'd thrown a few pitches, Mr. Malone, who helped out, said something to the coach, Mr. Wysocki. Mr. Malone was heavyset and sad-eyed. He looked like a melancholy bulldog. Mr. Wysocki was a sergeant in the Air Force, tall and thin and high-strung.

Mr. Wysocki nodded, said something back to Mr. Malone, and yelled out to me: "Wheel one in there, Hough."

I'd never heard the expression "wheel," but I knew what

they wanted. I wound up, reared back, threw my leg in the air like a big-leaguer, and flung the ball with everything I had. The batter swung and missed as the ball pounded the catcher's mitt. Not bad.

"Wheel another one in there," said Mr. Wysocki.

I did. Swing and miss.

"Come on in here, Hough," said Mr. Wysocki.

I went over to him and Mr. Malone. Mr. Wysocki wore his cap perched forward; you could barely make out his eyes under the visor.

"You want to take a crack at pitching?" Mr. Wysocki asked me.

"Sure," I said.

" 'Sure'?" He looked at Mr. Malone. "That doesn't sound very hungry, does it?"

"I mean *yes*," I said. "I really, really want to."

"Aw-*right*," said Mr. Wysocki.

That's how my short pitching career got started.

Best of all was pitching against the team called the Red Sox, who came from the scientific community of Woods Hole. The Red Sox, sons of oceanographers and marine biologists, were intellectuals, not ballplayers. It seemed that way, at least. Everyone murdered the Red Sox. They expected it. Their pitchers couldn't throw heat. Their hitters eyed the pitcher meekly, gripping their bats tentatively, like weapons they had no wish to use.

I loved playing them in their ballpark, the only times I was ever comfortable as a Little Leaguer on an opponent's turf. We drove over there knowing we were going to win big. The field was set back from the street down a gravel lane. Old lilac bushes grew along the lane, sweetening the evening air in early June. Along the third-base side were several towering elms with park benches underneath. On the first-base side was a tennis court, and now and then during the game I would look over and see women in tennis whites stroking the ball back and forth. Beyond the outfield lay a marsh, and beyond that, distantly, you could see the ocean, pale and shiny with the sun still hitting it.

In this lovely setting, against this docile team, I relaxed, had fun, played good ball. My big problem as a Little League pitcher was wildness, but against the Red Sox I found miraculous control. Effortlessly I laid the ball over the plate knee-high and hard. Their timid hitters waved late and missed. I remember a kid named Oaks, Bobby Oaks, who batted leadoff. He was very small, and they must have hoped he'd get some bases on balls. But he insisted on swinging. He'd swing at anything. He wore a happy, friendly smile, even at the plate. I remember him crouching with his bat cocked, smiling out at me from under his hat brim. He swung and missed, and still smiled.

I remember, too, a kid named Riley, who wore glasses and whose pale, freckled face looked fragile as eggshell encased in the wraparound batting helmet. Riley watched glumly as I wound up and pumped my fastball by him. An old man, who must have lived close by, was always sitting on one of the park benches and rooting noisily for the home team. He would yell at us, his deep hoarse voice carrying down strong across the field. When I was on the mound he would yell, *"Where'd you learn to pitch, Sears and Roebuck?"* He would ask this rhetorical question over and over as a game went along. *"Where'd you learn to pitch, Sears and Roebuck?"* I never minded. The voice was good-natured, and I took the razzing as a compliment.

Once, on a golden summer's evening in this pretty ballpark, I found myself pitching to Buddy, my best friend from next door. I was twelve; Buddy was ten, a first-year player who usually warmed the bench. We were way ahead, and their coach must have stuck Buddy in the game to give him some experience. Suddenly here he was, peering out at me with a smile slopped on his face. I never knew why Bobby Oaks smiled, but I knew why Buddy was smiling now. He didn't have a prayer against me. I was too old, too big, too good. It was so hopeless, it was funny. My heart sank. I didn't want this. Buddy's father was watching.

I thought about walking him, and half tried to. I threw indifferently, but the ball sailed through the strike zone, and Buddy waved dutifully and missed. Where was my wildness when I needed it? I struck him out on four pitches. He trudged back to the bench and sat down by himself. He'd forgotten to take off his helmet. His smile was gone. He was staring out past me, at the distant water, perhaps. I wondered what he was thinking. I knew he wasn't mad at me, but what? I thought of his father, up there watching. *What have you done?* I thought.

"*Where'd you learn to pitch, Sears and Roebuck?*" the old man yelled.

In junior high my arm went bad. Whenever I threw hard the pain would come. It would begin deep in the biceps and steadily swell, till it filled my upper arm. It was a cold, deadening pain. It would remain for hours afterward. The doctor took X rays and found nothing wrong. He advised me to take my time warming up. I did that, anyway. I was in eighth grade, and Mr. Kalperis had big plans for me. He'd counted on me to be his ace. The coach never said so, but I could tell he suspected I was a head case.

One day, our pitcher ran into trouble late in a tight game. I was playing first base. Mr. Kalperis came to the mound, took the ball from his pitcher, and turned to me.

"Think you can give me a couple innings?" he said.

What was I going to say? There was a bunch of girls from our eighth-grade class sitting on blankets on the grass not far away down the right-field line. In front of everybody, was I going to refuse to pitch?

"Sure," I said.

Mr. Kalperis summoned me with a toss of his head.

"Throw strikes," he said, slapping the ball in my glove.

"I will," I said.

It was a warm day, overcast. The grass was a dark, intense green. With a heavy heart, I began throwing my warm-ups. I knew how this would go. At first, a cold spur of pain deep in the arm. It would grow as I threw, till my upper arm was crammed with it. I would end up lobbing slowballs that would be rocketed all over the outfield. Or else I'd be wild. I'd walk everyone, a slow merry-go-round circling the bases.

I was still thinking these thoughts when I realized my arm wasn't hurting. I'd thrown about four pitches. No pain. I threw again, harder; no pain. My arm felt rubbery but powerful. I threw harder still: nothing, just snap, resilience. Joy filled me; I'd been reborn. I threw one more blazing fastball and told the ump I was ready.

The hitter dug in. Three or four kids were straddling bikes behind the backstop. I didn't know who they were, but they were heckling the opposing team, mostly the hitters. *"No-hitter, no-hitter, no-hitter!"* they sang. Or, *"Strike this chump out! Strike him out!"* The shrill voices wafted out, friends' voices. We had the hitter surrounded.

I threw. *"Swing, batter!"* yelled the kids behind the screen, and the batter did, and missed. The pitch was hard and high; he couldn't lay off. I struck him out. My arm felt weightless, yet strong. My pitches all wanted to climb, though I was trying to keep the ball low. But it didn't matter where I threw; they couldn't catch up with it. I struck out the next hitter, ending the inning. As I came off, I could hear the girls out in right applauding. Tall, dark Carla; Faith, blonde and beautiful. Reborn.

We were ahead by a run or two, and it was up to me to hold the lead in the seventh. No sweat. *"Strike this chump out!"*

one of the kids shouted. "*No-hitter, no-hitter, no-hitter*!" My catcher, DeMello, held the mitt low, urging me to keep the ball down. I couldn't; it sailed like a comet, unhittable. "*Swing, batter*!" They swung. The strength in my arm flowed from deep inside me, as new as new love. Somebody punched a harmless lucky single off me in that last inning, but that was all. I fanned the last hitter, a lefty, who swung through the high fastball.

The game was ours. It was mine. I was a new person with a new arm; an arm with greatness in it.

A week later Mr. Kalperis penciled me in as his starting pitcher. I warmed up slowly, confidently, lobbing the ball and retreating a step at a time. Then I snapped one hard, and in that instant the pain woke again in my arm. I threw; the pain hardened and grew a little.

It was a hot day, not a cloud anywhere. We were playing away. Tall oaks curtained the field. Those old ballparks were pretty. I didn't say anything about my arm, just kept warming up, feeling the pain get bigger with every pitch. The sun beat down. I was sweating hard.

I sat down on the bench and waited for the bottom of the first inning. Up on a hill I could see a brick school and more big trees. Survive, I thought. Just survive the game. The third out was made, and I picked up my glove and went out to pitch.

I threw my warm-ups gently, but the pain kept growing. The first hitter dug in. Leadoff hitters were always small. Most of them were spunky-looking little buggers. I pitched: ball one. I threw ball two. My upper arm was solid, cold pain. Ball three, I walked off the mound toward the plate and called my catcher. Jackie lifted off the mask and asked the ump over his shoulder for a time-out. The ump pulled off his mask and waved both arms. Jackie came jogging out.

"My arm's gone," I said.

He didn't say anything, just looked over and beckoned to the coach. Mr. Kalperis came out scowling. But as soon as he climbed the mound and looked closely at me, the scowl vanished.

"You're sweating," he said.

I felt my forehead, brought down a palmful of sweat. I was drenched.

"Are you okay?" Mr. Kalperis asked.

"My arm's gone," I said. "I can't pitch any more."

"There's no need to," he said. He kept staring at my face. "Can you stay in the game?"

I nodded. He patted my shoulder and sent me to right field.

"It's all right, Hough," he said as I left the mound.

Right field is a strange place to send someone with a broken-down arm. From right field you make the throw all the way across to third, corner to corner. But right field is where I went. It was shaded out there by the tall trees. A lawnmower droned up the hill where the brick school building stood, and I could smell the cut grass. The sweat dried on my face. I felt far away from everybody, detached, as if the game no longer concerned me. I felt forgotten. I stood in the shade watching the distant-seeming game and filling up with the sadness of knowing that God didn't want me to be a big-league baseball player.

I wasn't surprised to see Mr. Kalperis at my mother's funeral, although I didn't know of any connection between them except through her kids. He must have taught us all science as we came through ninth grade. I'm not sure Mr. Kalperis ever met my mother, but here he was.

He'd given up coaching baseball years ago in favor of coaching track and cross-country, which turned out to be his natural calling. His runners won state championships. They put our high school on the map. For some reason a lot of our high-school runners were from poor families. A lot of them had been in trouble in school and even with the cops. Mr. Kalperis had a way with these kids. They loved him and ran their hearts out for him. I remember my mother talking about this, saying he gave these kids value in their own eyes and in the eyes of others that they might never have had.

It was a dark afternoon, very cold. Scarves of old snow draped the churchyard. Gray ice stuck to the walks. The church was full. I remember the light dying against the stained-glass windows above the altar; tall, beautiful windows that have always depressed me. After the service everyone walked across the churchyard to the stone parish hall for a reception, if that is the word. The hall was brightly lit and soon noisy, as if people had checked their grief at the door. It was here that I discovered Mr. Kalperis.

I hadn't seen him in ten, maybe fifteen years. His black hair had gone gray, and his face was thinner. He still had the fine teeth, and when he smiled he reminded me of a benign, gentle wolf in a children's story. They'd just named a fancy new outdoor track at the high school after him.

He shook my hand, and I introduced him to my wife.

"Mr. Kalperis was my junior-high baseball coach," I said.

"You bet I was," he said.

"I was his ace pitcher," I joked.

"That's right," he said.

"I wasn't really," I said. "I had the sore arm. Remember?"

"Oh, but you pitched some great games for me," he said. He really thought I had.

"Just one," I told him, but I was glad he remembered it that way.

On the night of July 1 the Sox complete a three-game sweep of the inept Orioles, and Todd Benzinger hits his first major-league home run. Buckner, back from the disabled list,

hits two singles. Gedman gets a rare base hit. Clemens domi-
nates the Orioles, but in a puzzling, uncharacteristic way: he
doesn't strike out a single hitter.

The Orioles' first pitcher is another drifter by the name of
Mike Griffin. A week ago Griffin was pitching triple-A ball in
Rochester, New York. Tonight's sheet from the Orioles' PR
people describes Griffin as "a well-traveled 30-year-old right-
hander with a year and a half in the major leagues behind him,"
but neglects to point out that he has been accumulating that
year and a half in bits and pieces since 1979. Griffin gets them
in the first and squeezes out of trouble—singles by Buckner
and Owen—in the second. His luck runs out in the third. Benzinger knocks one high off the wall, an easy double. Baylor
drills the wall a few feet from the top, the ball popping back
so fast that Baylor has to stop at first. Evans ends the inning
with a fly ball.

An inning later Benzinger gets his home run. He is batting
left-handed. Griffin pitched him outside when Todd hit his
double. Griffin sensibly tries the other edge of the plate, and
Todd gets around on the ball and lifts it into the bleachers
above the Sox' bull pen. The crowd knows it's his first in the
big leagues and lets go a tremendous cheer as the ball clears
the bull pen. Benzinger lowers his head and runs the bases
through a steady, loving ovation. He accepts Morgan's handshake and a high five from Boggs, then descends the dugout
steps to a welcoming committee of his teammates. The crowd
cheers on, calling him back. Todd doesn't keep them waiting,
but bobs up out of the dugout promptly. He waves. Playing in
the big leagues is fun.

Meanwhile, Clemens is pitching a masterpiece, but without his most trusty weapon, the strikeout. Roger hasn't pitched
well lately. He hit bottom last week in Yankee Stadium. Baseball people are still buzzing about what happened. The Sox
led, 9–0, going into the bottom of the third. A nine-run lead,

with the best pitcher in baseball on the mound, and in a single inning the Yanks tied the score. They bombed Clemens, they hit everything he threw. He was gone before he could get the second out. The Yanks went on to win the game big. This would have been embarrassing enough against any team in any ballpark; against the Yankees in the presence of their merciless fans, it constituted the humiliation of Roger's career. It also killed what was left of his candidacy for the All-Star team, and this is going to cost him a lot of money. One of the terms of his contract settlement was an incentive of $300,000 for making the All-Star team. This looked like guaranteed money back in April. I would have said Roger would have to break a leg not to make the team. McNamara, having won the pennant last year, is manager of the All-Star team and will decide whether Clemens makes it or not. Already McNamara has been grousing about this responsibility. He has even suggested that the League ought to relieve him of the decision of Clemens.

A couple of nights ago Clemens ran into his friend Peter Gammons in the dugout. Gammons, who for years covered the Sox for the *Globe* and now writes for *Sports Illustrated*, collaborated with Clemens last year on Roger's autobiography, *The Rocket Man*.

"That'll teach you to have one bad game," Gammons kidded Clemens, referring to the disaster in Yankee Stadium and talk that Roger won't be an All-Star.

"They were glad," Clemens said, meaning his employers. "They were glad that happened to me."

Tonight, against the Orioles, Roger looks as if he has one thought: to regain his honor. You can see it in the way he moves: rapid and emphatic. After each good inning he comes down off the mound with a proud shrug of his big shoulders. His lion's heart is aroused. He gets the first ten hitters, walks a man, and mows down three more. He gives up a single and a double in the fifth, but not a run. For eight innings he shuts them out.

And yet without a strikeout. What gives? I look at my scorecard: through eight, half the outs are fly balls, half are hit on the ground. You couldn't ask for better pitching, yet Roger's game has a funny odor to it. In the press box, heads shake. "Weird," someone says.

Weird, yeah.

Lee Lacy sticks a base hit into center field to begin the Orioles' ninth. With one out, Eddie Murray gets a base on balls. Freddie Lynn lifts an easy fly ball to Burks: two out. The hitter is Ray Knight, Most Valuable Player of the '86 Series. Ray Knight, who hit a two-strike single against us in that nightmare tenth inning of the sixth game and who, in game seven, blasted a home run off Schiraldi, shattering our hopes—the first nail in our coffin. Incredibly, the Mets refused to give Knight the money he was asking, and so he came to Baltimore and is stuck with these bums. Last night Schiraldi struck him out. You couldn't have put a price on that strikeout last October. Now Knight singles to center, and the bases are loaded.

The Sox are leading, 6–0. They aren't going to lose. The only question is Roger's shutout. He flings himself off the mound and snatches up the rosin bag. He pounds his ball into his glove. The batter is Terry Kennedy, their catcher. Not a bad hitter. Roger throws a strike and a ball, and Kennedy, batting left, pulls a nice line drive down the right-field line, a clean single bringing home two runs. The crowd emits a low, disappointed sound. A few boos come ribboning down. For Kennedy, maybe. Or for the situation in general. Roger throws two strikes past Larry Sheets, but Sheets makes contact, knocks a fly ball to Burks. It's over.

Right away Bresciani lets us know on the press box loudspeaker that Clemens has come away from a game without a strikeout only twice in his big-league career. Both outings were brief: a two-inning relief job in '84, and an inning and a third last year, when he was forced out of a game when a line drive caught him on his throwing arm. But nine innings without a strikeout?

The writers go funneling out through the two press box doors, clutching their notebooks and scorecards against them and shoving pens and pencils into hip pockets. We join the crowds streaming down from the skyview boxes, and fight our way through the concourse to the clubhouse.

McNamara sips his Bud Light and tells us in his slow, pained-seeming way that the Red Sox now are playing as well as any team could. He has no idea why Clemens struck no one out and is unconcerned by it.

We spill out into the clubhouse and find Evans, who has stripped to his electric-blue Gore-tex tights. Dewey is having a great year and tonight is in a bubbly mood.

"We got our confidence now," he says. "You can feel it." He speaks rapidly, which is unusual for him. "If we can close to six, six and a half games out by the All-Star break, we'll be fine."

The reporters scatter, hunting Clemens. No strikeouts: what will he say? He absents himself; we wait. But here comes Benzinger from his shower, a towel tied around his flat belly. The kid is smiling. He has a high forehead—in a movie you might cast him as a boy computer genius, the forehead walling a big brain. His smile opens down as well as across, toothy. No Clemens, so the reporters converge on Benzinger, who is open to any question any time. While the feline Burks is aloof but courteous, Benzinger smiles, trades pleasantries, chats. Greenwell is somewhere in between, reserved but obliging. The triumvirate, dream outfield of the future: Greenwell, Burks, and Benzinger.

The TV lights hit Benzinger in the face. The home run? "It was an inside fastball," he says, confirming my observation. "They'd been pitching me away. I wasn't thinking about anything, going around the bases. I was walkin' on air."

He shakes his head and grins.

"After the home run, when I went out to center field they cheered me. Then, when I was moved over to left"—a late-inning shuffle to strengthen the defense—"I got more cheers." Big smile. "I wished I could go over to right, get some *more* cheers."

The reporters chuckle.

"You know," he says, "just about every day something new happens. I keep thinkin', What else can happen? And something does."

The TV people have enough. The lights die, the out-stretched arms shoving microphones withdraw. A few last questions, and the pack dissolves. Where is Clemens? Some of the deadline writers leave, some wait. The TV guys wait. Everyone hovers idly, ignored by the ballplayers.

Here he comes, finally. He is wearing shorts and a gray Puma T-shirt, very tight on his hunky shoulders. His hair is wet. The reporters home in. Clemens looks at no one, just barges past as if he were alone in the room. His face is set hard. He goes to his cubicle and begins digging around on the top shelf, hunting for something.

"Roger . . ."

"Roger, any particular reason for the zero strikeouts?"

Clemens, still digging, tells us over his shoulder, "I don't have any comments tonight."

The reporters look at each other and shrug. Nipper strolls up, wearing shorts and a polo shirt. The reporters are still thronging around Clemens, and Nip can't get through to his stall. Nip doesn't say anything, just sticks his hands in his pockets and waits.

A couple of stalls down, Crawford is stepping into his trousers. He sees Nipper waiting and sends a glare our way. Big, slow body, a big twangy voice.

"Tell 'em," he booms down to Nipper, "to get the fuck out of your way. It's your fuckin' locker, Nip."

Nipper tosses off a shrug, hands still in his pockets: It's

okay, Shag. Clemens finds what he is after, a letter, and turns abruptly back into the hovering reporters: make way. He heads for the trainer's room, looking at no one.

"Roger, just a couple of ques—"

"I'm not commenting," says the world's best pitcher, and is gone.

Someone says, "He *did* win the game, didn't he?"

Half an hour after a game ends, the husky bouncer is still sitting by the door in the little hallway outside the clubhouse. I say good night; he nods and yanks the door open. Now the big concourse is empty. The tide has swept out, scattering hot dog wrappers, squashed paper cups, and a million tatters of peanut shell. The cement floor and painted brick walls breathe their stored-up smells of cigar smoke and beer. Somewhere a slatted metal door slams, sending echoes shuddering up and down the concourse.

The narrow streets outside the ballpark are still wide awake. Vendors' radios spew FM rock. Frying sausages make the warm air sweet and sticky. People gather round the vendors' push-carts; they eat, swig beer, get loud. Outside the press gate the visiting team's bus waits at the curb. A gaggle of teenage girls keeps watch by the bus door, chewing gum and smoking cigarettes. What are they hoping for? Autographs? What? At the entrance to the Red Sox parking lot on Van Ness Street a larger assemblage has convened—college boys, fathers and sons, more teenage girls. They are all oddly quiet as they wait for the ballplayers to wander out and get in their cars, then come gliding out onto Van Ness. A cop keeps an eye on things, but these are orderly people.

There are still some cars parked along Van Ness on the other side of Yawkey Way. The big parking lot with the wire fence around it hasn't emptied, either. The traffic is packed solid in both directions on Boylston Street, and a lot of people prefer to wait till the logjam breaks up before heading home. A car radio plays softly in the dark on Van Ness. Men cluster around, talking loudly. Farther down, kids huddle by an open car trunk, digging into a case of beer.

My pied-à-terre is the Howard Johnson's around the corner on Boylston, but after the last game of each trip I drive all the way to Cape Cod—by choice, not necessity. I like the solitude of the road at this hour. I like coming in while the town is sleeping.

Out beyond the city the air changes. It becomes cooler, and sweet with pine and bayberry. I spin the dial of the radio, chasing good songs. Old songs, if I can find them. Late at night you can get stations from all over. Detroit, Richmond, Philadelphia, Baltimore. I was told once why this is, but I've forgotten. A good song on the radio at one in the morning along an empty highway sounds better than at any other time. Especially an old song. It sounds truer, wiser, more lovely. I drive the empty highway, chasing my songs across the dial, with the piney air blowing in, and I feel suspended in the darkness along an arc that joins Fenway Park with the house I grew up in. I'll stay there tonight and take the boat to the island in the morning.

The highway, Route 3, didn't exist when I was a little kid. By the time they put in the highway, my parents and I weren't going to ball games anymore. My sisters and brother were growing up, and I suppose it was no longer fair or even possible to single me out for a rare daylong outing.

I made a couple of trips to Fenway alone with my father. We went on Friday nights, after he'd put out the paper. He'd still be wearing his white shirt, his loosened necktie. There were grease-slashes on all his shirts where he'd brushed up against the printing press. My father would be tired on a Friday night in the summertime, but as soon as we were out on the highway he relaxed, turned jovial. We were a big family and he was a hardworking man, but now, for once, I had his full attention.

One time, he stopped the car at the beginning of the highway and asked me to drive. I'd never driven in the city. We changed places, and my father turned, reached down, and pulled up a brown paper bag full of bottles of beer. He placed the bag on the floor by his feet and took out a bottle. While I drove he drank, looking around before each swig to be sure people in other cars didn't see him. It was a golden summer's evening. I knew that what my father was doing was illegal, but that wasn't why I admired it. No, I liked this because it gave our trip a sort of truant quality. The two of us were skipping out on everything, going to the ball game.

I drove us into Boston, following my father's directions. He didn't worry, didn't criticize, just let me drive. We parked for a buck at a gas station on Boylston Street. It was a hot, hot night, and Fenway Park was jammed. We had terrific seats, under the grandstand roof behind the Red Sox dugout.

The town, even though it has grown so tremendously since I was a kid, is asleep when I drive in. The bars, jammed on summer nights, are closed. You come into town on what was pretty much a country road back then, the houses built close to the road with mailboxes out front. There were a couple of gas stations and a general store with gas pumps. Since then all the empty spaces, fields and wooded lots, have been built on. There's a bank, an Italian restaurant, another gas station. A road leads off to the skating rink, which was built when I was small. Now you pass old houses, rambling things with gabled roofs. They aren't lived in anymore; one is an antique shop, one a law office, one the Elks Lodge.

The lights have been doused at the Gulf station on the intersection. I'm almost home. I whip through the intersection onto a narrower street with more old houses, sea captain's houses with widow's walks. I cross the bike path—railroad tracks when I was a kid—and veer onto the winding road I grew up on. The ancient elms still grow up out of the sidewalk, muscling through the asphalt, warping it. Their branches arch in the distance overhead.

My father leaves the outside light on for me. It throws its pale nimbus out into the yard, where I once played baseball. I was once that small. I remember slugging the ball over the row of pine trees into the thickets and shag beyond the stone wall, a home run. Then we'd all have to go look for the ball. The house seems taller at night than by day. Moonlight runs down the steep sides of its shingled roof.

The dogs stir but don't bark when I walk in. Dogs always know family. The smell of this kitchen is as old as anything I know, a mellow fragrance of coffee and overripe fruit. My father has also left the light on in the kitchen. He has left a note on the table. *Try the stuffed tomatoes. They're good!* Or, *Cold cuts and cheese in the fridge.* There is a note and food every time. My mother's old province, his now. Whatever he leaves for me, I eat. The electric clock hums noisily. I am surrounded by empty rooms.

My sisters and brother and I used to eat supper in this kitchen every Friday night, on our own while our parents had drinks with my father's parents. I was the cook: canned stew or frozen chicken pies. I presided, made the rules, invented the games.

"This is venison stew we're eating."

"It is?"

"We're pioneers eating venison stew, and this is our stockade."

The three girls would nod and become very serious. The games had to be designed around my baby brother.

"This," I said, "is the papoose we captured from the Indians."

The girls got right into the spirit of things.

"Eat, papoose."

"If he cries, let's scalp him."

I had dozens of games. Hundreds.

I get up, put my plate in the sink. I open another beer. Snap off the light. The dining room smells of the dogs. The two of them sleep here on cushions soaked with their odor, the good muddy smell of dog. A laundry basket crowns the dining table. In the moonlight I can see folded sheets, pillowcases, balled socks, T-shirts.

The staircase, walled on both sides, is narrow and steep. The steps creak underfoot. At the end of the upstairs hall my father's bedroom door is open, and I can hear him snoring. He has left the hall light on. His snoring is robust, rhythmic. Strong.

This upstairs hallway is hung with framed photographs, family pictures going as far back as my grandmother Kurtz's wedding. The pictures cover one wall, hung randomly, crowding each other. There's a picture of my Little League team, the Hornets, the year I was ten, my rookie season. We won the town championship that summer, which I suppose is why the picture was taken. I'm in the front row, down on one knee, freckled and bucktoothed. Legs and arms like twigs, but I was wiry. At least one of these boys is dead, killed in Vietnam.

Over here is my father in a football uniform minus the helmet, posing in the three-point stance and smiling handsomely. Haverford College, 1942. He has wavy black hair, thick eyebrows, a fine straight nose. He and my mother were a stunning couple. At prep school my father was captain of his football and basketball teams, but he never played baseball. He followed the game, though. He remembers Williams, Pesky, Doerr. He remembers Joe DiMaggio.

And here is my mother carrying a sign on a long stick, STOP THE WAR NOW. She's wearing an Australian bush hat and beaming at the photographer, who seems to have caught her in the midst of a delightful adventure. Someone in town had decided to organize a march against the Vietnam War. The marchers gathered at the village green and paraded up Main Street; mothers and children, a sprinkling of men. It was a winter morning. Quiet. The brim of my mother's hat is pinned up on one side. She's enjoying herself thoroughly.

I always pause in the hall, snagged by one picture or another. My father snores on. I turn off the light and bring my beer to bed. The bedroom was mine for many years, till the girls got older and needed more space. Then I was moved downstairs. I hung baseball pictures all over these walls. I cut the pictures out of magazines and put them in cheap frames from the five-and-ten. The walls were riddled with my nail holes. Baseball, baseball, baseball. How did my parents put up with it? The games on the radio, the nail holes in the wall? Outside the bedroom window a porch roof slopes down; I used to spend hours bouncing a rubber ball off it, splitting shingles, shaking nails loose. I would throw the ball onto the roof of the house, and it would roll back, drop to the porch roof, and leap up unpredictably, almost as good as a fly ball. You could see what it was doing to the roof, but my parents never put a stop to this game of mine.

The bedroom has a shallow fireplace and smells of mildew. I drink my beer in the dark, propped up in bed. Often I won't sleep well. The beer helps sometimes, sometimes not. I've been an insomniac since my early twenties. When you get older you stop fighting insomnia, you stop raging against it. You let it have its way.

There was a kid who lived in our neighborhood whom we called Spike. Spike was huge, tall and blubbery, but he was a pretty good ballplayer. He couldn't run, but he could pound the ball a country mile. Spike liked to break things. He broke windows of empty houses, and I once saw him take a baseball bat to a rain pipe, blasting it off the side of the house with one mighty swing. Adults understandably disliked Spike, but to his peers he had a certain appeal. He had the courage of his convictions, such as they were. He was his own boss. In Little League he played for the Woods Hole Red Sox, and one night in their ballpark Spike put on one of the most magnificent displays of aplomb in league history. He was playing right field, and in the middle of the game he called time and went into the woods to take a leak. He yelled, got the ump's attention: time-out. The batter stepped out of the box. The pitcher held the ball. Spike laid his glove on the ground and shambled off into the woods as coolly as a big-leaguer visiting the dugout for a pair of sunglasses. It took everyone a moment to understand what was happening, and then a laugh went up on both benches and on the hillside under the old elms. There was a lengthy wait. Then out came Spike, not in the least embarrassed, moving in a swaying, fat kid's gait. He picked up his glove and nodded to the umpire: play ball. I mentioned it to him afterward, but Spike couldn't understand what was so funny. If you got to go, you got to go, he said.

Sometimes I lie awake in this old bedroom of mine till I hear a car go by, and then I know it's getting on toward morning.

Seven

Reggie and Robin and Me

THEY USED TO SAY THAT THE TEAM THAT HELD FIRST PLACE on the Fourth of July was going to win the pennant. I was a kid, but I could see that this axiom was an equal blend of logic and superstition. Obviously, if you're in the lead halfway through, you've got something. On the other hand, if you lead by half a game, a single loss can drop you to second place. Here's where romance entered the equation: whoever led the league on the Fourth of July was charmed. My father told me this way back, smiling in a way that meant there was more to it than met the eye. I liked it: the Fourth was summer at its most magical, a day of lasting light and infinite laziness. In those days the teams all played doubleheaders on the Fourth of July.

I haven't heard the old Fourth of July saying in years, probably because the season has been stretched, and the halfway point comes a good week later. In mid-July play is interrupted for the All-Star game. "The break," as it's called. There

147

are no axioms, no superstitions regarding standings, but certain facts speak loud and clear. The Sox, after that invigorating home series against the Orioles, have been traveling the West Coast, where they won three and lost eight. They cannot catch fire, cannot find that streak they've been chasing. Evans, pumped up and talkative after the third trouncing of the Orioles, predicted that the Sox would climb to within six games from the top by the All-Star break. But the distance has swollen to more than twice that: thirteen and a half games. The Sox have won forty-one, lost forty-seven. They are in fifth place, two and a half games in back of Milwaukee.

The second half of the season opens on July 16, a day that seems borrowed from September. The air has the cool taste of autumn, and an icewater clarity that distorts, shrinks distances. As a kid I hated these aberrant July days. They felt like school.

A little before six Boggs is sitting at the table in the clubhouse, signing baseballs. A whole box of them, each in its snug compartment, packed like eggs. Wade plucks one out, signs carefully, sticks it back in its place. He is leading the league in hitting by a mile at .375, but looks somber, quieted perhaps by the autumnal weather, perhaps by that thirteen-and-a-half-game gap. Except for Boggs and the writers clustered by McNamara's shut door, the clubhouse is empty. Wade signs and signs again, oblivious to the reporters, remote. It is as if he knows something that no one else can and it sets him apart, even from his teammates. He doesn't flaunt his isolation and doesn't rebel against it. He accepts it, it's a fact of his life.

The door swings open and McNamara strides out in his uniform. He strolls past us, eyes front. He doesn't look at us, doesn't nod. No one seems surprised. The reporters continue to stand around until the door bumps shut behind McNamara, and then, wordlessly, the whole pack takes off in pursuit. Out into the little hallway, down the half flight of steps to the tunnel. McNamara now is about halfway up the tunnel. He can hear the clank and thud of our footsteps, but he doesn't turn or break stride, just walks on to the patch of blond fall light and vanishes.

He is sitting on the bench when we get there, waiting for us. I'm reminded of a scene from a movie, but can't place it. A comedy, certainly. The reporters gather in a semicircle around McNamara, who sits with his back pressed to the wall, his cap pulled low.

"What can I do for you, gentlemen?" he says softly.

"What's the news on Crawford?" someone says.

These sessions almost always begin with a medical question. McNamara doesn't mind medical questions, and it's a way to get him talking, to get the conversation off the ground without ticking him off.

"Crawford's on the DL," McNamara says graciously. "He said he felt something like fire in his elbow when he threw in Seattle. He threw a slider, I think it was."

Everyone scribbles. Some hold their thin notebooks in the cup of their palm; others bend down with their notebooks laid against their thighs.

"What's the word on Stanley?" someone asks.

"Stanley's throwing normal. He's fine."

Everyone takes it down, and after this cordial beginning silence shoulders up between the manager and his audience. This doesn't bother McNamara. He squints past us to the field, to his players, who are hitting and fielding and sprinting up and down the outfield.

The silence lengthens.

Then. "What will it take," someone says carefully, "to get back into it?"

McNamara brings up a sigh. He is still watching the field. "Our pitching has to get more consistent," he says. "You people have been around me long enough to know I believe that pitching is the name of the game." Now he surveys the faces surrounding him, looking at us curiously and without affection. "We want to get up there," he says. "We want to get competitive."

"Can you?" someone dares, softly.

McNamara thinks a moment, as if baffled by such a question. He answers simply, and with some feeling: "Hell, yes, we're capable of gettin' back into this thing. We're not throwin' in the towel." He leans out, spits—watch your feet—and flattens back against the wall.

"You know," he says, "it killed us, what happened with Clemens and Gedman." Clemens and Gedman, Clemens and Gedman. The holdouts. Clemens missed exactly one start. Gedman joined the team on May 1. Clemens has had a lousy first half—for him—and Gedman keeps getting hurt. (He is hurt now.) Are their late arrivals to blame? Clemens denies that his is. Pesky says that injuries are part of the game. Everyone seems to have forgotten that Hurst was out of action, injured, for over a month last year. The team kept winning. Nipper's knee was slashed open in a collision at the plate; Nip was lost for six weeks, and the team kept winning. Oil Can went AWOL for two weeks; the team kept winning. Injuries are part of the game.

Someone asks McNamara about the kids, especially Benzinger and Greenwell. Will they play more in the second half?

"I'm gonna put my best men on the field," he says.

"You wouldn't want to start playing them prematurely," someone says.

McNamara squints at him. "What do you mean?"

"You'd want to wait till you're out of the race."

McNamara sends him a steely smile. "You're talkin' a language I don't understand. I don't *expect* to be out of it."

Tonight Clemens pitches, and 34,861 customers jam Fenway. The enormous crowds in this losing season don't seem to surprise anyone. I haven't heard anyone in the press box comment on them. There are plenty of reasons to come to Fenway this summer. There are the blossoming kids. There's Clemens. There's Boggs, swinging his way to another batting title. There's always the ballpark itself.

Tonight, there's Reggie Jackson. This is the last visit of the season by the Oakland A's, and Reggie's Fenway swan song. Yes, the big guy, Mr. October, is finally retiring. When Reggie bats in the top of the first—there are two out and two men on base—he receives a long, affectionate ovation. Reggie, who these days wears a fuzzy beard over his round jaw, touches the visor of his helmet in acknowledgment. Reggie's beard has come and gone over the years. The beard refines and dignifies him. It gives him a look of royalty. I check the A's roster and note that Reggie and I were born the same year, 1946.

Reggie was wearing the beard in 1973, when his A's beat the Mets in the Series. Reggie hit some monstrous home runs and played well in right field. He was Series MVP. I was in Washington, D.C., watching on television the night Reggie blasted three home runs on three straight pitches in the sixth and final game of the '77 Series. It was Reggie's first year with the Yankees. I was with friends in a little house without much furniture and no rugs, and I remember how the noise of the TV ran along the hardwood floors and was thrown back by the bare walls. Three pitches, three enormous home runs: we'd seen the impossible. I was again far from home in '78, when the Sox and Yanks finished the season in a tie and the next day played a single game in Fenway for the division championship. Reggie helped break my heart with a long home run into the center-field bleachers.

Now, Clemens strikes him out with a fastball that climbs out of the strike zone. Reggie hacks at it, changes his mind in midswing. The umpires call the half-swing a strike. Reggie accepts their judgment and stalks back to the dugout as I have seen him do it hundreds of times, striding rapidly, with a bounce, shoulders thrown back. He carries his bat in his fist like a yardstick. Reggie the Terrible, scourge of the American League. It's all over now, and as Reggie, the DH tonight, stalks back to the dugout, the crowd gives its old enemy a second fond ovation. Reggie looks up and around, and nods.

The A's are a couple of games out of first place in the Western Division and have the idea they can win it this year. Their most spectacular possession at the moment is the towering freckled rookie, Mark McGwire, who has hit thirty-three home runs. At this rate McGwire will break Roger Maris's single-season home run record. The A's have a posse of long ball hitters—McGwire, Reggie, Jose Canseco, Carney Lansford—kegs of gunpowder that can ignite at any time.

The Oakland pitcher is their ace, Dave Stewart, a leggy giant who seems to step a third of the way home as he throws. In the bottom of the first, Burks dribbles one to the shortstop and beats the throw, which bounces wild. Ellis scoots down to second. Stewart gets Barrett. He throws two strikes past Boggs, who then drives one over the center fielder's head, the ball sailing as if weightless, a glider catching a breeze, riding up over it. A long double for Wade, and a run for the Sox.

The A's score once in the second—Clemens isn't putting his fastball quite where he wants to—and the Sox get another in the bottom of the inning. Evans smashes one, low, down the left-field line, just fair, a rocket double. "*Dooooh* . . ." groans the crowd. Dewey takes third on a ground ball by Buckner and trots gracefully home on a fly ball by Owen.

The game flows quickly for a while, ruled by the pitchers. The A's get a run in the fifth on two doubles, but Roger promptly stamps out the fire. Reggie rolls one into right field, base hit, in the fourth. Nice round of applause. Clemens gets him on a weak fly ball in the sixth. At the end of six the score is tied, 2–2.

Their catcher, Mickey Tettleton, leads off in the seventh.

Roger walks him. The brilliant shortstop, Alfredo Griffin, punches a fastball with the bat handle, the bat splintering, the ball floating past Barrett and dying on the grass in very short right—a lousy little single on a fastball that had him stymied. Tettleton goes to third. Their center fielder, Luis Polonia, cracks Roger's first pitch on the ground at Owen, who muffs it. The ball ricochets from Spike's glove to his shoulder and off into the outfield. Tettleton scores: Griffin takes third.

Runners at the corners, none out; Polonia, of course, is going to try to steal second. Clemens smells it and picks him off. Polonia is running, thinking in his eagerness that Roger is throwing to the plate, and now is caught halfway between bases. He keeps running, and Buckner bounces his throw past Owen into left field. Home comes Griffin, to third goes Polonia. Things suddenly are flying apart. Roger gets the next hitter, but Canseco rams a hit into center field and Polonia scampers home. The A's lead by three, and you can't help thinking that the Sox aren't going to get those runs back. Not tonight. Not this year.

The crowd knows it, and when Tettleton hits one into the bleachers next inning, the mood swings way around, a wind blowing the other way, bringing bad weather. They begin booing in a random, capricious sort of way. They holler at players, including their own, mocking them by their first names. The bleacher crowd takes up the moronic diversion that has become custom out there, mimicking the television commercial for Lite beer, chant and counterchant. "Tastes great!" "Less filling!" "Tastes great!" "Less filling!" The mock argument goes mindlessly on, the two sides trying to shout each other down. Are they bored? Or is this a message to the home team, like yawning conspicuously at a poetry reading? Stanley comes in to pitch the ninth; there are scattered boos and no discernible applause. Steamer gives up a hit, then disposes of the next three hitters, including Reggie. The final score is 6–3.

Afterward, McNamara seems more deflated than testy. As

usual after a loss, the reporters put on mournful faces. This counterfeit gloom eases the flow of conversation but doesn't fool McNamara. What McNamara seems unable to understand is that the reporters, even the most cynical and acerbic, are pulling for his team. No one here wants to see the Sox lose. If that was understood, the reporters could be themselves.

The manager hauls up a sigh and summarizes:

"Roger threw all right. We had some golden opportunities that didn't materialize." He is unbuttoning his shirt. "We created our own problems."

There is, he notices, a stack of mail on his desk. He drops forward in the springy swivel chair and picks up the mail. He flips through the envelopes, pauses, looks up.

"Anything else?"

There isn't. We file out into the silent clubhouse. Gedman, on the DL again, sits facing his stall, hunched over a letter. Clemens is nowhere to be seen, nor is Boggs. The reporters descend upon little Spike, who is always good for a pleasant word or two. Spike, asked about his very expensive error in the seventh, is forthright and courteous.

"It was a tailor-made double-play ball," Spike admits. "The ball came up on me. I was down, and the ball came up. You know, it's sandy out there on that infield. I don't know why, but it is. It's like a *beach*."

Clemens comes out of the shower, swaggering just a little. Always. The reporters swarm around him. The hot lights flash on. "I threw the ball decent," Roger begins, conversationally. Tonight he is cooperative. Gracious.

Rice is in the cage, taking extra batting practice. For almost a month the days have been shortening, and tonight for the first time I notice that the shadow of the third-base grandstand has gained ground, has already slid beyond the cage, pushing the sunlight toward right field. The evening is clear and cool. I watch Rice: that short swing, restrained but vicious. A snake striking. He's having an awful year, seven home runs and thirty-nine RBIs at midseason. Somewhere along the line he hurt his knee, a quiet, nagging injury that allows him to play, but not terribly well. No one seems to know, exactly, what's wrong with him. Rice won't talk about it to writers.

He is a few feet away from me. I have seen the compact swing a thousand times. I know the handsome, shut face. He won't look at me, won't say hello, carries an indifference to me and my business that is so colossal, so absolute, that the sheer weight of it seems aggressive. Still, I admire the man. I would tell him, if I thought he'd care. I told Buckner. I said it simply, "I'm an admirer of yours," trying to sound dignified. Buckner didn't answer. He looked at me curiously, as if he wondered what I meant by it.

I watch Rice. It is one of those sweet moments. I love being here. I love watching Jim Rice hit from a few feet away. I lean closer. Rice flicks his wrists and bangs one on a rising line to center field. The ball gains altitude, slams into the empty bleachers. Rice watches it, then strolls out of the cage, one of the game's great sluggers.

I go looking for Pesky, who is a big admirer of Rice. An epigram from Pesky will cap this poetic moment. The dugout is empty. I walk down the tunnel, enjoying the clank of my own footsteps. I go into the clubhouse.

It is quiet and nearly deserted. Frank Malzone is sitting at the table, shooting the breeze with Buckner and Stanley and enjoying a big cigar. The equipment manager, Vince Orlando—a large gray crag of a man—is puttering. Orlando stops what he's doing. He is standing with an armful of towels, staring in my direction.

"Hey," he says. *"You."* The voice is a growl, hard and husky. It has gotten that way, I imagine, yelling orders through the blare of radios and clubhouse babble.

Malzone, Buckner, and Stanley all stop talking. They look over.

"You." Orlando is pointing at me.

Not at me. Impossible. I turn around. There's no one else in the room.

"Yeah, it's you I'm talkin' to," growls Vince Orlando. Gray hair drips down both his temples.

"Me?" I say.

Malzone, Buckner, and Stanley are all staring at me. Stanley is grinning. So is Malzone. Buckner just stares.

Stanley says, "You got grease on your face."

Grease? To be spoken to here is disorienting. I don't know what to make of it, don't know what to do. Nipper appears. He stops and stares at me. He wrinkles up his face, amazed, then smiles.

"You got grease on your face," he says.

"Grease?" I say. I touch my face.

"You won't get it off that way," says Buckner.

It hits me that this is a prank, a setup for something. You hear stories about clubhouse pranks. People being thrown in showers with their clothes on, or getting smeared with mustard. I rub my cheek, inspect my hand. Nothing. They all stare at me. Malzone grins. I want to turn tail and run.

"What've you been doin'?" Stanley says.

"Nothing. I . . ."

Buckner gets up from the table. He comes over, gaze riveted to my face.

"Jesus," he says. "You look like a fuckin' monkey, man."

"Maybe your pen's leaking," says Nipper.

"What does he write with, fuckin' bear grease?" says Buckner.

Stanley gets up. He comes over and stands with Buckner.

"Jesus," Stanley says.

"I don't know," Buckner says, and ambles away.

I glimpse Malzone, one of my boyhood heroes, grinning up from the table. Nipper comes closer, fascinated.

"It must be your pen," he says. I'm surprised how small Nip is. "Come into the bathroom," he says.

The bathroom? My mind races. In the bathroom I'll be jumped by Steve Crawford, who hates writers, and by Clemens himself, who surely isn't above a little rough pranking. They'll throw me in the shower. They'll steal my pants.

Nipper sees me hesitate and smiles. A friendliness in Nipper's Incan face, thin dark eyes over high bones, half convinces me.

"Come on," he says. "It's okay."

"Come on," Stanley says, big-voiced.

I don't know what else to do, so I follow them. I follow Al Nipper and Bob Stanley into the Red Sox bathroom, which is off-limits to writers. It is a long, glistening room with sinks and mirrors along one wall. It is empty. Silent. A final wild thought occurs: players hiding in ambush in the toilet stalls.

"Look at your face," Nipper tells me.

I stare in a mirror and almost stagger backward at the sight of myself. I have grease on my face, all right. Black, inky, smeared over my forehead and painting the right side of my jaw.

"Jesus," I say.

Stanley laughs good-naturedly.

"Check your pen," says Nipper, who seems determined to get to the bottom of this.

"My pen's blue," I say.

Nip lifts my arm, as if he thought I might be packing a shoulder holster. He's gentle about it, just trying to solve the mystery.

"The batting cage," I say. "I was leaning up against the batting cage."

Stanley laughs again and wanders out.

"I'll get you a towel," Nipper says, and vanishes.

I stare at myself. Christ, is this embarrassing. This would never happen to the beat writers. It wouldn't happen in a million years to Roger Angell. Just to me.

Nipper comes back with two white towels. One is soaked with hot water. "Here," he says.

I give him a grateful, defeated look and accept the towels.

"Take your time," he says. "Don't worry about anything."

He pats my shoulder, is gone. The wet towel scrapes my face clean. Stanley comes in, still with that amused smile.

"You get that grease off yet?" he says.

"I think it's from the batting cage," I say.

"Yeah?"

He wanders out again. I dry myself. The towels are fluffy, the kind you get in fancy hotels. I don't want to come out of here, don't want to see anyone. It would be a comfort, at least, to know what happened. I think back. The batting cage, watching Rice. The netting, thick rope, is black. Of course. They grease it to keep it from drying out. I leave the towels in the sink and pick up my notebook. The clubhouse is empty. Malzone is gone, leaving the acrid perfume of his cigar. I don't see Vince Orlando, but he must be around somewhere. The players have gone out to the field. This quiet makes me realize how lucky I've been. The clubhouse might have been full when I walked in with my face greased up. Laughter spreading like wildfire on all sides of me. Nipper might not have been here, or Stanley. It might have been Steve Crawford sitting at the table when I came in.

In the dugout I sit down with Pesky and Morgan. Morgan relaxes with his legs crossed. Pesky sits with both hands resting on the knob of his fungo.

"What's the matter?" he says to me.

"Nothing," I say.

"You look dejected."

"No," I say.

"You like that word, 'dejected'?" Pesky says.

"He loves it," Morgan says.

"I ain't as dumb as I look," Pesky says.

"You don't look dumb," I say.

Morgan says, "Who holds the record for goin' the most games without hittin' into a double play?"

Pesky thinks a moment, frowning. "Augie Galan?"

"Augie Galan," says Morgan, "is kee-rect. A hundred and sixty-two fuckin' games—is that unbelievable?"

"He must have hit a lot of fly balls," Pesky says.

"Must have," Morgan agrees.

"I mean, shit," Pesky says, "sooner or later you got to hit a ground ball at *somebody*."

"You'd think so," Morgan agrees.

Pesky shakes his head and spits.

"You hear the one about the three fliers who crashed in Africa?" he says.

"You already told that one," says Morgan.

"Well, I'm gonna tell it again," Pesky says.

It is an amusing dirty joke about an elephant's trunk. Each of the fliers loses an anatomical part in the crash, and a witch doctor performs emergency surgery. The witch doctor uses animals' parts to replace what each flier has lost. Pesky laughs at the punch line as if someone else were telling it and he were hearing it for the first time. He shakes his head and repeats the punch line: "Women love it, but every time I'm at a cocktail party, the goddamn thing keeps reaching for the peanuts."

Wherever you are, the saying goes, the ball will find you. I heard this as a kid, and sure enough, I saw it proven. Sooner or later, when a guy was playing a position he didn't know, he'd make the big error. In baseball, most errors are big. Muff a ground ball, throw one wild, and it usually tells. Wherever you are, the ball will find you, which means that sooner or later you will be challenged. You have to be able to field your position.

The Sox play the second game of the second half on the night of July 17, and in the tenth inning Mike Greenwell, who has never caught except for a single game in high school, straps on catcher's gear and goes behind the plate. Wherever you are, the ball will find you—especially if you're catching. The ball promptly finds Greenwell, and because it does, the A's win big. Everyone has his own idea as to when the Sox fell out of the race—many point to the night of June 26, when Clemens blew the nine-run lead in New York—but my pick is the two autumnal nights in July, the two losses to the revved-up young A's.

Oil Can, finally off the DL, starts for the Sox and gives up four runs in seven innings. A Boggs double off the green wall and a single clipped to right field by Rice get the Sox a run in the fourth. As the bottom of the ninth begins, the A's lead, 4–1.

It is far from over. Greenwell walks, and Evans hits one into the alley in left center, a double, Greenwell braking at third. Buckner walks on four pitches. The huge crowd, 34,543, is roaring. Suddenly there's hope in the air, where there was none last night. Maybe the crowd is with me in my hunch—that the season is being made or broken here. This game is our last chance. Baylor, who has been on the bench both nights, bats for Owen. The big man drives one into center field deep enough to allow Greenwell to jog home after the catch. Now comes a tall decision for McNamara.

Gedman is on the DL, and so McNamara has two catchers, neither of whom can hit a lick. Sullivan started this game; in the eighth inning McNamara sent Benzinger to hit for Marc, who was leading off. Benzinger walked, but nothing came of

it. Behind the plate went Danny Sheaffer, who has been shut-
tling back and forth between here and Pawtucket and whose
big-league average this year is .122. It is Sheaffer's turn to hit.
What to do? McNamara tells Romero to bat for Sheaffer.

He is now without a catcher, but it doesn't look as if it's
going to matter, because Romero strikes out. Two down. The
tying runs stay on first and second. People begin to percolate
to the exits. They should know better with Ellis Burks at the
plate. Ellis works the count to his advantage, three and one,
then hammers one the opposite way, right field, low and cleav-
ing to the chalk line. The ball skids to the barrier, caroms,
bounces around; Evans and Buckner score, Burks zooms around
to third. The game is tied. People scramble back to their seats.
The winning run is at third. McNamara won't need another
catcher if Ellis can score.

They pitch carefully to Barrett and walk him. The hitter
now is Boggs, our best bet, and the best bet in all of baseball,
to bring Burks home with the winning run. The A's summon a
new pitcher, Greg Cadaret, to deal with this crisis. When I was
a kid I knew every big-league baseball player—his team, his
position, and, roughly, his ability. Even National League players, even the Cubs and Phillies. I knew them from studying
baseball magazines and baseball cards. I absorbed the knowledge effortlessly, stashed it away with computer efficiency. Never
again would my mind work so well. I no longer collect baseball
cards or pore over baseball magazines; I have never heard of
Greg Cadaret. He comes from near the bottom of the barrel,
Oakland's fifth pitcher of the night. A lefty, of course, to pitch
to Boggs.

Boggs watches Cadaret throw his eight warm-ups. Wade
serenely chews his gum, studying the pitcher. He is the man
for this job and knows it. He takes a practice swing, slashing
Hriniak-style, and goes briskly in to hit. The crowd rises. Wade
watches strike one go by. He slaps the curveball foul into the

seats beyond third. Cadaret twists another curve, and Boggs hits it on the ground to the second baseman, easy out, extra innings.

Extra innings—and no catcher. Extra innings, and Mike Greenwell behind the plate. How long will it take the ball to find Greenwell? Bob Stanley has been pitching since the eighth, and beautifully. He has struck out three of six hitters, and no one has reached base. But now Terry Steinbach hits a double. The swift Griffin is up. Alfredo sees to it that the ball finds Greenwell, dropping a bunt a few feet in front of the plate. Mike flings away the mask, snatches up the ball, and lobs a curious arcing throw, pushing the ball like a shot-putter, over Griffin, over Buckner, over everybody. Steinbach scores; Griffin dashes to second.

McNamara trudges lugubriously to the mound in a windstorm of boos. Stanley leaves. More boos. Sambito comes trotting in from the pen. He throws two strikes past Polonia, who then singles to left, bringing home Griffin. On the next pitch, Polonia goes. Greenwell shoots to his feet, and when he cocks his arm to throw, the ball jumps out of his hand like a live fish. The boos come down thick. On the next pitch Polonia swipes third. Greenwell's throw is late and clumsy. Sambito strikes the hitter out, and McNamara returns to the mound to call for Schiraldi. The old, obligatory strategy, righty to righty, pitcher's advantage. So they say. Schiraldi walks Canseco on four pitches.

The rookie McGwire, another righty, finally does what we've all been expecting sooner or later, which is to launch one of his majestic home runs. This one nearly clears the screen. It is higher than I've ever seen a ball hit; it seems to climb forever and float down reluctantly, as if it had taken on weightlessness up there in the stratosphere. The rookie is about as tall as they come, and so are his home runs.

The next hitter is Lansford, another righty. Lansford sends Schiraldi's very next pitch into the screen, just about where

McGwire's touched down. Lansford's home run is another high one. Schiraldi walks Reggie, and McNamara has finally had enough. The boos fill the place as McNamara treks out yet again. He signals for Gardner, who always prances in across the outfield as if he can't wait to begin pitching. Gardner finishes them off, but not until two more singles have enabled Reggie to score the inning's seventh run. The game is gone, and so, for another year, is the pennant.

In his office afterward McNamara stands behind his chair, leaning on it with both arms folded. One side of his mouth is pulled over and down. The reporters file silently in, looking appropriately despondent. There are a lot of us tonight. Everyone finds a place, packed thick around the desk. Silence.

"Go ahead," McNamara says. "Ask your questions. I'll answer 'em."

There's a pause, and then: "John, has Greenwell ever caught before?"

"Not professionally. He *has* worked in simulated games." McNamara looks around him, at the faces hemming him in. "I was tryin' to win a baseball game, was all," he says.

"John, whose idea was it to put Greenwell back there?"

McNamara stares hard at the questioner. "I don't get the drift of your conversation," he says.

"Well, did Greenwell volunteer?"

"I talked to Mike. He said he could go back there."

"Would you do it again?"

McNamara sends the man a lightless smile. "Certainly," he says.

Greenwell's cubicle is the next stop. Mike can smile wryly at what has just happened to him. "Well," he says, "I caught in high school once when our regular catcher got hurt." He grins. "I didn't do as bad then as I did today." There's a pause as he thinks back. "I caught a few times in Little League. Oh, and I *have* been warmin' up some pitchers this year."

That's it?

"That's it."
The ball will always find you.

Meanwhile Reggie Jackson has been soaking up adoration. There is more tonight, it seems, than last. Tonight he is playing right field, his old position, and when he chugs out there in the first inning the crowd in the distant sections beyond the foul pole and in the bleachers above the A's bullpen welcomes him with a cheer. Reggie turns, lifts his cap high, holds it there as the cheering feathers down over him.

In the top of the second, Reggie walks out to hit against Oil Can, and the old ballpark resounds with his name, "Re-*gee*! Re-*gee*!" a breathy roar that is almost palpable, like puffs of wind. Reggie touches the visor of his helmet and, when he has the count his way, three and one, knocks a double off the wall. The crowd cheers and cheers.

The worse the game goes for the home team, the more vociferously affectionate toward Reggie grow the fans. He bats in the top of the ninth with the score 4 – 1. The crowd, figuring it is his last at-bat of the night, rises. They are booing Mc-Namara, booing Stanley, even booing Rice, but they give Reggie Jackson a standing O. Reggie strikes out, which is irrelevant at this point. Reggie has no more to prove than Williams did in the Old-Timers game. The crowd knows this, and as Reggie stalks back to the dugout they rise and say farewell—prematurely, as it turns out—cheering on and on. The people in the box seats behind the visitors' dugout yell their good-byes and wave to Reggie. He waves back.

The Sox surprise everybody by getting those three runs in the bottom of the inning. Even so, it takes a big inning by Oakland to bring Reggie to the plate in the tenth. The A's have scored six runs by the time Reggie bats, and the crowd has grown thoroughly disgusted with the home team. Reggie gets another standing O and a big cheer when Schiraldi walks him. More cheers when Gardner slings a wild pitch and Reggie gallops to second.

Reggie scores the seventh run of the inning on a hit by Steinbach. The game is in tatters, but the crowd doesn't seem to care anymore. It seems happy. Reggie crosses the plate, circles back toward his dugout. The people in the first row of the boxes between the backstop and the dugout are standing. They lean way out, and as Reggie comes by they reach, palms out, a row of high fives. Reggie veers over, slows, and works his way down the row, slapping each palm, painting delight across every face. At the top of the dugout steps he pauses, lifts his helmet high. The cheers flow down over him.

I ask Pesky if it was hard to quit.

"Sure it was," he says, emphatic about it. "You think you can still play. You feel like you always felt. You think you can play."

I saw how tough it can be to quit in what I remember as the hard Pennsylvania winter of 1966–1967, my junior year at Haverford College. I remember the frozen yellow-brown campus, scabs of snow and gray ice, shadows stretching out early as the sun finished shining against a classroom window. This was the moment of the day I'd been waiting for. A friend and I would get out of that last class as fast as we could and go straight to the field house, which was brand-new then, the result, I suppose, of a bequest by an alumnus longing for better teams. This field house, which reminded me of a gigantic airplane hangar, was affixed to the antique locker rooms by an unheated passageway made of corrugated metal. Winter blew through every seam and kept the metal subfreezing, creating a refrigerator effect. Swinging doors delivered you into the warm, dim world of the field house. At this hour the basketball team hadn't come down yet, and from behind the collapsible bleachers on the parquet court you could hear a volleyball game, stringbean intellectuals getting their phys ed requirement out of the way. You could hear them slapping the ball back and forth, and now and then a voice dully calling out a score. You could hear the whisper of heated air on the move; that, and the mushy slaps of the volleyball game. But in a moment—most afternoons, anyway—you would hear as well the *whap* of a baseball in a catcher's mitt. A big-league *whap*, ringing out like the crack of a pistol in the warm stale air of the field house.

That winter we had two famous pitchers—one of them bound for the Hall in Cooperstown—working out together in our field house. The two, Robin Roberts and Curt Simmons, had reached the end of the trail and were sharpening themselves for what they hoped would be one more big-league season. Simmons, actually, had a home, the Chicago Cubs, for whom he'd pitched in '66, but without distinction. The great Roberts, too, had been with the Cubs that year, but they'd dumped him. He was writing letters to ball clubs, trying to work up some interest, an invitation to spring training. They had run into our college athletic director at a sports banquet, and somehow the subject of the field house had come up. Maybe Robin Roberts had simply asked if he could use it. It was what he needed. Our athletic director had been a great tackle and placekicker at Temple; his game was football, but he seemed to understand that our field house and locker room, and even the frigid walkway, would be graced by the presence of Robin Roberts. It was as if Segovia had asked if he could practice in our conservatory.

I first heard about it one afternoon in the locker room when I was changing to go upstairs to the old gym to play some pickup basketball. A fat kid named Santini, who was a second-string lineman on our winless football team, mentioned it to me.

"You know who's down there?" he said, jerking his head in the direction of the field house. "Robin Roberts and Curt Simmons. Used to pitch for the Phillies?" Santini sounded only mildly interested. He was not interested enough to walk down there and watch them throw.

"Robin Roberts?" I said.

"That's what I said."

"Robin Roberts is in our field house?"

"He doesn't look like much," Santini said.

"You're a jerk, Santini," I said, and was gone, loping bare-legged through the cold streams of air working along the tunnel.

Some numbers: nineteen years in the big leagues, 286 wins, a 3.41 ERA. He won twenty games six times and twice led the league in strikeouts. Roberts achieved all this pitching for bad teams. His Phillies somehow won the pennant in 1950, but otherwise never came close. He pitched for the Orioles for a few years in the early sixties, before the Birds became an American League power. Robin Roberts was almost a right-handed Warren Spahn.

Simmons had pitched for the Phils almost as long as Roberts. They'd been together on that '50 team, which will be known forever as the "Whiz Kids." Simmons was a good pitcher, a winner. Durable.

Simmons was thirty-seven, the winter I knew him. Roberts was forty-one. They'd been pitching professionally since before I was born, and here they still were.

I entered the field house alone that first afternoon, heard the intellectuals playing volleyball, heard the baseball pound the catcher's mitt. I followed the sound, down past the basketball court, the collapsible bleachers, to the long net cage where the baseball team took March batting practice, hitting machine-thrown pitches, and where now Robin Roberts, in sweat clothes, toed an imaginary pitching slab, rocked into his windup, and threw.

It was pretty. He was slightly overweight, but it didn't matter. He threw with what seemed to be no effort at all, using every inch of himself, wasting nothing, fluid and never hurried as he wheeled and jackknifed down, bending his back over the throw, following through, his right foot off the ground now, the knee bent daintily. Five times he led the league in complete games, five times in innings pitched, and here was why, this smooth delivery, all grace and economy.

He was throwing to Simmons, who squatted at the end of the cage. Simmons was a lefty. He was wearing the catcher's mitt—they don't make catcher's mitts for lefties as a rule—on his right hand, wearing it backward. It looked clumsy, odd, a new contraption for snaring foul balls. But Simmons used it with perfect deftness. The ball smacked in there, *whap*, and stuck. Crouching, Simmons would peel it out casually and flip it back to Roberts.

Roberts threw a second pitch and then seemed to notice me standing there. He nodded from the other side of the netting and said hello. His face was quite pink and his hair jet black and combed over and back with a neat part. I'd seen the face on a dozen baseball cards, in a thousand magazines. He was sweating. He went back to work. The fastball sliced the air with a hiss. The curve bit down hard. I watched. I had this all to myself.

After a while he nodded to Simmons: That's it. Simmons got up, and they traded places. Simmons was bigger and better built. He had a crisp black crewcut and a swarthy face that was lean and handsome. Now he began to throw, easy at first, and for a moment—I'd become so attuned to Roberts's balletic delivery—I thought Simmons was clowning around. I thought he was trying to get a laugh from Roberts. His motion was jerky, nervous. He hid the ball in his glove like all pitchers, but too long, it seemed, rushing it out and getting off the throw a little behind the natural wheel of his body. Roberts's motion was supple, jointless; Simmons flapped his elbows, he yanked himself around.

But this was mostly illusion. It was what came of seeing

Robin Roberts perform from close up. Simmons actually was quite smooth, even elegant. You don't pitch twenty years in the big leagues if you throw like someone heaving spears at woolly mammoths. A couple years before, '64, Simmons had won eighteen games for the Cardinals.

Haverford College in 1966 had an enrollment of something like 450 students, all males. Simmons and Roberts were a secret I thought I had to guard. I told only my best friend, who was almost as nuts when it came to baseball as I was. Every afternoon we joined up and hustled over to the field house to hang out with Robin and Curt. We kept our mouths shut about it and had them all to ourselves. If word leaked out, we'd become mere faces in a crowd. That's what we thought, anyway. We didn't want people horning in.

The pitchers came to expect us. They learned our names and actually used them. Simmons told us stories about Leo Durocher, who managed the Cubs in those days. Roberts remembered his first game in Fenway after he'd come over to the Orioles. He said he'd given up a couple of home runs in the first inning, then hung on to win. He said he hated the wall. Once, as we watched him throw, Roberts snagged the cleats of his left shoe in the dirt and spun all the way down to both knees, losing the ball as he fell. It looked clumsy as hell, undignified, and he knew it and was embarrassed. You could see it—the already pink face flushing redder, and a quick, uncomfortable smile. There was nothing graceful about him down on both knees, or picking himself up. He retrieved the ball, bending slowly to pluck it up. Then, walking back, not looking at us, he said very quietly, "I did that in the Polo Grounds one time." He spoke so low that Simmons couldn't hear him sixty feet away. He reached the pretend mound, toed the pretend pitching rubber. Just as softly, and still without looking at us, he said, "Mays scored from third."

One day the college newspaper sent a guy down to do a

story. He stood for about ten minutes watching through the netting with as much dispassion as if this had been a couple of guys moving a piano and soon sauntered off. His story comprised a single column that ran maybe a third of the way down the page. As far as I ever knew, it inspired not one trip to the field house to watch Robin Roberts throw. Was everyone else crazy, or were we? Understand, I no longer bought baseball cards or studied *Street and Smith's Baseball Annual.* I had new gods named Fitzgerald and Hemingway, and I stayed up nights scratching terrible youthful fiction on yellow legal pads, driving myself as hard as I ever had practicing for the major leagues. And yet this is what I remember above all else about the winter of 1967, Robin Roberts and Curt Simmons. They were the top priority of every weekday. Crazy? The fascination was, is, ineffable. A mystery.

After they threw, they would jog laps around the perimeter of the field house. The dirt was soft, powdery, artificial-seeming. Sometimes I ran with them, trotting a little behind. They ran a measured pace, digging along steadily, building more sweat. A few times around, then I would go up the long cold tunnel with them, their cleats rattling *ka-plick ka-plick ka-plick* on the concrete floor.

Roberts told us of the letters he'd written, offering himself for a spring training tryout. He'd written to the Dodgers, I remember, and the Yankees. There were others. He would let us know when he heard back. They all told him no. He would shake his head, half smile, and say, "They aren't interested in my act." He had a wry, wistful way of telling things. He'd spent part of last season with Houston, which I hadn't known. I asked him how he'd done. "Not real good," he said. "I won three and lost five." He gave me a look, the slow beginning of a smile. "The funny part of it," he said, "I was tryin' to win *all* of 'em."

At the end of February, Simmons left for spring training.

He made the team, but around midseason the Cubs let him go to the Angels. His numbers that year were five wins, eight losses, with a 4.24 ERA. It was his last season.

Roberts, meanwhile, decided to try to pitch his way to the big leagues the hard way. The Phillies, perhaps for sentimental reasons, agreed to let him join their double-A team in Reading, Pennsylvania. One of the Phillies' radio announcers was Richie Ashburn, a former Phillies teammate of Roberts's. Ashburn had been one of the Whiz Kids. Whenever Roberts pitched that spring, Ashburn would arrange a telephone hookup with the ballpark and keep us listeners apprised of how his old buddy was doing. "After five innings in Lancaster," Ashburn would say, "Robin Roberts has given up two runs and three hits, and Reading leads the ball game, 4−2."

I saw Roberts one more time. Reading was in the old Eastern League and so was York, where my mother grew up, and where her mother still lived. The York White Roses. Their big rival was Lancaster, the Red Roses. My grandmother's house was a couple of miles from the ballpark, which was an old-fashioned, run-of-the-mill country ballpark at the edge of town— cement grandstands in the open air, spindly light towers, outfield fences plastered with local advertising. Pesky remembers it. He managed Lancaster for a couple of seasons, and he remembers coming over by bus, the hilly farm country and the mile-wide Susquehanna River. I waited till Reading played in York, and went to visit my grandmother.

We went to the ball game, she and I, on a Saturday afternoon drenched in the daffodil light of May. You could smell the black earth of that rich farmland, turned inside-out for spring. The day was cool, just right. My grandmother and I arrived a few minutes before game time and sat behind the visitors' dugout. Robin Roberts wasn't pitching that day, but I was determined to see him, one way or another. I'd ridden a train and then a bus, and I was going to see the man. So, before the game started I took a deep breath and worked my way down to the dugout. A fat usher was relaxing by the barrier. I asked him if Robin Roberts was in the dugout.

"Maybe," the usher said.

"Would you please tell him I'm here?"

"Tell him *who* is here?"

I gave my name.

"Go sit down," the usher said. "I'll tell him."

I noticed, coming back up, that I was being stared at. There were a lot of kids. Kids with their ball gloves. I sat down beside my grandmother. She looked at me, smiling in a querying way she had. She remained tall all her life and sat up very straight. A grandmother who took all her grandchildren to Europe and who liked baseball.

"Well?" she said.

"I don't know," I said. For one thing, my last name would mean nothing to Roberts. And I didn't trust that usher.

The York White Roses broke onto the field to a festive cheer from the small, minor-league crowd. Reading's leadoff hitter strutted to the plate. There was, I remember, a lot of swagger on those double-A teams. The ballplayers must have all figured they were headed for the big leagues in a couple of years; they were just kids and full of themselves. The game began, and my heart sank lower and lower. The usher lolled against the dugout and wouldn't look at me.

The half inning ended. The Reading guys spilled up out of the dugout, and then a head and shoulders appeared above the dugout roof: Robin Roberts, squinting up to see who, exactly, had sent the message. I shot to my feet. This was a small grandstand, no higher than bleachers overlooking the football field of some rustic high school. Roberts didn't have any trouble spotting me. He didn't look at all surprised, just beckoned me with a toss of his head.

He met me at the barrier. We shook hands.

"You didn't come all this way to see a minor-league ball game, did you?" he said.

"My grandmother lives here," I said. "I'm visiting her."

"Ah," he said, as if relieved.

His gaze was straying past me, to the crowd in the sunshine. He looked anxious, looked almost afraid of what he might see up there. He wore a regular Phillies road uniform. I suppose the club couldn't afford its own uniforms, or at least preferred to take leftovers from the parent big-league team.

"You're pitching well," I said.

"Oh," he said, in that wry, wistful way, "I'm gettin' a few of these boys out."

Boys. Yes. They were my age, and younger. And yet they had men's bodies, and an arrogant grace that was beyond me, unimaginable. They were a little more than boys to me, and I didn't understand, then, Robin's discomfort, a nervousness that had worked its way into his easygoing face. He was uncomfortable standing there talking to me; I didn't know why, exactly. I was sure it was only a matter of time before he'd be pitching for the Phillies.

"Curt had a nice game the other day," I said. Simmons had beaten Pittsburgh. They'd scored five runs off him, but he'd stayed in there and gotten the win.

Robin said, "Curt did?"

"He beat the Pirates," I said.

"Oh, yeah."

Play was resuming. Robin glanced over his shoulder toward the plate. Apparently they would play ball with him standing here. This was double A, and he was Robin Roberts. But I knew he wanted to sit down. He wanted to vanish; I sensed that much.

"Listen," I said, "maybe I could see you when you come to Pawtucket this summer. I don't live far from there."

Pawtucket then was in the Eastern League. It's all been changed. The old Eastern League is gone.

"All right," he said, without enthusiasm.

"Unless you're up with the Phillies," I said.

"You could write to me," he said. "Care of the ball club."

I said I would. I wished him luck.

"Thanks," he said.

It hit me finally that he looked tired. Not old, just tired. We shook hands.

"Good luck," I said again.

"Thanks for comin' by," he said.

I turned, climbed the cement steps. People stared. Kids. One kid at the end of a row asked me, "Are you a ballplayer?"

"No," I said, "I'm a friend of Robin Roberts."

I did write to him after I got home for the summer. It must have been mid-June. I didn't get an answer for a long time, till I began to think he'd had enough of me. I supposed he had better things to do in Pawtucket than have dinner with me. But in July, I heard from him. I have the letter, of course. It is written in ballpoint on stationery with his name, Robin E. Roberts, printed at the top, and a leafy-sounding address in Meadowbrook, Pennsylvania. Time has rubbed smoky brownish smudges into the paper. The ballpoint ink has been bled to a lead-gray. *"Dear John,"* he writes,

> *Thank you for taking the time to write. I don't believe I'll be in Pawtucket for quite a while.*
>
> *Good luck to you. Hope you are a very successful writer. I'm in fine health and so is my family.*
>
> *Ballplayers are just people. We play a boy's game all our lives. I'm finding it extremely difficult to separate myself from this boy's game. It's been good to me.*
>
> *Good luck, Robin.*

Eight
Good-bye, Bill; Hello, Big Sam

THE RED SOX HAVE RELEASED BILL BUCKNER AND CALLED BIG Sam Horn, gigantic Sam, up from Pawtucket. Horn has been bashing the ball in triple A. He is to become an instant folk hero in Boston, man-mountain and swatter of prodigious home runs, and he will erase the memory of the man he replaces on the roster—except, of course, for the Error. The Error, the Error. Error or no, Bill Buckner was a hell of a ballplayer.

Numbers: through '86, a lifetime major-league batting average of .292. Get out your record books and see how many guys hit .290 over the long haul. In 1980 Buckner led the National League in hitting at .324. Seven times he hit better than .300. In '85, his second year with the Sox, he batted .299. The man is no bum. And he said hello to strangers in the dugout.

Buckner's getting the sack comes as no surprise. The Sox remain in fifth place, thirteen and a half games back. It would be different if they were thirteen and a half back in second

175

place; a formidable task, to catch the leader, but not out of the question. As it is, they have four teams to overtake. Four teams, then, would have to go flat, blow big leads. I have heard Evans and Boggs talk about how the '78 Yankees came from fourteen and a half games back and won, but the Yanks were chasing one team. McNamara hasn't gotten around to acknowledging it in public, but he knows his team isn't going anywhere. It is time to turn it over to the kids. Let them play, let them learn. Buckner is thirty-seven. The ankle still bothers him. The writers have been asking Lou Gorman, the general manager, what the plan is for Buckner. Gorman's answers have been coy. Read between the lines. Buckner said he was sick of waiting and wished they'd get it over with. Finally, they have.

It is Friday, July 24, and a heat wave swamps Boston. I drive into a city buried in white smog, in vapors that can't budge under the weight of this heat. Ninety-six degrees, says the man on the car radio. I think of home. Of sea breezes and evening shadows.

At five o'clock the heat is moist, heavy. I find McNamara sitting on the bench with Cliff Keane, fat and owlish, sitting there with his hands planted on his knees. They are talking about the heat, naturally. Keane is remembering the first game he ever saw in Busch Stadium in St. Louis. He was covering the All-Star game. Cliff says he never knew a hotter day.

"They asked Casey Stengel how he liked the new ballpark," Cliff says. "Casey says, 'Well, I'll say this: It holds the heat pretty good.' " Cliff chuckles and repeats the punch line. "It holds the heat pretty good." He says much funnier things than this up in the press box, but what he says up there— caustic, irreverent stuff—wouldn't go over very well down here.

"Yeah, St. Louis," McNamara says. "I remember some hot days in St. Louis. One time when I was managin' Cincinnati, we went to St. Louis in an awful heat wave. I remember one afternoon some dumb bastard wanted to keep his feet cool, so he wrapped 'em in aluminum foil."

Keane nearly splits open laughing. "Who was it, John?" he says.

"One of my players," McNamara says. "I don't remember who it was."

The Sox are taking batting practice. Pesky is slapping ground balls to Rice near third. I don't know why Jim Rice is fielding ground balls. He is throwing them lazily across the diamond to the new guy, big Horn, who snags the ball casually one-handed, then rolls it in to Pesky. Rice is enjoying himself. He charges the grounders with a springtime verve, gobbles them up, but then only lobs them to Horn. "*Aw-rahhht*," he yaps. "*Aw-rahhht . . .*" As if he didn't have a care in the world.

Rice tells Pesky he's had enough and jogs in to hit. He is starting tonight in left field. Pesky circles the cage from the third- to the first-base side, makes sure no one else needs him, and brings his bandaged fungo to the bench. McNamara and Keane have vanished. Pesky sits down.

"Too bad about Buckner," I say.

"Well," Pesky says, "I'm afraid the time had come."

"He was hitting," I say.

"He was hitting *singles*," Pesky corrects me. He works his chaw for a while, contemplating the ball field. Then he turns to me, draws way back, and fixes me with his dark little eyes. "Do you think he was as good this year as last?"

"I guess not."

"Goddamn right he wasn't," Pesky says. "There's more to come, too," he says.

More changes, he means. Veterans departing, traded or simply let go; kids arriving from Pawtucket. Baylor has been mentioned. Horn's arrival has made Baylor expendable. Baylor can't play the field, and neither can Horn. Sam Horn is a born DH if there ever was one. A hitting specialist, a nonfielder. Already I have glimpsed him at first base, sluggish, indifferent, killing time. The only question is whether Horn can hit big-league pitching. Henderson, too, has become superfluous. Ellis

Burks has seen to that. Hendu, still blithe-seeming in the club-house with that slit smile, but never playing these days.

Pesky sighs. "It's tough," he says, "it's tough. Christ, when they traded me to Detroit, I couldn't believe it. I thought I'd be here forever."

The rooftop region of Fenway has obviously been built piecemeal over the years, as needed. There is no plan to it. Catwalks cut across tar roofing; steps ascend steeply to the sky-view boxes, the final word in construction up here. The press box reminds me somehow of a trailer, perhaps because of the steps up to the door, perhaps because of its long shape, or its added-on, temporary look, difficult to pin down. The lounge is a big square thing with frosted windows, as unmemorable from the outside as a Salvation Army headquarters or a city inocula-tion center, but on the inside, quite magical.

The magic is in the air as much as anything. It is in the snatches of conversation overheard, baseball talk, knowledge-able and passionate, rich in anecdotes. It is in the faces in the crowd: Frank Malzone, Paul Blair, Ken Coleman, Ned Martin, Billy Martin, Bobby Murcer, Phil Rizzuto, Hawk Harrelson, Don Drysdale, Ernie Harwell, Al Kaline, Birdie Tebbetts, and even, once, Ted Williams. The pictures on the walls add to the spell. Carl Yastrzemski, in color, belting one. Mel Parnell in the clubhouse after he threw his no-hitter, sweaty and smil-ing, flanked by Sammy White, his catcher, and the manager, Mike Higgins. Ted Williams posing in a dugout with Joe DiMaggio. A funny one: Williams in the clubhouse in shorts and shower clogs, demonstrating the famous swing for the pho-tographer, the young body supple-looking as a cat's. Then there are two red numbers on white flannel, in frames. Number nine and number four, the only two the Sox have retired, Williams and Joe Cronin. By the door hangs a smallish photograph of a young infielder bending down as if to field a ground ball but staring at the camera. The kid has the dark good looks of a movie actor. Pesky tells me he was twenty-one then. He remembers the picture being taken.

The lounge otherwise looks pretty much like any nice cafeteria. The young women who serve you are extremely pleasant. The tables have red-checked tablecloths. In the lounge in Shea Stadium, I can't help remembering, certain tables were reserved for broadcasters and other bigshots. There's none of that here. Lou Gorman, Haywood Sullivan, even the venerable and elegant Mrs. Jean Yawkey all pick up their food and find an empty seat, just like the rest of us. There is a bar, presided over by a paunchy, white-haired bartender named Arthur, whose smile is tough and crinkly and who knows his baseball, like everyone else in here. A TV on the wall blares the pregame show on the cable sports channel. Some of the old-timers, like Malzone and Pesky, prefer to stay right here after the room empties, to smoke their big cigars and gab and watch the game on television.

Usually, I eat alone. I've made a few friends up here, not many. The beat reporters hang together, share information; a fraternity that doesn't cotton particularly to writers who work outside the daily grind. It works both ways: I find myself hanging back, going my own way. Better to be a fly on the wall than part of the network.

One day in the dugout Leigh Montville, a columnist for the *Globe*, notices the name on my pass and sticks out his hand. He has read a novel I wrote about a big-league umpire and remembers my name. Montville is about my age. He is literate, unaffected, easygoing.

Through Pesky and Morgan I meet Ed Bridges, a freelance reporter who also tapes radio interviews for WSRO in Marlborough. He makes himself at home here, bantering with players and reporters, shooting the breeze with Morgan and Pesky on the bench. He is a smallish man with a foxy twinkle and a good earthy sense of humor. Ed has been around.

Steve DeMarco, who covers the Sox for the *Woburn Daily*

Times Chronicle and who seems to travel outside the elite circle of the big dailies, introduces himself to me one night when we find ourselves sitting side by side in the press box. Steve is in his twenties. He sheds an initial shyness and peppers me with questions about my work. How long does it take to write a book? How do you find an agent? How are royalties computed?

Then there is the distinguished Ken Coleman, who has been broadcasting Red Sox games since I was a sophomore in college. The Voice of the Red Sox is one of the best in the business. I introduce myself to him in the lounge one evening. He welcomes me with a courtesy that is almost Old World in its gracefulness, though I soon see that Ken Coleman has what my mother used to call "natural manners." Later I give him a paperback copy of my novel. He likes it and we are friends, colleagues in the word business. The Voice of the Red Sox is a broad-shouldered little man with an athlete's prowling walk, a good ballplayer himself once upon a time. He's been coming to Fenway since he was a boy, and had his own dreams of playing in the big leagues.

One more friend: Jim Samia, the public relations assistant. Jim is a few years out of U. Mass, a tall reed of a kid who lopes around on endless errands of diplomacy. Often I hear writers and photographers complain about the PR people with other teams, who they say are capricious and niggling. The Red Sox' PR triumvirate—Bresciani, Spofford, and Samia—are reasonable, cordial men who don't speak the language of self-importance.

Sherm Feller, the public address announcer, makes it his business to find out what I'm doing here. Feller has been growling the lineups and pitching changes at Fenway for twenty years. Behind the scenes he has become a hoary and comic institution. He is a large man with a face like the root of an old oak. He is gregarious, opinionated, blunt, and funny. His wit is more sledgehammer than rapier.

On the hot night of July 24 he sets his tray down across the table from me and sits. He has already ordered me, more or less facetiously, to put him in my book. No problem with that.

"Too bad about Buckner," I say.

"It's a big mistake," growls Sherm. He stabs his food, wolfs it down. "They're gonna miss him. He can still hit, ya know. And I'll tell you this: Evans is no first baseman."

I agree. Boy, do I agree.

At the next table Lou Gorman sits down with three or four well-dressed, important-looking men. The moon-faced Gorman always enters the room beaming. As he moves about, he doles out handshakes, slaps on the back, hearty nods, working his way slowly among tables like a jolly Boston politician.

He lowers himself into a chair, and before he can take a bite Sherm Feller interrupts him, leaning over and clamping a knotty hand on Gorman's dove-gray coat sleeve.

"What the hell ya doin'?" Sherm bellows kiddingly. "I wish you'd consult me before you make these big moves." He means dumping Buckner.

"Hey, I tried to call you," Gorman says.

"I went to law school, ya know," Sherm says.

"Did you?"

"Two years," Sherm says.

"I'll be darned," Gorman says.

Sherm turns back to me, to his food.

"I'll tell you this," he says to me, "they never should have sent Glen Hoffman down."

I cannot remember when Hoffman was dispatched to Pawtucket. He is gone, is all I know.

"Hoffman's a good shortstop," says Sherm. "A *good* shortstop. And he can hit. I can prove to you that he can hit."

I wonder how. No matter; it's the opinion that counts. You can't love baseball and not hold these opinions. I am learning this summer that people in the game dispute our right to question their work—our right to ideas of our own. But how can we not be opinionated, caring so deeply, loving the game so deeply? What do they expect?

"If you want to keep Owen at shortstop," Sherm continues, "I got another idea. Play Hoffman at third, put Boggs at first." A nearly revolutionary thought. Sherm seems to have forgotten that they never should have let Buckner go. He has released Buckner himself and installed Boggs at first. "Why not?" he says, noting my doubtful look. "Boggs was a first baseman in the minors, ya know. Hell, if you can play third, you can play first."

"That's probably true," I say. I wonder if Lou Gorman, seated maybe five feet away, is listening to all of this. Maybe Gorman doesn't mind. Maybe he understands.

"I'll tell you another thing," Sherm goes on, bending to his food, "we should have picked up Ray Boone."

He means Bob Boone, the veteran Angels' catcher who was a free agent in the spring. Ray Boone was Bob's father, a first baseman with the Tigers and White Sox in the late fifties. I saw Ray Boone play here.

"As soon as Gedman refused to sign, we should have grabbed Ray Boone. The guy hits .265, .270. He can field. He's reliable. *And* he's got balls."

"He wanted a lot of money," I say.

"He's *worth* a lot of money." Sherm wolfs a last spoonful and rises. "Time to go to work," he says. He slides past Gorman's table, gives the GM a pat on the shoulder.

"You consult me next time," he says, and grins. He's missing a tooth here and there.

"You bet," says Gorman.

The opponent tonight is the Seattle Mariners, and the Sox beat them, 5–4. Hurst starts and finishes. With two on in the top of the third, a fast young outfielder named Otis Nixon, who has spent most of the season in the minor leagues and who is hitting .164 in the bigs, sticks one into the screen—his first major-league home run. Hurst doesn't have much of a fastball tonight—not that he ever is blinding—but he is pitching cannily, throwing at different slow speeds, floating it by them. Nixon got lucky. Hit a mistake, as they say. Hurst gives up one more run in the sixth, and that's it.

The Sox win it on a late home run by Baylor. It is Don's first home run since June 23. Boggs, Barrett, and little Spike all contribute two hits. A neat, close game.

Marc Sullivan bats in the second inning with Owen on first base and one out. Marc knocks the first pitch straight to the second baseman, easy double play. They are throwing him curveballs, I notice. He attacks them with a stiff, muscle-bound swing, as if he were slashing with a broadsword or battle-ax. He is hitting .167. In the fifth again with Spike at first, Marc scoops a high pop-up that drifts down foul to the catcher. The crowd gives him a fierce booing. Sullivan takes the short walk back to the dugout with his muscle-strapped jaw clenched tight. He pulls off his helmet and flings it against the back wall. He rams his bat violently into the rack. In the seventh he gets himself in a hole, no balls and two strikes, then strokes a low line drive over second base, a big-league single. All *right*, Marc. I'm pulling for you, kid.

With a man on first in the sixth inning, John Christensen of the Mariners sends one low toward Rice in left field. The ball is coming hard but fading down; Rice slides, slaps down at the ball, doesn't touch it. It bounds past him, and Christensen has a double. They boo Rice, and up in the press box faces scrunch as if a bad smell had wafted through.

"He's become a liability out there," someone says, and heads nod agreement.

McNamara seems unimpressed with his team's win. He has chosen again to receive us on his feet, draped wearily forward on the back of the chair. He pulls a long sigh and says, "Ask."

Buckner is gone; tonight, Todd Benzinger played first base, Evans was in right field. So the first question is, Who's on first?

"Benzinger," says McNamara. "He's played first more than Dewey has. When he plays, that's where he'll play. We'll leave Dewey in right field."

McNamara says little else of interest, and the reporters funnel out and go to Hurst. Bruce is cheerful after the win. So cheerful, in fact, he can still imagine a championship.

"I haven't raised any white flag yet," he says. "I'm not ready to give in."

The reporters listen with straight faces to this optimistic declaration, as unblinking as courtiers humoring a slightly bonkers king. Some even jot it down. Then we move on to Baylor, who won it with his home run.

Baylor is sitting in his canvas chair, bending down and tugging on his shoes. He pays no attention to the reporters. We wait. Baylor ties his shoes, sits up. A dark blue polo shirt clings across his huge chest, with tiny gold letters proclaiming Mercedes Benz on the pocket. Baylor stays in his chair. Someone pokes a microphone under his chin and asks him something. Baylor begins to talk, softly, thoughtfully, not looking at anyone. The reporters all dive down, heads cocked over, trying to hear. Baylor finishes; the mike pulls away. Baylor stands, towering over us all. Another question; he speaks, but softly. At the back of the pack, people stretch to hear. A minute or two, and Baylor has had enough. He barges forward, broad as a door, spilling people out of his way, and is gone. Immediately the writers huddle. The few who could hear Baylor read their notes to the many who could not. I decide I can do without the utterances of Don Baylor, rare though they may be, and call it a night.

At ten-fifteen the next morning Bill Buckner is fielding ground balls at first base, getting in a last workout before he empties his locker. The morning is hazy, not a breath of wind. The heat is smothering. Rac Slider is providing the ground balls. Buckner is wearing a gray T-shirt, regular uniform pants, and the high-top shoes he made famous last autumn. Sweat darkens the shirt up the hollow of his back. He is chewing gum. The traffic is thin down on the Turnpike, no more than a whisper beyond the green wall. The grandstand sweeps around empty.

"About fifteen more, Rac," Buckner calls in. "Then I'll get out of here."

Rac nods, slaps another ground ball. Buckner scuttles to it, snares it one-handed. He looks stiff-legged, gimpy, but I wonder if I'm imagining this. I wonder if the lame man playing first base in the '86 Series, the man hauling himself around the bases with that bobbing limp and elbows pumping, is so imprinted on my mind that I can't imagine a fleet, agile Buckner. Is he limping now, just a bit? I don't know.

Slider raps another. The ball skips at Buckner; he jerks the glove in, up, missing. The ball shoots past him, rolls into the empty outfield. Buckner shakes his head and half smiles under the droopy mustache.

Now Joe Morgan comes out of the tunnel and bounces up the steps, punching his fist into his glove. Morgan doesn't say anything, just jogs out to second base. Slider hits another, and Buckner snaps his throw to Morgan on the bag. Joe stares at the ball, then lobs it in to Slider. I sit back, listen. I've never heard Fenway Park so quiet. The ball whacking Morgan's glove rings out, carries. Romero and Schiraldi come out of the tunnel. They climb into the heat, the waxy glare, and trot to the batting cage. They stand there, chatting quietly and watching Buckner.

"One more, Rac," Buckner calls in.

Slider flips the ball into the air, hangs it there in front of him, and waltzes into it swinging the fungo, easy, a gentle downward slap. Buckner springs to his right, squares away, takes the ball knee-high as it jumps off the velvet-smooth dirt. Still leaning, he pegs to Morgan, whipping the ball underneath his chest with a sharp snap of the wrist. It is over.

"Thanks, Rac."

He waves. Slider nods pleasantly, strolls away with his fungo. Buckner walks over to the cage, to Romero and Schiraldi. He talks awhile with Romero and Schiraldi. He shakes their hands. He throws an arm around Romero, pulls him in against his shoulder, says one last thing and comes away.

I get up off the bench. Buckner comes stiffly, sideways, down the steps.

"Bill," I say. We're alone in the dugout. Buckner stops, squints at me. I say, "I'm the guy who had the grease on his face."

He snorts a laugh. "I remember *that*," he says.

"It was from the batting cage," I say. "The netting. They grease it."

"Oh yeah?" He studies me, wondering maybe what this is leading up to.

"I just want to say good-bye," I tell him.

He studies me and then, finally, offers his hand. I take it.

"What'll you do?" I say.

"I'll wait," he says. "Someone'll pick me up."

"They will," I agree.

"Well . . ." he says.

"I want to tell you, you're a hell of a ballplayer," I say. *"Really."*

The grin slants up, brief. "I appreciate it," he says.

"Good luck, huh?" I say.

"You too."

I listen to him go up the tunnel, clank and thud on the loose plywood, loud at first, shrinking. A distant bump and clunk, then nothing.

Meanwhile McNamara has written the name of Sam Horn on the blackboard inside the clubhouse door, batting fifth, after

Rice and in front of Evans. And so today is the kid's first big-league game. Sam Horn is twenty-three.

The temperature at game time—the PR guys always announce it over the press box loudspeaker immediately after the first pitch—is ninety-eight degrees. The windows are sealed and the air conditioner is going, a tired old system that labors on and on but cannot drive the heat from the room. A good crowd, 32,040, carpets the grandstand and bleachers. All season, these big crowds.

Oil Can is the starting pitcher, and again Can is perplexingly off his game. The Mariners score a run in the first, two in the second, and one in the fourth, after which Can tells McNamara he thinks it would be a good idea if he called it a day. McNamara lifts him. He summons the young lefty, Bolton, to pitch the fifth. The skinny blond is surely the most anonymous member of this ball team, and no one expects much. He shuts them out the rest of the way.

The Sox, meanwhile, are feasting. Nineteen hits, eleven runs. A slaughter. Burks hits a single, double, and home run. Rice clips three singles, Evans three. Owen hits two singles and a triple. Rich Gedman drives one into the bull pen, his first home run since the last game of the World Series.

None of four Seattle pitchers can stem the assault, which seems to feed on itself. Hitting, they say, is contagious. It is a good day, then, for the debut of Sam Horn.

He comes to bat in the first inning with Rice at first, two out. The crowd murmurs, stirs massively: this is history. The man was made to slug baseballs; you can see that in the shoulders like two knobs of mountain, and in the slow, confident way he lumbers up there, bent forward off giant haunches. The bat looks like a toy in his brown fist. His size and serenity promise the long ball. The crowd welcomes him with a Horn-sized cheer. It is love at first sight.

Sam bats left; if he were a righty he could probably pop the ball one-handed over the left-field wall. The pitcher is a righty, Scott Bankhead. The presumption in the big leagues is that any slugger will kill the fastball unless you surprise him with it, or unless you are Roger Clemens. Bankhead is no Roger Clemens, and he feeds Horn slop, benders and change-ups. Horn, eager, swipes too soon, missing, nicking lazy foul pops into the seats along third. Bankhead tries to tease him into swinging at some bad, low pitches, but Sam lays off. The count stretches full. Horn anticipates the fastball, but Bankhead just floats it in there. Sam swings hard, way too early—strike three.

He bats in the third with Rice on first and one out. Bankhead throws a fastball outside; Horn tries to pull it, does, weakly, a ground ball to the second baseman. Easy double play. The crowd emits a collective sigh, a sound of letdown. *Damn.*

Rice is on again in the fifth when Horn's next turn comes. Bankhead has been shelled out of the game; a lefty, Stan Clarke, has succeeded him. McNamara lets Horn hit anyway. The crowd turns quiet, nervous. Come on, Sam. Clarke feeds him slow stuff, and Sam swats and misses twice. He looks at ball one. Come *on*, Sam. Clarke zips a fastball outside and a bit high, and a marvelous thing happens. Sam Horn steps to the ball and taps it; it flies off his bat, climbs to left center field, climbs and climbs, finally vaulting the green wall at its right end, directly above the 379-foot mark. I hardly believe my eyes; I mean, he *tapped* it, as you or I would knock a tack snug. The crowd is standing, letting go a pent-up roar before the ball ever clears the wall. The roar builds, crescendoes as the home run plunks the screen. Horn circles the bases with little dance-steps, fists working close to his shoulders. The cheering holds and holds. Horn collects a high five from Joe Morgan at third base, another from Evans, who is waiting to hit. Greenwell, who follows Evans, is on his way to the on-deck circle; grinning, he offers Sam a hand palm-up, *low* five. Horn slaps him five and takes little jump-steps down into the dugout out of sight. The crowd won't sit, won't stop cheering. They want him back.

You would swear it couldn't get any louder, but when Sam climbs up into view it jumps deafeningly. Horn is smiling. He waves, then goes back down, peeling off his batting gloves.

He hits again in the seventh, and you can see a new confidence, a briskness in the way he digs in and swishes the bat, coolly threatening the pitcher. He is more patient this time with the slow curves, and he gets a walk. In the eighth inning he taps one 420 feet to center field, an immense parabola to the deepest valley of Fenway, a home run in any direction but this. Nixon scoots back, turns near the wall below the bleachers, and gloves the giant fly ball.

McNamara afterward is understandably more concerned with Boyd's mediocrity than elated by the big win. What is wrong with Oil Can? McNamara wouldn't be human if he weren't already thinking about next year. Next year he will need the Can. Now, McNamara shakes his head, sadly puzzled. "Oil Can just isn't makin' his pitches," he says. "I wish I knew why. He's losin' some confidence. He told me between innings, he says, 'I'm strugglin' out there. I'm strugglin'.' "

Tom Bolton, who day after day undresses alone and unnoticed on the far wall behind the brick pillar, today finds himself surrounded by reporters, and with a TV light shining in his face. Bolton looks as happy and self-conscious as a kid at his own birthday party. He is stick-thin, with a schoolboy face that looks razor-chafed, and a wispy attempt at a yellow mustache. Today he pitched beautiful big-league baseball. He tells us now that it is his first win in the majors. No one realized it.

"I had a good sinkerball," he drawls. The voice is Tennessee-flavored. "My breakin' ball wasn't workin'." He grins. "This was my sixteenth day not pitchin'. You tend to get a little rusty after sixteen days."

On then, to Horn. He has not yet taken over Buckner's locker. He is undressing at a temporary stall against a pillar in the middle of the room. The reporters engulf him. Sam, who has stripped to his T-shirt, gazes around at the crowd, showing no emotion in particular. He carries, I notice, some extra bulk over his belt.

"Sam, what were you thinking when you rounded the bases after your home run?"

"Well . . ." The big face with its flat, sloping forehead knits up. The voice is soft, slow, silky. "I was tryin' not to act too excited. I was tryin' to act, *you* know, cool."

Everyone scribbles.

"Sam, when did you find out you were going to play today?"

"Oh, I found out last night." He grins. "I had a very nervous night. Had a nervous *day*, too."

"How 'bout the curtain call, Sam? Ever do that before?"

"No, I'd never done it before." The smile spreads up his face, which is shaped like a very wide heart. "I was happy," he says. He thinks some more. "Yeah, I liked that."

It's time to talk to the kids.

Mike Greenwell sprawls in his canvas chair, stripped to his underwear. He sips thoughtfully from a can of Budweiser.

"Grab me after batting practice tomorrow," he says.

The following night I wait in the dugout while Greenwell hits with Hriniak under the bleachers. I watch them emerge, white-clad and graceful even at this distance. When I was a kid, just watching a big-league ballplayer walk made me want to be one. They come in unhurriedly, conversing. Greenwell brings his bat. Hriniak talks, gesturing, hacking air with his big red hand. I wonder what Walter says, whether he repeats himself or if his theories have such endless ramifications that in an entire season he cannot touch upon them all. They march in step. Greenwell doesn't look at me as they go by. *Here we go again*, I think, remembering Boggs. But Mike rams his bat into the rack and comes down the bench to where I'm sitting. He drops beside me wordlessly.

Greenwell is twenty-four. He is my height, six feet, but much broader, of course, through the chest. He isn't as boyish-looking as Bolton and Benzinger, perhaps because of his thin split mustache. He's a quiet kid. Serious.

He didn't grow up rich, but he grew up comfortable. He was born in Louisville, Kentucky, and grew up in North Fort Myers, Florida. He speaks in rapid bursts, with a faint Southern twang.

"I had five older sisters, a brother, then me. My mother works for the telephone company. My father, he's retired now. My brother had a tryout with the Reds, but he didn't pursue it. We weren't a particularly athletic family, except for me. My father played a lot of softball, but that was it."

He recites his exploits in a matter-of-fact, believing way, as if it all made perfect sense. Four years of varsity baseball at North Fort Myers High School, quarterback of the football team. Benzinger, too, was a high-school quarterback. So was Hriniak, at Natick High, a football powerhouse in Massachusetts. When Greenwell was a junior, North Fort Myers won the state baseball championship. This was Florida, mind you. They went to Nashville to play in a regional tournament. "I had a real good tournament. In one of the games, I hit two home runs." On it goes, on and on. In his senior year he was on an all-star team that played a team from the northern half of the state. "I had a home run and a single in *that* game." Not long after he signed with the Red Sox. He was eighteen.

"I spent four and a half years in the minors. I never did play double-A ball. I jumped from A to triple A. They say that the biggest jump is from double A to triple A, and I got a lot of confidence from skipping double A. Confidence is everything, you know. My first three hits in the majors were home runs, and *that* gave me confidence. Playin' in the World Series gave me confidence, even though I didn't do anything except pinch-hit three times. Yeah, they did get me all three times, but it was a learning experience. The Series wasn't as hard on me as on the older guys. I was down when we lost, sure, but I was just beginning, I was barely a part of it. See, I expect to play in another World Series. I fully expect it."

I ask him if he feels anything, playing in Fenway Park. Any magic, history, ghosts.

"Well, the fans here are probably the most knowledgeable fans in baseball. That's number one. You're playin' in front of people who really know the game."

Bob Stanley and Jim Rice would laugh.

"As far as the tradition goes," continues Greenwell, "there's *one* tradition I'm aware of, and that's the great left fielders. You had Ted Williams, then Carl Yastrzemski, then Jim Rice. I want to be the next Red Sox left fielder. I want to come after Jim Rice."

We chat on. These interviews don't yield much. Ballplayers, understandably, get sick of talking to strangers. Understandably, they say as little as they can get by with saying. Greenwell answers a question, waits for the next. It was like this with Boggs, except that Boggs's answers were shorter, drier, stingier. The minutes are flowing by, and I'm running out of ideas, of questions. How can I make the most of this? The knowledge is always with me that next year I'll be up in the grandstand again.

Greenwell tells me that he knows he has to work hard to remain in the major leagues, and that the injuries on the team— he means Rice—were unfortunate but a piece of luck for him, personally. It has been the diminished availability of Rice that has given Greenwell his chance.

Now it is about thirty-five minutes until game time. My questions are petering out, getting triter. Enough. I thank Greenwell for his time. "No problem," he says, and pops up. "Good luck," he says, and gives me a friendly slap on the knee with his glove as he leaves.

———

It isn't something Ellis Burks wants to do, sit down and be interviewed, and he avoids it as long as he politely can. I stick to the strategy of requesting the interview in advance, which gives them space to maneuver in. I speak to Burks after a night game, as I did to Greenwell, and Ellis consents to a chat after batting practice tomorrow. Tomorrow comes, one of those steamy midsummer days, and as I wait for Burks in the dugout I congratulate myself on my tact and skill. Burks, however, comes in from the outfield without awarding me so much as a glance. He shoves his bat into the rack and turns toward the tunnel. I bounce up, overtake him, touch him lightly on the arm.

"Uh, Ellis . . . ?"

Ellis regards me with hooded eyes; sleepy, smart eyes. Sly. The thin arches of his eyebrows look painted on. Here is a man, you just know, who will always do the smart thing.

"Uh, we were going to talk for a few minutes?"

Burks smiles faintly, as if the idea amused him. "*Man,*" he says, "do you know how *hot* it is?"

"It *is* hot," I agree, knowing that my interview has just gone up in smoke. Even so, I give it the old college try, as my father says. "We could *talk.* . . ."

"I got to go change," Ellis says.

"Well, some other time," I say, sure that the time will never come.

Ellis slinks away, vanishes into the tunnel.

"He's a good kid," Pesky assures me. "Great kid. Smart. He just don't like to talk, is all."

"Fuck it," I say, and am pleased to be feeling a little anger. Boggs told me to get to the ballpark at three if I wanted to talk, then didn't sit down with me till four. I'm sick of this stuff.

"Try him again," Pesky says. "He's a good kid."

I do. I find Ellis on another evening standing near the

batting cage with his bat on his shoulder. Number twelve. Skinny legs, slightly bowed, very long. Built for speed.

"Uh, Ellis, I was wondering . . . I was trying to arrange to sit down with you for a book I'm working on?"

Ellis stares at me, and his face slowly lights up, sly, amused, and just a touch apologetic. "*Man*," he says, and snaps his fingers. "Didn't we do that yet?"

He knows we didn't, and knows I know it, but the little act tidies things up between us.

"No, actually, we didn't," I say.

"*Damn.*" Burks is twinkling. "How long you gonna be around?"

"Three days."

"I'll git you," he says. "Promise."

He does, finally, on the third evening. I've about given up when he plops down beside me, landing sudden as a cat from out of nowhere. I look around for my notebook.

"Writers are a pain, huh?" I say.

"Well," he says, "it tends to take you away from your job, but then, they got a job, too. I got a job, they got a job."

Burks was born in Mississippi and grew up in Fort Worth, Texas. Horn grew up in Texas, and so did Schiraldi, Owen, Baylor, and, of course, Clemens. Ellis's father is an electrician, and he is an only child.

"I never played organized ball till I was thirteen. Hardly ever *played* ball till then. It was my parents' idea. It was summertime, and they recommended for me to go out for Pony League. I guess I was bored or somethin'. I went out for Pony League, and people said, 'You got great instincts.' So I pursued it."

He played shortstop in high school in Fort Worth.

"Best on the team? Naw. I was no shortstop. But then coaches and scouts started recommendin' I play the outfield. Things changed then. I begun thinkin' I had no limitations.

None. My idol was Bobby Bonds, you remember him? I told my friends I was gonna be just like Bobby Bonds."

Bobby Bonds was an outfielder who could run *and* hit the long ball. This is rarer in baseball than one might think. There was Mays, of course. Mantle, for a time. In the long history of the Red Sox, only two men, Jackie Jensen and Carl Yastrzemski, have ever hit twenty home runs and stolen twenty bases in a season. Jensen, Yastrzemski, and, soon, Burks.

"When you sign with a big-league team," Burks says, "you set a timetable for when you'll break in. I signed in '83 and said I wanted to make the big leagues in '88. That was my year. So I'm a little ahead here."

He didn't know anything about the Red Sox before he signed with them. They were just a team from far away who came periodically to Texas to play the Rangers. Fenway suits him; he likes the wall. And he feels the way Greenwell does about the fans. "They appreciate talent," he says.

I surprise Burks, startle him really, by abruptly ending the interview. I do this on impulse, shut my notebook and give a companionable dismissive slap on the knee.

"I appreciate it, Ellis," I say. "Thanks a lot."

Burks looks at me, surprised. He starts to speak, stops, then, "That's it?"

"Sure," I say. "Thanks, huh?"

"No problem," he says.

I watch him move away, deliberate with that long-legged feline prowl. There were other questions, but it was satisfying somehow to end it so early, so neatly. I like Ellis Burks, and I like Mike Greenwell. I hope life here doesn't change them.

"How much you think I'd be worth, playin' these days?" says Pesky.

"A .300-hitting shortstop?" I say. "Good glove, good speed?"

"Half a million?" he says.

"Shit, more than that."

"I don't know," he says.

"Claudell Washington gets a million," I say. *"Claudell Washington."* Steve Crawford gets eight hundred grand, but I don't mention Crawford.

"I wouldn't be worth what Boggs is, but I'd be worth half a million, anyway."

"More," I say.

"Well," he says, "I would have invested it, bought annuities. If I'd had what these guys have"—he nods at the field, covered with young ballplayers—"I would never have had to worry when I was through. I could have taken care of my son, my wife, and never had to worry."

Pesky's parents emigrated from Yugoslavia not long after the turn of the century and settled in Portland, Oregon. Their name was Paveskovich; Johnny shortened it after he made the big leagues. He was one of four kids. His father worked in a sawmill. One day during the Depression Johnny was walking home from a job he had on a farm—he was always working—when he noticed a bantam rooster scrabbling in a front yard close to the road. Hunger got the better of him—real hunger—and Johnny grabbed the bird, shoved it under his coat, and brought it home. His mother demanded to know where he'd gotten it. Johnny said he'd found it running loose in the road miles from anywhere, but his mother knew a lie when she heard it. She didn't even ask whose rooster it was, just told him to take it right back. He did.

Pesky's father used to say a strange thing to him.

"If you play ball," he said, "you'll be a bum. All your life, you'll be a bum."

Nine

Nothing to Play for but the Game Itself

ANOTHER KID HAS ARRIVED FROM PAWTUCKET, JOHN MAR-
zano, a catcher. Marzano is twenty-four, like Greenwell and
Benzinger. He is here because Gedman's season has been ter-
minated by yet another injury. Up in Toronto the other day
Gedman was putting a tag on the Blue Jays' big slugger, Jesse
Barfield, who slid, catching Gedman's left thumb with his foot.
Barfield was safe. The thumb was broken.

It is as if the gods of baseball were punishing Gedman,
making an example out of him, for refusing to sign his contract.
He'd slumped in '86, and yet they were offering him a raise.
He wanted more. Hubris. He joined the team May 1, ignored
in the free agent market, and almost immediately hurt his back.
Later he was on the disabled list with a damaged groin. When
he did play, he looked like a bewildered rookie: eight passed
balls, countless lousy pegs to second, a batting average of .205.
This is a man who, two seasons ago, hit .295 and blasted eigh-

teen home runs. The home crowds don't boo Gedman. It's strange who gets booed and who doesn't. Gedman, with his stoic proletarian face and dogged play, has absolutely no flair. Stanley has none, and they love to boo him. Rice has enormous style, though it is subtle. They also boo Rice.

The fans may like John Marzano, who grew up in the Italian section of Philadelphia and who plays with Gedman's stubborn hustle. Marzano is beefy, not tall, with a broad flat nose and wide jaw. The face is open, neighborly. His speech is chirpy and grammatical. Marzano went to Temple University for three years, which no doubt polished his syntax.

It is August now, and the powerful Blue Jays are in town. The Jays are in first place, a half game ahead of the Yankees, a game and a half ahead of Detroit. On paper the Jays are the best team in the game. At almost every position, a star. So there is excitement in the ballpark tonight. The lounge at dinnertime is fuller than usual, noisier. If the Sox could win all three games they would be, if not in the race, at least in sight of it.

The raised stakes seem to have depressed McNamara and to have made him crankier than usual. Nonetheless, he plants himself on the bench during batting practice, offering himself to the writers, who of course converge from all directions with that magical knowledge they have, as if the manager's willingness to chat went shimmering out in brain waves. Quickly, McNamara is surrounded.

The usual leadoff medical question is asked. McNamara tells us that Nipper is on the DL. Someone is always on the DL.

"John, are you going to play Toronto especially tough?"

The dour face creases up in disbelief. "We play everybody tough," he says.

"John, do the, uh, players still have feelings about George Bell?"

Bell is the Blue Jays' left fielder. A couple of years ago a Sox pitcher named Bruce Kison bounced one off Bell's shoulder, whereupon Bell made a crazed dash for the mound and upended himself, throwing a cleated karate kick at Kison's face. The kick missed. The dugouts poured players for the obligatory brawl.

McNamara nearly shouts his answer. "The George Bell incident was two years ago, for Christ sake!"

The questioner persists. "Do you think the players respect him more now that he's come into his own?"

McNamara's answer is a wintry blue stare.

The writer says, "Do you think there's less dog in him now?"

Another long stare, then: "I never said there was."

"I know you didn't *say* it . . ." The writer shrugs, and gives up.

McNamara stares at him, stares and stares until it is clear the subject has been dropped. Silence takes over. McNamara squints out at the field, content not to talk. The writers drift away one by one. Cliff Keane comes strutting over, jockeys himself down the steps and plops down beside McNamara.

"You got your hands full tonight, huh?" rasps Keane.

" 'Lo, Cliff," says McNamara.

They sit awhile, thinking their own thoughts. McNamara's face softens, goes wistful with Irish melancholy. Suddenly he raises an arm, points past Keane's nose to left field.

"We haven't had anyone out *there*," he says, adding a vehement dip of his head.

"I know it," Keane says.

"And we haven't had anyone behind the plate," McNamara says. He speaks with feeling, almost pleadingly to Keane. "People don't understand how it affects the pitching, not having your catcher back there. They don't *see* it."

"People don't know their ass from their elbow," Keane says.

Pesky, sitting with his fungo between his knees, says, "Williams used to say pitchers were the dumbest bastards who play the game." Pesky shakes his head, spits a brown oyster. "*I* don't think pitchers are dumb, but Ted sure did."

I ask him about that new invention, the split-finger fastball.

"*What* new invention?" says Pesky. "Split-finger fastball? Sure, that's a forkball. Preacher Roe threw it." He hunches forward, digs the packet of Beech Nut out of his hip pocket. "People say, 'You never saw a slider in your day.' Shit." He shoves in a new chaw. "What do they think Allie Reynolds threw? Bob Porterfield, guys like that? They threw the slider, you better *believe* it. There's nothin' new in this game, that's the beauty of it. We used to nick the ball, too. They didn't invent *that*, either. *I* used to do it myself. I used to file my belt buckle to a nice point. The ball would come to me, and I'd give it the treatment."

He shows me how he would take a throw close to his belly then turn the glove, cupping it over his buckle as he cut the skin of the baseball once, twice, and out again as natural as you please.

Joe Morgan sits down as Pesky is finishing the demonstration.

"And what the fuck is this?" Morgan inquires amiably.

"We're talkin' pitching," explains Pesky.

"Ah," says Morgan.

"I'm showin' him how I used to nick up the ball," Pesky says.

Morgan pushes back his cap. "How many no-hitters you have thrown against you, John?"

"In the majors?"

"Of course."

"One."

"Who?"

"You tell me," Pesky says. " 'Fifty-one, in Yankee Stadium."

"Allie Reynolds," Morgan says.

"Goddamn right," Pesky says. "I took a soft oh-for-four."

"That Reynolds could pitch," says Morgan.

"He struck me out looking in the ninth," Pesky says. "Cal Hubbard was the umpire. The pitch was up here."

Pesky scrapes his chest at the letters, just high, drawing his hand across like a knife.

"I turned around, I says, 'Christ sake, Cal, I want him to get the no-hitter, too, but make him earn it, huh?' The score was 8–0. If it had been a 2–1 game, I would have squawked."

Morgan sits with his legs crossed, head tilted back, pensive. It is hard to tell if he's listening. Half-listening, maybe. Pesky himself has turned thoughtful. His gaze widens; it is 1951, and he is hitting against Allie Reynolds.

"Well . . ." he says. He draws his hand across his chest again, perhaps an inch lower. "Maybe it *was* a strike." Again the hand comes up, flat, and this time slowly, slowly, traces the flight of the ball. "It was right here," Pesky says, "so maybe it was a strike."

Morgan nods, just slightly, and says nothing.

Clemens pitches the first of these three games with the Blue Jays. The game's best pitcher has hit his stride. He has won eleven, and the earned-run average is 3.27 and falling. Back in June the writers were asking Roger what was wrong, what was different this year, and Roger insisted nothing was. He said he wasn't hurt and was throwing as hard as he ever had. His record suggested otherwise, but it begins to look as if Roger was right. It is one of baseball's mysteries, why a healthy pitcher lacks his good stuff some days. *He didn't have it today*, people will say, as if they were shedding light on the game rather than stating the obvious. Why didn't he have it? No one knows. We do know that when a good pitcher doesn't have it, watch out the next time, and the next. Proficiency will tell. The American League has begun paying for Clemens's deficient spring.

Tonight, he blinds the game's most potent offense. A home run in the fifth, bases empty, by the second baseman and number-nine hitter, Garth Iorg, is the Jays' only run. Garth Iorg: sounds like science fiction, a warrior from another galaxy. Iorg hits the high fastball into the screen. Otherwise, Roger blinds them.

The Jays have a tall, lean rookie slugger named Fred McGriff, the DH tonight, and Clemens fans the kid three times with fastballs shoulder-high. McGriff cannot lay off. Roger gets way ahead in the count, then throws it like a fat dare up where McGriff can see it only too well. McGriff has a rippling, big-league swing, classy but too late to get Roger's high hard one. Down he goes three times. Clemens strikes out eight in all.

Clemens gets into very little trouble. The talented oddball, Bell, leads off the second with a cheap double to right. Bell breaks his bat—you can hear it in the press box, fibrous as celery—and the ball drifts low and dies on the line. Clemens disposes of McGriff, but Jesse Barfield hoists a high, high pop fly to short right. Benzinger is playing deep for the big lefty. Todd comes in, leaning as he runs, leaning and leaning till he drops to his knees, snaring the ball just off the ground, tumbling, losing it. The ball squirts in front of him. Bell shoots over to third. They give Benzinger an error. Runners at first and third, one out. Willie Upshaw, another big hitter, pops one high off his bat handle to Boggs. Ernie Whitt, still another, sails an easy fly ball to Benzinger, and the inning is over.

The Jays tap a pair of little infield singles in the third. Both runners steal on the new kid, Marzano. Clemens whiffs

Rance Mulliniks, the number-three hitter. Bell chops a ground ball to second.

Except for the Iorg home run, there is no more trouble.

The Sox score two in the first, one in the sixth, and bust the game open in the seventh and eighth. Boggs and Greenwell each whack three hits, but these two displays of excellence go all but unnoticed beside the show put on by big Sam Horn. Sam begins his game with a strikeout. He knocks a gentle fly ball to Barfield in right in the third. Then he bats in consecutive innings: the sixth, seventh, eighth. Greenwell is at first in the sixth. Horn hits the first pitch over Barfield's head, slaps it effortlessly, a tremendous fly ball that the wind grabs, slows, and bats down just short of the bull pen. The ball hits the pen on one bounce. Horn thinks it's gone and goes into his home run cruise; he has to scramble to reach second. Next inning he drives the first pitch high off the wall. The wind is pulling the flags hard from left to right and in, and Horn outmuscles it. Another double, and if not for the wind, a second home run. Next inning, Horn gets his home run. There are two out. Two strikes. The bases are loaded. The pitch comes inside, and oh, does he pound it. The home run climbs, a perfect arch, over the bull pen, into the bleachers, way up there, Ruthian, classic. The crowd surges up, lets go a wild ovation, an insistent racket that you can imagine lifting the roof off the grandstand. Sam skips bulky-legged around the bases, fists up near his shoulders, and goes down the dugout steps to a thicket of outstretched arms. Of course the crowd wants him back. Thirty thousand people, roaring for one more glimpse of Sam Horn. Happy to oblige, Sam climbs several steps, till they can see him above the dugout roof. He lifts the helmet off his close-cropped head, holds it high. The cheering swells in an arching crescendo. Sam Horn smiles.

After the game McNamara pronounces Clemens's return to form: "Roger is back where he was."

All around the room heads nod agreement.

"Uh, John, considering how many pitches Roger threw, did you think about taking him out after eight?"

"You see anyone warming up?" McNamara says. The question is rhetorical and goes unanswered. "You want me to get lynched?" he says, dropping a faint smile.

The reporters chuckle sympathetically.

"Maybe," says McNamara, "some people do."

A large obliging laugh goes up. McNamara's dry smile lengthens. He stares at his bare desk. The smile is proud and sad and lonesome. Some of those people are right here in this room, says the smile.

"So I'm gonna be in a book, huh?" says Sam Horn, leading me up the tunnel toward the clubhouse.

"That's right," I tell him.

"Imagine that," he says.

I suspect he can, now, and could not a month ago. I bet he can imagine almost anything these days.

It is four o'clock, and Sam is in his street clothes, pressed gray slacks and a white shirt with puffed sleeves, elegant, almost foppish. He walks bent forward off those mammoth haunches.

"Big night last night, huh?" I say.

"Oh, yeah," he agrees, sort of sighing it. The voice is soft, a shimmer. Like a baby's.

"That first double," I say, "I thought that was out of here."

Sam is climbing the half flight of steps. He grabs the pipe rail with a fist like a canteloupe and hauls himself up the last three stairs.

"I hit it hard," he admits. "It had plenty of steam on it, but it didn't have no height. It had a top spin on it."

"Ah," I say.

Horn barges into the clubhouse with me at his heels. He stalks across the room to his dressing stall, Buckner's old locker.

"Pull up a chair," he says.

I look around, find a free-floating canvas chair. I drag it over and sit.

"Could I ask you about—"

"Excuse me," he says, and walks away. I wait while he digs his mail out of the cubbyhole in the honeycomb by the bulletin board. He plods slowly back, flipping through the stack of envelopes. He stops in front of me, flips his way through the stack, and lays it on the shelf of his cubicle. Slowly, slowly, he tugs his shirt free. I have to look way up to see his face.

"I'd like to ask you a little about your childhood," I say. "About playing ball as a kid. You see, I—"

"What'd you say this book was about?" He eyes me warily, unbuttoning his shirt.

"It's about, uh, the Red Sox, and . . . It's about playing ball as a kid. Were you always big?"

Sam is frowning, thinking things over. He undoes the bottom and last button and peels back his shirt. He seems to swell out of it, mountainous. "At first I was kind of short," he says. "Then all of a sudden, I just *grew*." He hangs the shirt neatly, carefully, and sits down. He collapses forward and begins untying his shiny black shoes.

"Can I ask you about growing up?" I say.

"All right," he says. He sounds doubtful.

I elicit some bare-boned facts doled out with reluctance, as if the words were bills surrendered out of his wallet. Sam was born in Dallas, grew up from the age of eight in San Diego. His father was a construction worker. He has two athletic sisters. In Little League Sam pitched and played the outfield. In Senior League he pitched. At Morris High School in San Diego he pitched, played football and basketball. I try to imagine him at fourteen and fifteen, gigantic on the mound, the ball a white marble in his immense paw. He wouldn't have any fancy stuff, just raw speed. Kids who had never spoken with him, kids from other towns, would know his name: Horn. *Did you hear*

*what Horn did Friday night? Struck out fourteen guys. We're goin'
against Horn tonight—shit, we're dead, man.*

"When you were playing ball in those years," I ask him,
"did you fantasize about making the big leagues?"

Sam is carefully bunching his socks and tucking them in
his rowboat shoes. "Sure," he says, bending way down to place
the shoes in the bottom of his cubicle. "We all did."

He stands up. He wraps his fist around his mail, sits down,
and lays the pile in his lap. With his little finger he slits open
the top envelope.

I press on. "Do you have any feeling about playing for a
team with so much tradition and history?"

"Well, I *am* aware the Red Sox have been a traditional
team throughout the years." He has begun reading the first
letter. I wait. He reads on.

"The fans have treated you well," I try.

Sam finishes the letter, folds it, and returns it to its envelope. He slides the envelope under the pile. "They've been
very warm to me," he says. He isn't looking at me. Not at all.
"It makes it a lot easier," he says. He tears open envelope
number two.

A good question occurs to me. An important question,
really. "Would you like to play the field?" I ask.

Sam now is deep inside the second letter, as determinedly
submerged as a philosopher dissecting Plato. He hears me,
though. He looks up—not at me—considers the question.

"I'll do whatever will help the team," he says, and reads
on.

It is time, I decide, to take the hint. I close my notebook.
"I appreciate it," I say.

Horn finally glances at me. "Sure," he murmurs silkily.
"You got it."

Got what? I wonder. I get up, push the chair where I
found it. Boggs is sitting sprawled low in his chair, reading mail.

At the varnished table Evans is signing baseballs. The place is quiet.

In the dugout I find Pesky and McNamara having a chat.

"How's that fuckin' Pulitzer Prize book comin' along?" Pesky greets me.

McNamara squints into the distance, showing nothing.

"Okay, I guess," I tell Pesky. I sit down beside him, away from McNamara.

A kid comes down the steps, somebody's son or relative, about ten years old. He's got a glove and ball. He's got a deck of baseball cards. His gaze freezes on McNamara; he hurries his glove and ball under one arm and begins a rapid search through the baseball cards. He finds the card he's looking for, John McNamara, manager, Boston Red Sox. He extends the card gingerly.

"Mr. McNamara? Could you sign this, please?"

"Whaddaya say, kid?" greets Pesky.

"I'm fine," the kid says.

McNamara accepts the card. "You got a pen?" he says.

"How the hell can he sign it without a pen?" Pesky asks the kid.

The kid smiles and reddens. He draws a ballpoint from the hip pocket of his jeans. McNamara lays the card on his knee and inscribes it carefully, conscientiously.

"Say," he asks the kid, "can I borrow your baseball?"

The kid nods vigorously and hands over his ball, which is scuffed and dirt-stained. McNamara gets up with the ball and goes to the bat rack. He chooses a fungo, drawing it out with a flourish, as if unsheathing a sword.

"What's up, John?" says Pesky.

"Those fuckin' guys in right field," McNamara explains.

We all look out there. In the brilliant light of the sun that still hangs above the roof along third, three players are sitting on the grass, propped back on their hands, faces lifted to the light. I can't make out who they are. Starchy-white uniforms, emerald grass.

Pesky chuckles. McNamara climbs the dugout steps with the fungo and the kid's old baseball. He tosses the ball up nose-high and strides into it as it falls, swinging for the sunbathers. He pulls it, though, a ground ball that slithers way to the left of them. Benzinger is out there shagging batting practice fly balls; he thinks McNamara's ground ball is for him. Benzinger charges it, scoops, and pegs it in on one nice bounce. The three sunbathers haven't moved.

McNamara hangs the ball in the air again and this time swings under it, lifting a lazy, spinning fly ball that arches down about three-quarters of the way to Benzinger. Todd gallops in, graceful across the wide lawn as only a young athlete can be, scoops, and flicks the ball on the run to McNamara. The sunbathers remain oblivious.

"Son of a *bitch*," McNamara says. And: "*Hey*. HEY!"

He lifts his arms straight up, lowers them, throws them up again. The sunbathers have begun noticing him. They look for their gloves on the grass and pick themselves up with no alacrity whatsoever. McNamara stands there glaring at them. They all turn and break into a slow jog toward center field. You can read their numbers now: Clemens, Hurst, Sambito. McNamara sends them a final stare, then hands the fungo down to Pesky. He tosses the ball to the kid. The kid looks amazed by all of this. McNamara holsters both hands in his hip pockets and stalks away to the batting cage.

Now I can laugh. "He couldn't get it out there," I say.

"Well," Pesky says, loyal, "he hasn't hit fungoes in years. He's out of the habit, is all."

Horn emerges from the tunnel with his bat and glove. He whams the bat into its slot in the rack.

"Hit me some grounders, Johnny?" he says.

Horn lumbers up the steps. He fits the mitt over his right

hand. Pesky, slender still and with an athletic, a *cocky*, little body, climbs the steps with a surprising stiffness, unsure of his legs. He circles the cage to the third-base line, where he can hit ground balls to Horn at first.

Pesky drills the ball gently at Horn, feeding him predictable, choppy bounces. Hitting is Sam's pride: the colossal home runs are his monuments. He doesn't seem to dislike fielding, but seems indifferent. Wade Boggs, who has willed himself to become one of the better third-base gloves in the league, dirties his uniform every day in a passionate and solitary quest to improve. Boggs takes a hundred ground balls a day. Horn takes fifteen.

His legs are slow, they are thick and heavy; Sam springs sideways toward the ground ball with gravity sucking at those legs. He squares around and braces himself, waiting instead of charging. At the last second he thrusts the huge glove down, calculating that the ball will find its way into it. It does, usually. Sam's head is up a bit; watch Owen or Barrett, how they bend to the ball, studying it all the way into the glove. Mean, tricky hops warn Sam off, freeze him before he bends all the way down. He clenches up rigid as oak and swipes at the funny bounce, which may shoot low or over his shoulder like a bullet. Sam barely sees it, just swipes with that big mitt, almost always missing. Missing doesn't seem to affect him. He might shrug. He might smile. Or nothing—as if the ball and not he were at fault.

He takes the fifteenth ground ball—the big mitt drinks it—and waves to Pesky that he has finished. The kids have begun to gather at the ends of the dugout with their balls and scorecards.

"Sam . . . Sam . . ."

"*Sam can I have your autograph pleeeeze . . .*"

"*Sam you're awesome pleeeeze . . .*"

Horn goes to the barrier.

"How ya doin', fellas?" he says. He clamps his mitt under his arm, accepts the first scorecard, and scribbles his name.

A lefty, Jimmy Key, starts for the Jays tonight, so Mc-Namara benches Horn and Greenwell, who both bat left-handed. Playing those misty percentages. Greenwell is hitting .332, and after thirteen games Horn's average is .362. The righty hitters who replace them are the forgotten Henderson, whose average is .221, and Baylor, .233.

The Sox' starting pitcher is Bob Stanley, whose mere name, pronounced by Sherm Feller over the PA system, elicits a gale of boos. Why do they boo Bob Stanley, one of the most pleasant men on the team? Because he's overweight? Because he gets paid a million a year? Why boo Stanley and not Crawford? Booing Stanley has become an irresistible sport in Fenway, an addictive little pleasure turned ritual. They still cheer Henderson to the skies, though Hendu has been an utter flop since his glorious October. I can't imagine them booing Horn, though it's early yet. And they boo Rice, one of the most magnificent athletes ever to play here.

It's no mystery why they boo Marc Sullivan, who is behind the plate tonight. Haywood's son is now hitting .168. Early yesterday he and Barrett were taping a television ad for Team Picture Day, when the picture will be handed out free to everyone who comes to the ball game. Sullivan and Barrett were sitting on the top step of the dugout holding the picture between them and trading wisecrack lines printed on cards held for them by a woman in the dugout. Sullivan would point at the photograph and say Barrett looked like the batboy, then Barrett would point and say Sullivan would look better with his mask on. That sort of thing. They had to go through it quite a few times, and once between takes Rice happened along. Rice sat down beside Sullivan, threw his arm around him, and addressed the TV camera. "Hi, I'm Marc Sullivan. My father,

Haywood, sits up there." Rice pointed at the owners' skyview box. "Right up in that box," Rice said.

Sullivan seemingly untroubled by the subject of Rice's needling, gave it right back: "Yeah, he's sitting up there wonderin' why he signed Jim Rice."

Rice stood up, came down the steps, and said serenely, throwing it back over his shoulder. " 'Cause I can play."

"Play what," Sullivan said, "golf or baseball?"

Rice kept walking. "Either one," he said. "Don't matter."

Tonight, after Stanley shuts the Jays out for two innings, Sullivan bats with Henderson at first and Baylor at second. He is booed, of course. Not a cheer in the ballpark for this earnest and friendly kid, who works at his hitting, works and works and works. *"You're playin' for the family!"* bawls a loudmouth somewhere behind home plate. If we can hear it in the press box, Marc can hear it on the field. Key throws two quick strikes, slow curves that Marc only watches. A wind of boos. Then Key tries to slip a fastball past Marc's letters and Marc clobbers the sucker high off the wall, hits it so hard that only Baylor has time to score. Sullivan legs it to second. A large, generous ovation.

The Jays get a run in the third: a single, a sacrifice, a single. Evans, playing first, takes a ground ball wide of the bag and lobs the ball behind Stanley as Stanley scoots over to cover, an error that ends up costing nothing but does go to show, yet again, that the league's best right fielder is no first baseman.

In the top of the fourth with two out, Barfield unloads one high to right center field. Watch Burks, not the ball: Ellis gallops after it, angling back to his left, not quite sprinting, timing it so he and the ball will intersect, running with the fluid rhythm of a big cat, reaching and pulling the ball out of the air just before it can hit the center-field wall. A sweet, sweet catch. The Jays are out.

In the fifth, with runners at second and third, one out, Stanley wins a sizzling duel with Upshaw. A big moment: the Sox have scored two more and lead, 3–1. The Jays have the tying runs in scoring position. The count goes deep, three and two. Upshaw starts fouling them off, just touching the ball, just getting that little piece of it. He keeps fouling them off; Stanley keeps pouring in strikes. Then Bob puts him away with a fastball, fires it past Upshaw, who swings from the heels and gets nothing. Cheers for Bob Stanley. He throws two strikes past Lloyd Moseby. Smart, tough pitching. The crowd is with Stanley, cheering him. He tries his forkball, which twists down, and which Moseby nevertheless whistles into center field knee-high, a convincing single. Both runners come home. Booing erupts, and we are back to normal.

With one out in the sixth, Barfield slugs a towering home run into the bleachers. Barfield trots the bases listening to boos not meant for him. Stanley walks Mulliniks on four pitches, and the crowd is not only booing but hollering, sounding volatile and dangerous as a lynch mob. Iorg is the hitter. Mulliniks runs with the pitch. Iorg swings, misses, and lets go of his bat, which sails to the edge of the mound and goes dancing on past Stanley, who must jump to avoid getting whacked across the knees. Sullivan, meanwhile, has thrown Mulliniks out. Stanley grabs the bat and flings it angrily toward Iorg. The bat slides short of Iorg, who walks out to fetch it, but the crowd liked seeing Stanley heave it, and sends down a cheer. Stanley stalks to the mound, but it isn't Iorg he's mad at, it's the booing. Iorg is angry, too—his jaw is clenched—but at himself, for failing to put wood on the ball with Mulliniks running. Stanley glares in for the sign. He wheels, throws, and whiffs Iorg. God, I love baseball.

Bolton jogs in to pitch the seventh. The game is still close, 4–3. Kelly Gruber, the Jays' ninth hitter tonight, hits Bolton's second pitch over the left-field wall. Bolton walks Upshaw on four pitches. He gets Moseby, but Ernie Whitt singles, and McNamara trudges out to change pitchers. Sambito trots in, surrenders a sacrifice fly and a double by McGriff that nearly leaps the center-field wall, a monstrous poke. The little cannonade produces three runs, and we can pretty much kiss the game good-bye. Schiraldi pitches the ninth and surrenders one more run. The Jays win it, 8–3.

McNamara shortens tonight's postmortem by undressing in front of us. He sits in one of the chairs to the side of his desk, and begins with his shoes. "Stanley did his job," McNamara sighs. "He kept us in the game." He tugs off the stirrup socks, peels down the long tube socks. I'm struck by how white his big feet are.

But why did Stanley come out of the game after six?

"His elbow was tightening up. I asked him how he felt, and he said he was tired and his elbow was tightening up."

We sift out into the clubhouse, which is silent after the loss. Is Stanley still here? Yes, he is. I wonder why. I wonder why he hasn't gotten the hell out of here before the reporters can descend with their microphones and notebooks. He is sitting in a canvas chair in his corner behind the brick pillar. There are no lights back here, and he sits in near-darkness, sunk low in the director's chair facing out from the corner. He has had his shower; his hair is damp, his darkish skin has that scrubbed look, that sheen. He is wearing a blue polo shirt. His dark glasses hang by one stem hooked inside his shirt collar. The reporters crowd around, looming over him in his chair.

Someone says something I can't hear. I wedge in, stretch my neck. I can see Stanley, flopped deep in the chair with his hands clasped on his gut. He stares with wide, sad eyes through this forest of people.

"If I make one mistake," he says slowly, "I hear about it." The voice is deep and resonant. "I walked McGriff. He was the first guy to reach base, and they booed me."

There's a pause, but no one prods him with a question. The reporters all simply wait, motionless and silent. The scene has cast a spell: this man sitting weary and bitter in the shadows, his broad face the perfect tragic mask, tugged down at every corner. The silence stretches out but is not at all uncomfortable.

"It starts before the game," Stanley continues. "I'm down in the bull pen warmin' up, they're yellin' at me. They're booin'. This one guy was screamin' at me. *Screamin'*. You guys wouldn't believe what I hear in the bull pen sometimes."

He breaks off, stares awhile. The reporters wait patiently.

"It's been a tough year," Stanley says. "The toughest, I guess." A smile leaks through, slow and wry. "Next year I'm gonna be Comeback Player of the Year." He snorts a laugh, and lapses again into silence.

Then, "You know, my kids don't come to the ballpark anymore. They used to. They used to come all the time. A kid should see his dad play ball, right? I mean, they're gonna remember it sometime. But when this booing started, and the *stuff*, the insults, that was the end of it. I don't want my kids to hear the stuff I listen to."

Again he stops, and in this new silence the reporters begin to slip away, scattering in different directions. It is time for some to begin writing. Some need other interviews. Several of us linger by Stanley, who continues to stare straight ahead. When he speaks again it is in the same flat, weary way.

"I guess," he says, "you have some good years, and they keep expecting it."

I think about Henderson, who had a good month, period.

"I'll tell you this," Stanley says. "They're wastin' their breath. They—are—*wasting* their breath." He looks up, sees us writing. "Wasting their breath," he says.

The evening before the third game with the Blue Jays, word goes around that Oil Can Boyd is through for the season.

A shoulder injury. So the Can, who last year won sixteen and lost ten, concludes his season with a single win, three losses, and a fast 5.89 earned-run average. In the golden late afternoon—it is August 12—McNamara strolls out alone, sits in the dugout, waits for the writers to come to him. He draws a small audience including a photographer, a stranger here, faded jeans and a beard of dark curls, who sits on the dugout steps straight in front of McNamara and begins, across maybe ten feet of space, to snap pictures. He takes picture after picture, brief *whirr* and *snip*, again and again.

"Boyd is out for the year," begins McNamara, intoning as if he were reading a release, "and should be able to come back in the spring. From what I was told—" He fixes those ice-blue eyes on the photographer, who keeps shooting, *whirr*, *snip*, *whirr*, *snip*. ". . . from what I was told, there was a small tear."

He leans forward and shoots out a soggy wad of tobacco. The photographer sights and clicks off another picture.

"Clemens had the same thing in '85," resumes McNamara. "It shouldn't surprise anybody. Remember, these guys have been pitching competitively—"

The photographer is shooting again. Aiming, shooting; aiming, shooting.

". . . have been pitching competitively," McNamara pushes on, "since they were eight or nine years old. There's tremendous wear and tear—"

He breaks off and glares at the photographer, who is beginning to comprehend, and who lowers his camera hesitantly, as if considering whether he ought to keep it up there to protect his nose. He is smiling nervously, dopily.

McNamara, in a voice like steel, says, *"You are annoying me, sir."*

The photographer's smile wilts. "Excuse me," he mutters.

"Now, where was I?" says McNamara.

———

The sun has gone below the grandstand roof. The dugout is empty except for me, Pesky, Morgan, and Ed Bridges, who remembers when Pesky was hitting leadoff in this ballpark. Pesky tells a joke about a man who gets sick on an airplane in the ten-gallon hat of the Texan asleep in the seat beside him. As he tells these jokes Pesky sometimes gets laughing so hard he can barely get out the punch line. Ed Bridges, who has his tape recorder, asks if he can interview the two of them. Ed tapes these interviews for WSRO in Marlborough.

"Turn the fuckin' machine on," Morgan says.

"Wait a minute," Ed says. "Wait a minute. No swearing, now."

"Shit, we won't swear," Pesky says.

"You don't mind if I listen, do you?" I ask.

"Why not?" Ed says.

"You just stay the hell out of it," Pesky tells me.

"This is gonna be some interview," Ed says.

"Turn the fuckin' thing on," Morgan says.

Ed does. "Ed Bridges here," he says, covering ground quickly, "in the Red Sox dugout, sitting between two of my favorite immortals, Joe Morgan, third-base coach for the Red Sox, and John Pesky, who is all things to all men."

Pesky chuckles. Morgan grins.

"We'll begin with Joe Morgan," Ed rushes on. "Joe, what do Red Sox fans have to look forward to for the rest of the 1987 season?"

"Well," says Morgan, "you've seen the kids, and you're gonna see a lot more of 'em. I hope the bull pen gets better. Take it from there, big guy."

Bridges turns the other way, pushes the recorder toward Pesky. "John, you're a *little* guy." Pesky laughs, nearly choking on his tobacco. "What do you have to say to Red Sox fans?"

"Well," says Pesky, "I have to agree with Mr. Morgan. I

never disagree with Morgan. He's the trivia buff around here, he keeps me in stitches during batting practice. Anyway, I agree with Joe, the young guys are gonna have to do it. But you know somethin', Ed? Even though we're fourteen games out, you just can't tell what's gonna happen in this game. I haven't given up yet."

There is an incredulous pause. Ed Bridges fights back a laugh, finds his tongue and says, "That's good to hear, John."

Pesky laughs, Bridges laughs. Morgan smiles, the smile spreading wider and wider. This is no ordinary moment in radio journalism.

"Joe," Ed says, "last year you were very proud of the fact that when the season was over you were able to buy your wife a fur coat. What are you gonna buy her this year?"

"Nada," says Morgan. "You know what that means, don't you?"

Pesky motions that he wants to say something, and Ed swings the tape recorder over. "He's gonna buy her a trap," Pesky says, "so she can get her own."

This breaks everyone up, even Morgan.

"Traps cost money, Joe," Ed says, finally.

"It'll be an expensive trap," Morgan agrees, "but I got my pickup truck, so I careth not."

"You careth not?" says Ed. He shakes his head at Morgan's diction and plunges on. "Joe, you've always had a lot of publicity, because in the wintertime you were plowing snow on the Mass Turnpike. What are you gonna do this winter? You gonna go back to plowing snow if we don't win the pennant?"

"Last year," Morgan says, finally sounding serious, "was the first year in my career I didn't work."

"You mean, didn't work in the baseball season?" Ed says. "Or during the winter?"

Pesky loves this one.

"Both, sir," answers Morgan.

Ed turns again. "Let's have a little more prognostication from you, Mr. Pesky."

"The only thing I'm concerned about now is Oil Can Boyd," Pesky says.

"The press release did say he wouldn't be back this season," Ed says. "That *is* a rather unfortunate blow to the team."

"How much more time we got?" Morgan says.

"We have approximately one minute, Mr. Morgan."

"Then we got plenty of time to find out how good you are," says Morgan. "Tell me: who hit the first night-game home run? And if you don't get that one, who hit the first home run right-handed and left-handed in the same game?"

A blank silence.

"In what ballpark, Mr. Morgan?" Ed says finally.

"One of 'em was in Crosley Field, the former. The latter I would guess was in Wrigley Field."

"Do you know the answer, Mr. Pesky?" Bridges asks.

"I'd have to say Augie Galan."

"That," says Morgan, "is the answer to the second question. Now, who hit the first night-game home run, John?"

"I have no idea," Pesky says.

"Brooklyn Dodgers," prompts Morgan.

"Who was a switch-hitter with the Dodgers in those years?" Pesky wonders aloud.

"No," Morgan says, "he wasn't a switch-hitter, not the guy who hit the first night-game home run."

"That's right, the first night-game home run, uh . . ."

"This is Ed Bridges in Fenway Park with Johnny Pesky and Joe Morgan."

There's nothing funny about the ball game, a 10–4 shellacking by the Blue Jays. Young Jeff Sellers pitches for the Sox and gets hit hard in the first, fourth, and fifth innings. McNamara lets him finish the first inning, though he gives them five hits—two of them doubles—and four runs. The Jays rattle the ball all over the place.

They score two more in the fourth, and Sellers pitches straight into big trouble in the fifth. Bell smacks a single, and McGriff walks on four pitches. McNamara lifts Sellers. The Jays are leading, 6–2; they haven't run away with it, but will if Bell and McGriff should score.

The man chosen to prevent this is Crawford, the big Oklahoman whose dislike for writers exceeds even McNamara's. "They're all assholes," I heard him say once to a white-haired old-timer who was condoling with him over some cutting remarks by Dan Shaughnessy in the *Globe*. "Call him 'Shag' if he wants you to," wrote Shaughnessy, "but for heaven's sake call him a taxi. Get him out of here." I remember Cliff Keane cackling over the line in the press box. Shaughnessy looks deceptively boyish. Freckles spatter his cheeks, and he has amber Huck Finn curls. But this is a hard-nosed sportswriter who can't be bought off or bullied. McNamara can't stand him. Recently Shaughnessy has been referring to Crawford as "the Bombino," because of the frequent bomblike home runs that result from Crawford's pitching.

So here is Crawford—Shag, his teammates call him—to keep the Sox in this game. He must pitch to Barfield, one of the league's feared sluggers. The white-haired old-timer who was condoling with Shag over Shaughnessy's recommendation that he be dispatched once and for all in a taxi, told him: "You're a big-league pitcher, Shag. I don't care what anyone writes. You're a big-league pitcher." Here is a big-league task, pitching to Jesse Barfield with two men on base. The count goes long, three and two.

Shag throws his fastball, and Barfield wallops it. He hits it over the wall, over the screen above the wall; up, up, and away into the night. This is more than a fly ball: Barfield drills a hole in the sky. Three-run homer. The crowd—bigger than thirty thousand for the third night in a row—subsides with a sullen groan. With the horse a mile out of the barn, Crawford shuts the door, pitching three easy outs.

He gives up another run in the seventh, and in the eighth Gardner takes over. Wes gives up two singles in the eighth, a double and a single in the ninth, but the Jays somehow fail to score. Not that they need to.

In the press box, Jim or Josh or Dick Bresciani always alerts us when a pitcher begins throwing in the bull pen. *Steve Crawford is warming up for the Red Sox. Tom Bolton is warming up for the Red Sox.* These announcements have taken on a doomful color, as if the PR guys had flicked on the loudspeaker to inform us that the country had gone to war. *Joe Sambito is warming up for the Red Sox*: it sounds melancholy. *I'm afraid Joe Sambito is warming up for the Red Sox. I hate to tell you this, but Steve Crawford is warming up for the Red Sox.*

After the game Sellers converses in an easy, unruffled sort of way with the reporters, not at all discouraged by what has been happening to him on the mound. "I had good stuff to-night," he insists. "I was poppin' my fastball. Of course, they're a good fastball-hittin' team." They sure are. Sellers is a sturdy towhead. He has taken his shower and is wearing the usual polo shirt, a pair of plaid Bermuda shorts, and white leather Pumas. He looks like a high-school kid working around a marina or caddying. "I don't get discouraged," he tells us calmly. "I've had some tough times, that's no secret, but I'm a big-league pitcher. It's only a matter of time."

The Bombino, of course, is nowhere to be seen.

It is August 25, cool, darkening early. The evening has a loose feel to it, an absence of any urgency. The Sox are stuck where they were, thirteen and a half games out of first place, and there is no longer a possibility of winning. There is really nothing to play for but the game itself; to augment your statistics, to please the crowd, to have fun. The veterans are tired. The kids are enjoying every minute.

Oil Can Boyd is here tonight. He saunters out of the tunnel in a white shirt open wide at the neck, black slacks, white moccasins, and a brown leather pillbox hat on the thin bullet of his head. The hat makes Can look foreign. Moroccan, perhaps. Can is also wearing his glasses, which somehow shrink his already tiny-seeming face. The smallness of Oil Can tugs at the heart. There's a poignant fragility about him, as if his bones were hollow, like a bird's. He takes a perch on the bench and commences to study the busy field, where his teammates are taking batting practice. Before you know it, four or five writers have gathered around. Before you know it, the Can is talking.

Music. The monologue purls, eddies, floats high, dips low, slides, stops, gallops on.

"I was throwin' a week or two after the World Series, really puttin' it *down*, and my arm didn't *feel* right, you know? I went home and told my wife, she said, 'Well, what you expect? You ain't thrown in two weeks.' But I know my arm, I can throw ten pitches and I'm ready to *go*. . . .

"I was down to the university one day, throwin' easy. There's guys there, always is, want to see me throw. Want to see me spin some curves, do my thing. I say, 'Naw, I don't feel like it,' but they're insistin' about it, so I throw a few. My arm just . . . didn't . . . feel . . . right. You know? I thought I was just tired, I just come off a long ball season. . . ."

Bruce Hurst meanwhile has come loping in from center field, where he has been running his sprints. Hurst drops beside me on the bench, keeping an appointment. I have decided that if anyone on this team feels the pull of its history, it would be the thoughtful and candid Hurst. Bruce is a Mormon; his heart is an open book, generous and well meaning.

Oil Can, about ten feet down the bench, is saying, ". . .

come to spring training, I was poppin' that first day. I was *smo-kin'*, boom-boom-boom. Next day, I couldn't pick my arm up. But I thought whatever it was, I jus' needed to throw. I never been hurt before, see. I didn't know what bein' hurt *was*. . . ."

Hurst listens, smiles. "We miss Oil Can," he says. "You've got to run on all cylinders." He looks out, thinks about this. "Don't let me use that as a crutch. The fact is, we haven't played well. You can talk about Oil Can and Roger and Geddy forever, but the fact is, we haven't played well."

". . . changed my delivery," Can is saying, "come around at a different angle to take some of the pain off. This was pain comin' from all *over*. . . ."

Hurst's voice is curiously high from so tall and strong a man. "A World Series," he says, "is a tremendous strain emotionally. Not only do you have to rest up from it, but because of it there are all these demands in the off-season, interviews, speaking engagements, and so on. When I went to spring training, I felt like I'd never left. I felt like I'd never gotten a break. I was there two weeks before it hit me I was *in* spring training."

"McNamara," I say, "was talking about how the team has missed Gedman. He said people don't realize what it's done to the pitching."

"Well, it's true," Hurst says. "There's a lot of ego, a lot of stubbornness, involved in calling pitches. The catcher thinks he knows best, I think I know best. We don't want to give in to each other. But when you work with a catcher awhile, you can get over this. You can get on the same wavelength. Together, you remember hitters, you find yourselves in agreement on what to throw."

"Can't you just shake off the sign?" I say.

"Yeah, you can shake off the sign and throw the pitch you want," he says, "but when you do that you often tip off the hitter. You're either shaking off the fastball or the curve, and the hitter can often figure it out."

I ask him if he ever feels as if this team is fated.

He shrugs, and the gentle Mormon voice stiffens just a bit. "The Boston Red Sox of 1946," he says, "are different from the Red Sox of 1967. The Red Sox of 1967 are different from the Red Sox of 1975." It sounds rehearsed, or as if he were intoning from a written page. He has obviously said it before. "The Red Sox of 1986 were different from all those other teams. We use different gloves. We wear different uniforms. They were wool, we wear polyester. Are we snake-bit?" He puffs his cheeks, blows the thought away. "Nah."

"The way I was throwin' at certain periods of time," Oil Can is saying, "I thought I was okay. But then the way my control was goin' the last couple games, I *knew* somethin' was wrong. . . ."

"I wanted to be a big-league ballplayer," I blurt.

"Oh, yeah?" Hurst smiles, interested.

"When I was about fourteen," I tell him, "reality set in on me."

Hurst grins. "Reality sets in on all of us," he says. "It just happens later to some than to others."

"I suppose," I say.

"Listen," he says, "when I was in high school, every time I pitched, I'd throw a one-, maybe a two-hitter. I went to college, and now I'm pitching four-hitters. I got to double A, and I'm pitching *six*-hitters. Now I'm in the big leagues, and if they get nine hits a game off me, it's probably a good night."

". . . could always put the ball where I wanted to," says the Can. "I'm a control pitcher. . . ."

"Are you in your prime?" I ask Hurst.

He looks at me. "How long does your prime last?"

"Well . . ." I say.

"A year or two?" he asks.

"Longer," I say. "Five, six years."

"Yeah," he says slowly. "Yeah, I'm in my prime."

"I think so, too," I say. "What personal goals do you have at this point?"

"Well, whenever you start pursuing personal goals in this game, it seems to me you get on the wrong track."

He means it. His eyes are large and clear. Decent.

I thank Hurst for his time and wish him all the luck in the world. He smiles, says he was glad to talk to me. As he leaves, crossing in front of me, he gives me a friendly slap on the knee with his glove, exactly what Greenwell did.

Oil Can, meanwhile, is winding up his aria.

"It's my arm," the Can is explaining, "not wantin' to go along with my mind. I want to throw the slider down and away, but my arm says, 'Dennis, I can't *put* the slider down and away.' It ain't like when you get hit around 'cause you ain't got your stuff. My arm don't feel good, that's why I couldn't get 'em out. I never had to say that in my life. I know it's kind of contradictable: if your arm don't feel good, you shouldn't be out there in the first place."

The writers are no longer jotting, but they're listening with their heads tipped down and with lambent smiles, as one listens to pleasing music.

The Can has exhausted the subject of his injury. He and the writers watch the field awhile, companionably silent.

Then Can says, smiling, "I come back to see if anybody *changed* while I been gone. Want to see if the guys still doin' it right, takin' their four swings, like always. Who knows? Maybe they moved the mound back or somethin'." Can chuckles, a slithering sound.

Another comfortable silence.

"This is the time of year I like pitchin'," says the Can. "A cool, nice night."

The Sox whip Chicago tonight, 7–3.

John Marzano hits a home run, his fifth, a rather soft fly

ball that floats down just over the green wall. The stocky, al-most pudgy, college boy still looks as if he belongs on a campus ball field, but he is holding his own in the big leagues. He knocks a single to center field tonight as well as the home run.

Sam Horn builds the legend higher with a pair of titanic home runs, one with Greenwell on base. They are pitching Sam inside these days, which is a way of approaching the prob-lem, but not necessarily solving it. In the second inning Sam taps Rich Dotson's inside fastball into the bleachers above the Red Sox bull pen, the usual arcing mortar-shell trajectory. Right field in Fenway bellies out deep, the bull pen wall running finally to 380 feet from home plate. Just to plant one *in* the bull pen is a piece of hitting. These blasts of Horn's sail high over the pens. They bury themselves in the crowd a quarter, a third, of the way up in the bleachers. Sam's second home run is more prodigious still. It hits above the Sox' bull pen just to the right of the vertical yellow stripe marking the outermost reach of the playing field, 420 feet from the plate.

Afterward the topics in the clubhouse are Horn's home runs and the wound sustained by Al Nipper, who had to depart in the fifth. Nip was pitching to Donnie Hill, who whacked the ball on one hop into Nipper's crotch. Nip sat down as if he'd been kicked with a jackboot. The ball trickled away; Nip struggled on floppy legs to his knees, found the ball, and lobbed a sick Wiffle-ball toss toward Evans, much too late to get Hill. Nip then rolled over like a dead man on the grass. Everyone came running. Nipper lay there a long time with the trainer crouching over him. He did eventually climb to his feet unas-sisted and attempt to pitch on. The White Sox rapped three straight singles, and Nip walked their number-three hitter, Harold Baines. Nip obviously didn't feel well, and McNamara lifted him.

"Nipper pitched very well," McNamara says afterward, "till he got mangled." Everyone writes this down. "It's tough,"

McNamara says. "I been hit in the nuts myself a number of times." He looks around the room, blue eyes brightening. "I guess you'd better say 'groin,' huh?"

It gets a laugh.

"How long has it been," McNamara asks us, serious again, "since you've seen two home runs hit that hard in the same game?"

A long time. Maybe never.

A few minutes later, Nipper is talking about the injury in that thoughtful way of his. It seems that luck saved Nip from castration. He tells us that he forgot to wear his cup tonight and remembered the omission only after the fourth inning, when he sent the batboy in to fetch it.

"Good thing," says Nip solemnly, "or I wouldn't have any nuts right now."

And the mighty Horn? He's happy. Stripped to the waist, he lifts his bat out of his locker and raises it like a champagne bottle.

"This bat been here for three weeks," he says. "I ain't broke it yet, can you believe that? I just keep swingin' it."

He shakes his head, amazed by it all.

Ten
The Fitzgeraldian Beauty
of Carlton Fisk

ONE SUMMER I WAS A REAL BALLPLAYER. NOT FOR A GAME; FOR a summer. I was fourteen, in my second year of Babe Ruth League, and suddenly, more often than not, I was getting around on the fastball. Always a decent fielder, I was now proficient. No: I was expert. The coach, Mr. Lebherz, took one look and installed me—I swear it—at shortstop. All summer I played shortstop and batted third.

Babe Ruth League was a delight after the tribulations of Little League. It was pure baseball, pain-free baseball. Gone were the avid fathers, the know-it-all fathers clamoring for victory on the Little League field. These fathers would holler at umpires and urge their kids on with an intensity that scared me. Some teams had two coaches—*two*. These hungry coaches and these fathers evolved a policy toward the end of my Little League career: if you hit a home run, the coach or a father—even if you weren't his kid—would buy you a banana split at

227

the Dairy Queen down the hill across Main Street. This standing offer dogged me; I was tall for my age, I had long-ball potential I wasn't fulfilling. Show us what you're made of, the grownups were telling me. I never got a banana split, and when I see one today I think of Little League and my failure to hit a ball over the red slatted snow fence that circled the outfield, an addition the year I was twelve. I wish they'd never built it. It was that goddamn fence that started them thinking about home runs and banana splits.

The following summer came Babe Ruth League, real baseball on a big-league diamond, pitchers who could throw the curve. Where were these baseball-mad fathers? It still puzzles me. The hill rippling up on the first-base side of Guv Fuller Field was sun-dusted, empty. Oh, a few parents came. Quiet people. Some kids on their bikes with nothing better to do. Our uniforms were gray flannel bags such as Ty Cobb and Christy Mathewson wore. The loose shirts, which buttoned up the front, had no lettering and no numbers on their backs. Plain gray uniforms, plain baseball. The game had never been as much fun for me as it was that summer, and never would be again.

It's odd how the seasons of your childhood, which follow one another in such rapid succession, can seem so far apart, so disparate. This was the summer after I'd pitched my arm to a dangling rag for Mr. Kalperis on the junior high team, a month or two since I'd been ground down enough to abandon dreams of the big leagues. That spring and that summer seem years apart in my memory. The summer rises out of the mists like Bali Ha'i. Perfect. I was working my first summer job two days a week at the newspaper office, and I liked even that. I liked slipping papers, inserting one section into another, and sweeping the oil-blackened hardwood floor with the big push broom. I liked joining in getting out a newspaper. I liked making real money. The summer afternoons danced to the rhythmic grinding of the old press, a clanking dinosaur with a powerful sweet smell of grease and printer's ink. And when the clanking roar finally stopped, the silence seemed like nothing you could remember, a sudden new idea of God's. Many evenings I went to play ball with hands still smudged with newsprint ink, smoky stains that had somehow spread up the insides of my wrists. I was proud of those smudged hands.

I still got around on a bicycle. I rode to the games with my glove and cleated shoes dangling off the handlebar. Our first baseman was a tall kid a year ahead of me named Bob Carey, who lived halfway up Main Street. Carey didn't have a bike, and after a ball game I would walk my bike with him as far as his street. Sometimes we detoured down the hill to the Dairy Queen and bought cherry or lime dips, huge things for a quarter, the syrup or whatever it was hardening instantly over the ice cream, plasticky shades of green and red. Then we walked up Main Street, dawdling along in the gathering violet darkness, licking our ice-cream cones and talking dirty nonsense. Carey had a rubicund, impish face, a nose like a cherry and yellow hair scythed flat on top, a fashion in those days. He was a cutup, a joker, and he amused me walking home after the ball games. A lovely song called "Mission Bell" was big on the radio that summer, and when I hear it now I still think of the newspaper office as it was then, of playing baseball as dusk fell on country ball fields, and of Bob Carey.

And when I think of that summer, I go directly to the night of Harris Shenker's near-perfect game. Carey hated Shenker. We all did.

Not personally. We'd never spoken to him. He was a summer kid from New York or Providence or somewhere; we knew him only from playing ball against him, which we'd been doing for years, going back to Little League. He was a burly ox of a kid, the Sam Horn of our league, too big for the rest of us. He had immense feet and a head that seemed too small for the rest of him. He swaggered. He smiled with cool disdain.

His fastball, zippy as it was, looked heavy somehow, as if it would knock the bat out of your hand if you did manage to connect with it.

Shenker could hit, too. He tormented me for the first time one evening in Little League when I was ten. I was out in right field. Shenker, who batted left, was up. The coach waved me back, back, back. Everyone in the ballpark knew Shenker was going to hit it at me. The sun was in my eyes. I backed up some more. My heart thudded. Everyone was aware of me out there, the only hope against Shenker. Shenker swiped effortlessly and sent the ball my way; I backpedaled, finally spun around, nearly tripping myself, and saw the ball crash down and go bounding away. I chased it dutifully, though Shenker could have strolled around the bases. He struck me out all three times that game.

We had another grudge against Shenker, besides his invincibility, that summer of his near-perfect game. We assumed we did, at least. Carey was spreading it around that Shenker was dating a local girl named Sandra Sylvia. *Sandra Sylvia*: this was unbearable. She was two or three years ahead of me in school—older than Shenker—a silent, heart-stopping presence in the school corridors, lugging her books against her breasts, eyes front, lipsticked mouth locked shut in the fine strong wedge of her chin. She didn't go giggling through the hallways, yakking and waving to half the school. She went unsmiling and undistracted, as if she had no friends. There was a wonderful dignity in her manner, as if she were too old for all of this, a woman. She had golden caramel skin and her hair was sandy, the color of her name. And now here was Carey telling us that Shenker was taking her out. How had he even met her? I tried to imagine them together, Shenker and Sandra Sylvia; in the movies, at the A and W Root Beer, in the backseat of somebody's car at the drive-in. I asked Carey about three times if it was true, and he swore to God it was.

We were playing on our home field that night. After five innings everyone was conscious of the no-hitter. Shenker was relaxed and smiling: he expected it, saw no reason, if he was careful, why we should get a hit. He would swagger to the mound, dragging those big feet, and snatch up the ball in a decisive, impatient sort of way. He wanted the no-hitter: you could see it. It would be in the newspaper, of course—my father's newspaper. He could boast about it to Sandra Sylvia.

I made the mistake after my second at-bat of telling Mr. Lebherz I could hit Shenker. I can't imagine why I said this, but it does show what kind of ball I was playing that summer. The morale on our bench had collapsed; I heard the silence and saw the long faces, and blurted that I could hit this guy. Mr. Lebherz was a young lawyer, easygoing but smart. He stored up my remark, and when I stepped up to hit in the last inning, the lone remaining obstacle between Shenker and the glory of a perfect game, the coach told the entire ballpark what I'd said.

"Come on, Hough," he barked. "You told me you could hit this guy."

The words floated, perfectly audible, out over the darkening field. An explosion of laughter: their coach. A summer fellow, young, the kid brother of a well-known Boston politician. His laugh was windy, derisive. Their catcher added a laugh of his own.

"I doubt that," the catcher yelled, looking over at Mr. Lebherz.

More laughter; a snicker here, a whinny there, across the field.

Shenker, to his credit, only waited, grim and hungry, to pitch.

Mr. Lebherz had raised the stakes, and it lit a fire on our bench. The guys had been sitting slumped and silent, helplessly watching the perfect game unfold like some bad dream coming true. But this laughter, bush-league stuff, put the spunk back in us. It showed how sure they were of the perfect game— utterly—and apparently we were just sage enough to know you can't count on a thing like that. Shenker hadn't gotten me out yet, and that summer I was a pretty good hitter.

The guys started hollering encouragement.

"Come on, John, *babe*!"

"Come, John*eee* . . ."

"You can do it, buddy!"

What sweet noise. I'd been pretty calm through all of this— more evidence of what kind of a ballplayer I was that summer—but the sudden energy on our bench, my teammates' shouts, went to my head like a belt of schnapps. Confidence is everything, says Mike Greenwell.

The catcher sank into his crouch, chortling still at this notion of mine that I could hit Shenker. A summer kid, I didn't know him. Their whole team was summer kids. Let them laugh. Shenker kicked at the dirt, raking the mound to his liking.

I didn't wait. Shenker's first pitch was low and outside, a good pitch on the corner, and I got all of it. I saw the yellow flash of my bat, felt the stingless impact of a hardball jumping off fat wood, saw my line drive climb toward right center. I remember Carey, glimpsed out of the corner of my eye as I hauled ass to first, bouncing off the bench and hollering, gesturing, willing my drive into the alley, howling when it struck grass and bounded through for extra bases. I rounded first while Carey sprang up and down on long rubbery legs like a pogo stick. I slowed into second base—they'd run the ball down—for the easy double.

The score was something like 4−0; we had no chance to win it. Still, this was victory. Our guys were hollering, they were sending laughter across to Shenker's coach. Their guys had all lost their voices. They looked down, pawed a little dirt, said nothing. Shenker took a walk around the mound, rubbing the ball between both hands. He looked thoughtful. His face was sun-darkened, like varnish, and I remember the lines running down it, etching a chagrin that was near to pain.

"No big thing, Harris," the catcher yelled, a breezy lie that fooled no one.

Least of all Shenker. He looked suddenly tired out there. He laid the next pitch over the middle of the plate—I had a view from second base—but the hitter swung late anyway, bumping a little pop fly to the first baseman. The game was history.

I walked my bike with Carey as far as his street. Carey was jubilant over what I'd just done. He kept telling me I should have seen the look on Shenker's face. He looked *sick*, Carey said. That night I was a hero to Carey, who was a year older than I, and who, when we'd both gotten to high school, would just about forget he knew me.

I said "So long" to him where his street dipped away from Main beside the darkened appliance store. Time to mount my bike. It was the hour when the summer bars came alive, places with names like the Driftwood and the Oar and Anchor, which hired cops to keep order on the sidewalks out front and keep traffic flowing. Live music roared inside, rock bands whose muffled din—it would swell suddenly, come whooshing out, when the doors swung open—was as suggestive as some heady perfume leaking its scent on the summer night. I rode home past the bars, circling out to avoid the clusters of people on the sidewalks out front, guys in shorts and Madras shirts, the women very jazzy-looking with their waxy suntans. I slid by on my bike with none of the usual pangs these places excited in me, a mix of helplessness and longing. That night I almost pitied the people I saw, steeped as they were in the pleasures of sex. I had what I wanted: now, this summer, always. I'd hit a double off Shenker.

———

I saw Carlton Fisk's immortal World Series home run on black-and-white TV in my parents' living room. The video of Pudge dropping his bat, urging his line drive fair with both arms, shoving gobs of air sideways left to right, *get* over, *get* over, urging and urging and then the leap, arms stretched high, is a national treasure. Twelfth inning, sixth game, 1975. End of the greatest game, perhaps, in World Series history. Greater even than the sixth game in '86.

My mother put her hand over her mouth. She said, "*Wow*," and then laughed, pitching her head forward, hugging her stomach, and finally straightening up to look at my father and me with eyes just shining. She was in her nightgown and bathrobe, on the sofa with a quilt pulled up over her, her way always of watching late-night television. We had a cat then, who would lie on the quilt where my mother could reach her, purring as she slept.

My father sat in front of the fireplace, bent forward with his elbows on his knees. My father is detached from rooting; he doesn't catch pennant fever. "Wow," he said, like my mother, but softly, wonderingly, as if he'd just seen his first Rembrandt.

I sprang to my feet, waking the two old dogs snoozing by the fire. I was raving. *"Oh yes oh yes oh yes, oh my god I don't believe it, I love you Pudge, I love you!"*

And I did. I loved him for hitting the home run, and for the way he danced around the bases. I was grateful to him with a gratitude that would flow forever, like a spring. My father eyed me, amused by my reaction to a baseball game. Who can explain it?

Anyway, twelve years later I'm sitting in the Red Sox dugout with Johnny Pesky when, sudden and immense as a landslide down the steps in front of us comes Fisk himself, garbed in a White Sox uniform. The Red Sox let Pudge get away in '81. Wouldn't give him what he was asking, which ought to have been anything. Tragic, but never mind. What's done is done.

Pudge lands in front of Pesky wide as a door, strapping, grinning the all-American grin, wholesome yet knowing. He's not golden, as I'd imagined, but hewn instead from some tawny hardwood, a muted tan. His hair is a lightless brown. He is forty. A year younger than I, and look at him.

He and Pesky shake hands. Their hands come together with a smack.

"Hey, Johnny."

"Hey, you son of a bitch." Pesky grins.

"*Real* good to see you," Pudge says. He stands there with his hands on his hips, a knee canted out, all that size and power elegantly at ease. He is rinsed in grace, a Fitzgeraldian hero who will never lose that unspecific beauty that has been given as if by the touch of a magic wand.

"So how you doin'?" asks Pesky, beaming. He was a coach on that '75 team.

"Well, shit," Pudge says, "one day I play, the next day I don't. I never know from one day to the next. It's messin' me up."

"Well, shit," Pesky says sympathetically.

"They don't know what to do with me, I guess." Fisk smiles, shrugs those shoulders. "What the hell."

"How's the family?"

"Terrific," Pudge says.

I bump Pesky with my elbow.

"Introduce us, will you?"

Pesky does.

Fisk buries my hand in his. He smiles. Perfect.

"I just want to tell you . . ." I blurt, and pause, groping for a way to say this. Pesky sends me his sideways look, mock stern, and Fisk waits patient and grinning. ". . . you're just about my all-time favorite. I mean . . ."

"Ah, shit," Pesky snaps. "You said the same thing to me."

"I did not," I say.

Fisk is grinning. "I bet he says it to everyone."

"He does," Pesky says. "It's disgusting."

"I don't."

"He's full of shit," Pesky tells Fisk.

"Oh, well," Fisk says.

"You playin' tonight?" Pesky asks.

"I'm catching. Can you believe it?"

Just like old times, I think. For some years Pudge has been playing mostly in left field, saving his legs.

"I got to get over there," he says. He grabs Pesky's hand again. "It was nice meeting you," he tells me.

"I'm rooting for you tonight," I tell him.

"I appreciate that."

"Don't believe him, Pudge," Pesky says.

Clemens pitches tonight, and against him Pudge Fisk launches two beautiful home runs, gets a base on balls, and scores his third run of the night. The White Sox win it, 5–3. Our three runs come instantaneously in the seventh, when Dewey Evans smashes one of his line-drive home runs into the screen with two men on. Home run number thirty for Dewey in this year of years. Boggs gets three hits in four at-bats, which goes unremarked. So does Evans's home run. After the game everyone is talking about Fisk.

Pudge hits his first round-tripper in the second inning. Nobody has scored yet, and Clemens has mown down the first five Chicago hitters. I'm pulling for Fisk; it can't be helped. He stands erect at the plate, holding the bat vertical and high. It is right for him, natural, a batting stance with aplomb. No crouching, no coiling: Pudge stands tall and calm, elegant under fire. When he played here he wore number twenty-seven, and in Chicago he chose number seventy-two, reversing the digits; a gesture, of course, that Pudge let us interpret as we pleased. I saw it as the sort of symbolic inversion that signifies sadness, like flying the flag at half-staff. Pudge had left his heart in Boston.

This first round-tripper is slugged high and far, the ball drifting against the blue-black sky above the light towers. The count is full; Clemens throws the fastball, which Pudge is certainly expecting. But as McNamara says, it's hard to get hold of Roger's heat even when you know it's coming. Pudge jogs the bases deadpan, erect with his arms held low. Elegant. The crowd gives out an ambiguous cheer. It has that fluffy, sarcastic quality, like cheering a manager for pulling a pitcher who's getting bombed. Brilliant decision, says the sarcastic cheer. Brilliant decision, letting Pudge Fisk go to Chicago.

In the fourth with a man on base, Pudge cracks one into the screen beside the foul pole, a straight shot, almost identical to his World Series home run. Pudge doesn't wave the ball over, or leap, or exult, just trots the bases as another, larger cheer flows down. The score is 3 – 0. In the seventh, none out and a man on second, Clemens walks Fisk on four pitches. Wary of him. Donnie Hill, who last night pasted Nipper in the nuts, hits a double, and it is 5 – 0.

In the chilly silence of McNamara's office afterward someone ventures, "Fisk has really proved to be a nemesis, hasn't he?"

"You aren't shittin'," says McNamara.

And in the clubhouse after McNamara's postmortem the talk is still of Fisk. The reporters go to Evans, Fisk's teammate in '75, a veteran who himself is pushing forty. Evans receives us sitting, as usual, stripped to his electric-blue tights. Dewey will talk politely, thoughtfully, to the reporters, but he won't stand up to do so. He sits, always with a paper plate of pasta on his lap—lasagne, rigatoni with meat sauce—slowly eating, quietly answering questions. You have to lean down to hear the low, resonant voice.

"All I can say is, I don't know if *I'll* be playin' when I'm forty," muses Evans. " 'Course, I try not to think about it. I try to think about tomorrow."

He eats.

"Two home runs," he says, and shakes his head wonderingly. "Tonight was the best I've seen him swing the bat in a *long* time."

Before I leave—before I go out into the neon-lit darkness and greasy air of Yawkey Way—I go into the visitors' clubhouse to congratulate Fisk. Perhaps he'll remember me from his talk with Pesky. The visitors' clubhouse is half as large, at best, as the home clubhouse. It is too small to hold so many big men; it is uncomfortable in here, overcrowded, too loud. The players ignore me, as players always do, but in such cramped quarters it seems stiff and overdone.

Fisk is stripping. I pick my way over, but before I reach him a Boston reporter gets there and strikes up a conversation. The writer, one of the older guys, isn't doing a story, just chatting. I stand back, waiting my turn. The guy laughs, Fisk laughs. It is very chummy. Fisk finishes undressing and still the guy hangs on, asking this, asking that. Fisk is in shape, all right: all flat slabs of muscle. He sees me waiting, but figures I'll be patient or is too polite to shut the guy off. I have the feeling Pudge thinks the conversation has gone on long enough, but I could be imagining this. I look at my watch: eleven-thirty. I have the long drive to Cape Cod ahead of me. The reporter gabs on, the selfish bastard, and I give up and walk away from my hero forever.

It is September, and the Sox have let Baylor and Henderson go. Baylor has joined the Minnesota Twins, who are in first place in the American League Western Division. Hendu has jumped across to the National League, to the Giants, who lead their division. Hendu arrived too late to be eligible for postseason play, but if the Twins get there Baylor can play. It's hard to imagine the Twins beating the Eastern Division champs, but who knows? Baylor may find himself in the World Series again.

So they are gone, one a blithe, one a brooding, presence. Hendu always wore the wide kid's smile with the slit between his upper front teeth. He always looked cheerful and game. He bopped around the clubhouse to the music on the radio, or to music in his head, jiggling his big shoulders. Baylor never smiled. I remember the furrows roughing his forehead, the intelligence burning darkly in the narrow triangles of his eyes. He seldom looked at writers. They simply didn't exist.

I never spoke with either man. Baylor's pensive, mirthless facade warned me off. As for Hendu, there was a good story there, as my father would say, but could I have coaxed it out of him? The man had hit .400 in the Series. He had hit that incredible ninth-inning home run against the Angels, the swing that saved the season. For two weeks of games as big as games can get, Henderson was magnificent. And now he is just so-so. A bench-warmer. Has Hendu, at the age of twenty-nine, gleaned any poignant insights? Has he been humbled? Is he defiant? A stranger to him, I don't ask. I lack that boldness, that willingness to go where I'm not wanted. When I was in college I worked for my father in the summers as a reporter. Among many things, I covered the police; and the chief, who was nearly as prickly with reporters as John McNamara, surprised me once when he was off duty and had had a couple of drinks by confiding to me that he liked me. "What I like about you," he went on, "is, you're not *pushy*." Biggest insult you can give a reporter. You can bet no one would say it to Dan Shaughnessy.

I've always loved September baseball. Pearly afternoons, early shadows moving out to cover the pitcher, scraping back sunlight till the pitcher and finally all the infielders are standing inside bright blue night while the outfielders wait in golden daytime. Nip-and-tuck pennant races. Braves and Dodgers staying dead-even all through the month. Dodgers and Giants in '62. And how about '67? A three-way race, undecided until the last day of the season. We always went to Fenway in September, my parents and I, grabbing one last game before it all ended. It was in September that we saw Larsen beat the Sox, his perfect game waiting just around the corner. It was in September that we saw Bill Fischer stride in from the Senators' bullpen to pitch the eleventh. Fish got two quick outs, and then Jackie Jensen, the golden boy of his day, stuck one into the screen, home run. *Eleven innings*, I thought, and felt lucky.

It is September, and the Yankees are sliding out of the race, leaving the Jays and Tigers to fight it out alone. The Yanks are five games out. They have a chance, but it is slim. They arrive in Fenway at the end of the first week of this do-or-die month for three night games. Big games for the Yanks. If they can win all three, or even two, they can go on hoping.

The first night darkens way early. The air is thick and carries the threat of rain. A storm is making up somewhere close by, and its electricity wanders over, makes the rain-scented air nervous. By and by, snake tongues of lightning flicker in the distance.

"The trouble with winning the pennant," McNamara is saying, looking doubtfully out at the scratches of lightning, "is you got to manage the All-Star team. And you take more fuckin' abuse for who you play, who you don't play, who pitches, who doesn't pitch. It isn't worth the aggravation, I'll tell you." He punctuates this with a squirt of tobacco. "What these people don't understand is, one outfielder has to play the whole game. I went to Winfield, and I asked him. I says, 'Dave, you want to play the whole game? You don't *have* to, now. It's up to you.' Dave said yes. You know Winfield: he loves to play. Was it my fault the fuckin' game went extra innings?"

What's he so hot about? The All-Star game is ancient history. As a point of honor, McNamara avoids criticizing baseball people, at least in public. It is, I suppose, hard to bear when others snipe at *him*. He can't forget it.

"And then Jimi Williams was bitchin' because I used Henke for two innings. Christ, Henke didn't mind. Henke said he actually needed the work. Look how he's pitched since then, does it look like it's hurt him?"

The reporters shake their heads, no. There are sympathetic murmurings. McNamara leans forward, scrutinizes the metal wall of the sky.

"Lousy weather comin'," he observes, and brings up a weary sigh.

But the storm changes its mind, slides off in another direction. The ballpark fills. Hurst is pitching, and although Bruce was expansive and seemed generally content when I talked with him, his season has gone sour. He has lost his last three starts, and his earned-run average has fattened up to 3.91. The big crowd is salted with Yankee fans, and Bruce makes them happy immediately by walking the Yanks' leadoff hitter, Ricky Henderson. Next up is the much admired Willie Randolph. The old pro gets behind, two strikes, then dumps one over the wall. A cheer goes up, avid and biting, as Willie jogs the bases. Don Mattingly drives a double down the right-field line. Winfield pumps a single to left, scoring Mattingly. Hurst gets the side, but it is 3–0, a night's worth of runs—usually—against Bruce Hurst.

The Sox score twice in the second, twice in the third.

The Yanks keep gnawing away at Hurst. He pitches out of a jam in the second, but in the third gets hit all over the place. The Yanks score twice and would probably draw more blood, except that Mike Pagliarulo gets himself thrown out at the plate trying to score from second on a single. In the fourth Bruce gives up four more hits, two more runs, and is through for the night. He flings himself off the mound, comes in on long, flouncing strides, hanging his head. There are no boos.

The Bombino replaces him and pitches decently until the

eighth. Then, with one out, Pagliarulo clunks a double off the wall. Rick Cerone bombs a home run; the ball jumps off the bat and jumps high into the screen, nearly over it.

In the ninth, Rice muscles a home run into the bull pen with no one on base. They were booing him earlier, but the home run wins him a cheer. It doesn't change anything. The Yanks win it, 9–5, and stay alive for another day.

McNamara seems baffled by Hurst's dismal showing. He frowns, shakes his head, trying to make sense of it. "It doesn't *appear* that he's doin' anything different. . . ." The manager thinks some more. He shrugs. "I just don't know," he says.

Someone asks one of the year's dumbest questions: "These games mean a lot to you, don't they, John? You try to win them just as hard as if you were in the race, don't you?"

McNamara sends the man a pitying stare, then looks around the room as if he were wondering whether he heard right.

"Yes," he says finally, "I try to win every game as hard as I can. Wouldn't *you*?"

We bustle out, looking for Hurst. There are, perhaps, eight of us; we don't see Hurst and there is a pause, a moment of hesitation as everyone looks around for someone else to interview, the next best thing. But before the pack can disperse, Hurst comes out of the trainer's room, looking very melancholy. He comes right at us, rapid on those long legs. We fall back, give him room. Hurst stops by the mail cubbies. He puts his back against them and stands with his legs braced apart, his hands stuffed in the pockets of his shiny red Adidas windbreaker. His dark brown hair has been blown dry. The reporters encircle him. Bruce looks sadly out over our heads.

"Uh, any thoughts on tonight, Bruce?"

"I'm a bad pitcher," Hurst says. The light, soft voice has gone lifeless. "I haven't pitched well in months. I stink."

He drops his head, hangs it. He keeps his hands holstered in his jacket pockets.

"Is control the problem?"

"I stink, that's the problem."

"Have you looked at films of yourself?"

"It doesn't matter," Hurst says dully, and shakes his head slowly, back and forth, back and forth. "It just doesn't matter."

"When was the last time you pitched well?"

"It doesn't matter." Lifeless, leaden voice.

Silence. Hurst straightens, lifts his head, squares his back against the cubbyholes. He gazes past us. The dark, gentle eyes look teary.

"Why doesn't it matter?" someone ventures.

"It just doesn't." Hurst sighs. "This is all so boring," he says.

"Boring?"

"Yeah. It's really boring."

Bruce waits, but there are no more questions. The reporters spin off in different directions, giving Hurst clear sailing to the door. He looks around warily, as if someone might be lurking with a knife. There's nobody. Hurst beelines for the door.

Hurst gets spanked in print in the morning papers for his hangdog deportment and sodden answers, but the way I see it, the man was upset and still did his best to face the music. He didn't snap at anyone. Didn't cuss us. His heart was heavy. He did his best. The writer for the *Globe*—not the redoubtable Shaughnessy but a kid with the aristocratic byline of Kevin Paul duPont—ridicules Hurst, which seems shortsighted to me, as well as unjust. Hurst will talk, give you the time of day, do an interview. A real gent. Why alienate him?

There is other talk of Hurst. The next afternoon Evans and Hriniak are sitting in the dugout, relaxing awhile in the shade before heading out to the cage under the bleachers to work on Evans's swing. It is three-thirty. Several Yankees are taking extra, early batting practice. Ron Kittle is one. He takes his licks, then strolls over to the Sox' dugout to pass some time with Evans and Hriniak. Kittle sits down, uninvited, on the dugout steps.

He's a big, rangy slugger, an outfielder who is used mostly as a designated hitter.

"Hey, Dewey. Walt," he says. A Southern boy. He looks like a big blond farmboy.

" 'Lo, Ron."

"I'll tell ya," Kittle says, "Hurstie ought to order me a taxi today. I'm the only guy he could get out last night." It's true, more or less. Hurst whiffed Kittle twice. "He didn't have any fastball," Kittle twangs on. "He had a batting practice fastball, is what he had."

"Well, he's had that before and done okay," allows Evans. Dewey is squinting past Kittle to the sun-washed outfield. "He hadn't pitched in nine days," Evans says.

"He sure ought to call me a taxi," Kittle says.

"Maybe he was tryin' too hard," says Evans. "Maybe he was tryin' to muscle the ball up there."

"May*be*," Kittle says. "All I know, we was takin' batting practice. 'Cept me. Shee-it."

Evans continues to study the field. Kids, just up from triple A, are shagging for Don Mattingly. Teams are allowed to expand at this time of year, to take on fresh blood.

"I hope Hurstie's okay," Kittle says.

"He's all right," Evans says.

"Look at this," Hriniak erupts, nodding toward Mattingly. "One of the best fuckin' hitters in baseball, and look at him. Workin'. He makes two fuckin' million a year, he doesn't have to be out here. The man works. That's why he's a great hitter, he *works*." Hriniak isn't interested in pitching. Just hitters.

Silence. The *plock* of Mattingly's bat hangs loud on the summery afternoon.

"Another thing," Evans says. "Hurstie got some bad calls from the ump last night. I think it upset him, threw him off."

"Oh, yeah," Kittle agrees, "I could see that. He threw me one breakin' ball, a *good* pitch, and the ump called it a ball."

Evans nods.

"Shall we get to work?" says Hriniak.

"I guess we better, Walter," says Evans.

"I'll see y'all later," Kittle says.

You get used to the beseeching shouts for autographs along the railing on either side of the dugout. Kids crowd the barrier as long as they can, which is until the ticket owners show up and the ushers boot the kids out. They clutch their pens and scorecards, their yearbooks and baseballs, and they scream at every ballplayer who slants by on his way to and from the dugout. They holler, squeal, beg. *"Sam. Please. Please Sam pleeeeze . . ."* The ballplayer might scoot over and sign for a minute or two, and he might not. The same guy will take the time one day, and be stone-deaf to the kids the next.

Tonight Rice is standing with a bat on his shoulder near the first-base line when Boggs pops out of the dugout and trots toward the cage.

"Wade!"

"Wade!"

Boggs keeps going. Rice's back is to the kids.

"Pleeeeze . . ."

"Wade! Wade! Come on Wade . . ."

Rice whirls around. "SHUT UP!" It jolts the kids like a cuff to the ear, freezes them. This has never happened before. They all stare at Rice, a peanut gallery of silent faces stretching along the barrier. Rice inspects his work, these stunned faces, a miracle. Rice nods as if to say, That's better. He comes toward the dugout with his bat, toward the kids, who watch him uneasily. One brave voice pipes up, very polite:

"Jim, can I have that cracked bat?"

Rice slows, but keeps walking. "It's not a cracked bat," he tells the kid. "It's a *good* bat."

"Well, then," persists the kid, "can I have your autograph?"

"When I come back," says Rice, stern as a schoolmaster. He ducks into the dugout, is swallowed by the tunnel.

"What about Woodward?" someone asks McNamara. "Is Woodward pitching Thursday, or is Stanley?"

Woodward is one of the triple-A kids fresh from Pawtucket.

"I don't know *why*," McNamara says loudly, face souring up, "this is such a big fuckin' *deal*."

"I didn't say . . ." begins the reporter.

"Yes, Woodward is pitching Thursday," McNamara says. "Stanley's goin' back to the bull pen. Okay?"

The reporters look uncomfortable. They frown, they smile nervously. McNamara is wearing his jacket, glossy blue, with the red sock slapped on front. He sits with his arms folded, squinting out.

"John, did Bruce's comments upset you?"

"What comments?"

"The stuff in the papers today."

"What did he say?"

The writer hesitates.

McNamara says, "I don't read your papers. How many times I got to tell you that?"

I wonder if this is true. A boycott of the sports pages.

"Well," the reporter says, "Bruce was upset."

"Upset?" says McNamara.

The reporter tries to smile. Maybe he wishes he'd never mentioned it.

"Look," McNamara says, "Hurst went through this at the beginning of last year. It's no big deal. Now, are you guys finished?"

We sure are. McNamara gets up, climbs the steps, and stalks to the batting cage.

The air turns heavy, moist. Just after darkness falls there is a sudden hard shower. The rain leaves the grass slick and shiny. It stains the infield dirt. The ballpark fills up, of course. Nipper pitches against Don Gullickson, who has just arrived from the other league in a straight trade for Dennis Rasmussen, pitcher for pitcher. Gullickson is the better pitcher; the Reds unload him plus his fat salary, hoping that the younger Rasmussen will get better someday. The Yanks are hoping Gullickson will pitch them to the championship.

The game zooms along for three innings. The air is a damp blanket, and it knocks down the fly balls. In the bottom of the second, Rice comes to the plate with Evans at first, one out. With two strikes Evans takes off with the pitch, which sails high; Rice slaps at it, missing, and Rick Cerone guns Dewey out at second, double play. The crowd bellows furiously at Rice.

Marzano singles home Benzinger in the third, the kids again getting it done. In the top of the fourth, Pagliarulo hammers one into the Sox bull pen. Nice game, 1–1. In the bottom of the inning Boggs singles. Dewey comes up, takes a ball, takes a strike, and then the sullen sky lets go.

The umps wave the game to a halt. The players sprint for cover. The grounds keepers come charging out, shouldering the rolled tarp along ahead of them. John Kiely, the organist, strikes up "With a Little Bit of Luck." In the press box everyone stands, stretches. A crowd collects at the little bar in back, where the press box attendant, Jim Gately, dispenses soft drinks and beer on tap.

"They'll wait two hours," someone says. "They won't call this game unless they absolutely have to."

It is ten of nine. The rain sails down through the white sheen of the light towers, buckets of water, tons of it. A hard, steady rain. Well, I think, why wait here? Around the corner is my motel, my Fenway HoJo. I could, from the HoJo parking lot, throw a baseball against the brick flank of the ballpark, right over Van Ness Street. There's a radio in the room, Ken Coleman will let me know when the game resumes. Hell, I'll hear the cheering.

The rain is melting the big crowd. Yawkey Way is bustling with folks going home. They scatter to their cars. People with kids, mostly. In three minutes I'm in my motel room. Ground floor: I can look out past the curtain and see the rain falling through the city lights, see it dancing on the HoJo parking lot, nicking the puddles.

On the radio Ken is signing off for now, sending the broadcast back to the studios. I spin the dial and run into Little Richard bawling "Tutti Frutti." Wonderful. I always bring a bottle to a hotel, and now I pour myself some bourbon, neat. I lie down with a novel, my drink, the music. The novel is by a woman who is very good, but whose male characters don't work for me. This starts me thinking: ever since Hemingway, the men have been getting nailed when they write women badly, but no one dares suggest that women, too, have trouble writing characters of the other sex. After Little Richard, Buddy Holly sings, and then the Temptations. What a radio station. At ten-forty the rain is still nicking the puddles. This is a long rain if I ever saw one, an all-night rain. I read a little more, drink a little more, and go back to the window: rain. Doubleheader tomorrow, I think, and hit the hay.

But they do play baseball over there, and I sleep through it, a few hundred yards away. I sleep through a battle and never hear the cheering—perhaps because the crowd has thinned to almost nothing by the time the long game is over. They play in slop, mud, water; Piniella, the Yankee manager, rages at the umpires for allowing the game to go on, and gets himself thrown out. It rains again, and they wait another hour and resume again. On and on it goes, until sometime around two-thirty. The Sox, with nothing to gain, outlast these desperate Yankees. The Yanks, who need the breaks now, don't get them: the umps take a home run away from Mike Easler, fair for sure, I hear.

I don't know what I've missed till I buy the *Globe* in the lobby next morning. It stops me in my tracks, reading the headline. I'm ashamed. It comes back to me how contemptuous I've always been of fans who leave early, giving up the last of the ninth so they can get a jump on the traffic, or abandoning the ballpark in droves when the game becomes a rout. Fair-weather fans. Besides, you never know what might happen. You never know.

Last night I was a fair-weather fan. Never again.

The rain clears out, leaving the air moist, weighted. In the afternoon the sun shines. It doesn't feel like September. In the ballpark, early, you can smell the frying odor that hovers on the streets outside and is breathed from the vents of Fenway, a fatty sweetness, meaty, spicy, oily, essence of fast food. It hangs on the sodden air. Artery-clogging stuff, deadly stuff. What does the team doctor think, the renowned Arthur Pappas, wandering through the clubhouse after a game, when the table is spread with sausage and breaded veal cutlets? Why doesn't he say anything?

Tonight Sam Horn, who seems less and less interested in the art of fielding ground balls, takes possession of the batting cage early, to work on that mighty swing. He goes out with the teacher, Hriniak, who says a few cautionary words about head position and then stalks rapidly to the mound, shoulders bobbing as he walks, springing along, impatient to pitch to big Sam. Walt puts on his old glove, leans down, and digs a ball out of the box. Sam scrapes a foothold in the dirt.

"We're gonna have a contest, Sam," Hriniak says. He is smiling ever so slightly. "You got six outs. I got brand-new baseballs. Brand-new white fuckin' baseballs. You hit till you make six outs. Got it? I'm the judge."

Horn grunts assent. He swishes the bat slowly, getting a bead on Hriniak. John Marzano, who will hit next, arrives behind the cage.

"You ready, Sam?" Hriniak calls in.

"Oh, I'm ready," Horn purrs. His eyes have grown large. Hungry.

Hriniak goes to work. Quick, jerky motion, yanking the arm around low, stiffly, zipping the ball in there.

Horn hits his first pitch into the right-field grandstand, a good way up. The ball rattles around among the empty red seats. Hriniak says nothing. He chooses another baseball and zips it low and inside; Sam smoothly pounds it into the bull pen. Hriniak says nothing. Horn drives the next pitch into right field, low.

Hriniak watches it land, bounce high. "Base hit," he says, and plunges his hand into the round box. Sweat slicks his face, wets his yellow hair. He tries the outside corner; Horn wallops it off the wall. You can hear the tinny clunk. Sam lifts one into the center-field bleachers, a majestic fly ball that takes its time, lazing down finally perhaps fifteen rows up.

"I guess outs don't come as easy as they used to," remarks Horn after watching this one find the seats.

Hriniak hoots a laugh, mock-outraged. "*What?*" he yells.

"I didn't say nothin'," croons Horn.

Hriniak looks at Marzano. "What'd he say?" Hriniak asks him.

"Nothin'," says Marzano.

Hriniak's smile lingers until he throws again, when his face goes taut with effort. Horn hits this one off the wall. He is in a groove, a rhythm, smashing the ball, timing every pitch just right. Hriniak finally gets the first out, an immense fly ball to center field, a ball that rubs the sky before descending. Sam rockets the next one into the center-field bleachers. He hits one on two rabbit-quick hops between second and first.

"That's an out," Hriniak says. He is sweating hard.

"Tough out," Horn says to Marzano.

"What'd he say?" demands Hriniak.

"I didn't say nothin'," Horn tells him.

"Nothin'," says Marzano.

The contest continues. Horn keeps launching them: bull pen, bleachers, *clunk* off the wall. This ballpark, now, is too small for him. Hriniak is bearing down, whipping the ball, trying different spots. Nothing works. He changes speeds. Horn's bat finds every pitch, meets the ball so regularly, so flush, that it begins to seem as if some trick were being played with magnets. Horn, yes, is making it look easy. He blasts another. And another. Hriniak hasn't gotten a third out. He'll never get six. We'd be here all night.

He watches Horn sting one down the right-field line, fair ball, and abruptly comes down off the mound. He waves Sam out of the cage. Sam ambles out with his bat, his weapon, on his shoulder. Hriniak comes halfway in, breathing hard and pouring sweat, all crackling movement, bottled-up energy.

"You beat me," he tells Horn, looking Sam in the eye.

"That's what I want to hear," says Sam.

Walt is smiling, but it is the forced smile of the gracious loser. "You beat me," he says again, "but I'm gonna fuckin' bury your ass tomorrow."

"We'll see 'bout that," drawls Horn.

You would think after watching this that Sam Horn would be in any lineup in the big leagues tonight—and tomorrow night, and the night after. But Sam isn't playing tonight, even though Charles Hudson, a righty, is pitching for the Yankees. McNamara has too many good hitters; he can't fit them all in.

Greenwell is batting .342 and has finally won an everyday job. The good old platoon system: against lefties, where he is at the theoretical disadvantage, Mike is hitting .364. Benzinger has begun a hitting rampage. Even with Henderson gone, and Baylor, McNamara has a superfluity of big hitters. Tonight, Rice is the DH and Horn is on the bench.

So Sam takes batting practice with the subs half an hour or so after his duel with Hriniak. The subs get less time to hit than the starters, fewer swings. For both subs and starters, the hitting schedule is rigidly observed. Time is precious. Swings are precious. Don't cheat.

Eddie Romero, waiting to hit, says, "That's seven."

"That's *five*," says big Sam, cocking the bat again.

"*Seven*," says Romero, and spits. His forehead is knitted, and he is looking hard at Sam. Romero speaks in bursts, with a Spanish accent. "It's not my fault you hittin' 'em up in the screen," he says, and spits again.

Sam *has* fouled a couple up into the netting. The pitch glides in and Sam cuts and fouls another one straight up. "*Damn*," he whispers.

"That's eight," says Romero.

"Six," Horn says.

He blasts a fly ball to center field, watches it arc down and graze the wall below the bleachers, and comes out of the cage.

"Nine swings, you had," says Romero. He's got his eyes on Horn, is following him. Sullivan is hitting. Romero is staring at Horn from the other side of the cage.

"What are you, a calculator?" says Horn.

Hriniak watches the two of them silently. Walt is faintly smiling. His gaze shifts back and forth as the two answer each other.

"I don't need no calculator to count to seven," says Romero.

"I don't, either."

"Seems like you do."

Horn says, "I don't need this, motherfucker."

"You were in there too long," Romero says evenly, "and my name ain't motherfucker."

Hriniak, looking amused, says, "He's the captain, Sam."

Horn spins, walks away muttering.

A little later McNamara is sitting on the bench with a couple of writers on either side. I'm at the end of the row. McNamara is relaxed tonight, in a friendly mood. He's telling us about his son, Mike, an officer in the United States Marines, who has been posted to an aircraft carrier in the Persian Gulf. The Gulf is a dangerous place these days, and McNamara is worried. He expresses his worry in a wry and manful way. Mike wants him to come visit him on the aircraft carrier for a week in January. McNamara isn't so sure he wants to accept the invitation, not because he's afraid, but because "I think I'd go fuckin' nuts on a boat for a week."

Pesky comes bustling out of the tunnel with his fungo.

" 'Lo, John," he says.

"Hi, Johnny," says McNamara.

Pesky comes down the line, saying hi to everyone.

" 'Lo, Paul."

"Hi, Johnny."

" 'Lo, Carl. 'Lo, Dave."

"Hey, Johnny."

Pesky gets to me, says, "Fuck you, Hough."

He sits down beside me, resting both hands on the knob of his bat. McNamara glances at me, wondering who I am to rate this special greeting.

Pesky says, "You got that Pulitzer Prize book done yet?"

McNamara glances at me again.

"Not yet," I say.

"What the hell's takin' you so long?" says Pesky.

Frank Malzone comes out, smartly dressed, as always. Black

patent-leather boots, gray slacks, white polo shirt with a cigar stuck in the pocket.

"Hello, Dago," Pesky says.

Malzone grins, sits. I can still see him at third base: stocky, bandy-legged. I can see him standing bowlegged with his glove up under his chin, socking his fist in the glove. He walked like a sailor on those loopy legs, strutting, shoulders thrown way back. Now he carries quite a belly. Always smiling, toothy. For many years he was the best third baseman in the league.

Malzone played for Pesky when Pesky managed here, '63 and '64. They look the same age, though Malzone is robust, husky. Their conversation swings this way and that, lazy dugout talk. McNamara excuses himself and goes out to watch his players hit. The writers drift away. Somehow Pesky and Malzone are on the subject of Dick Stewart, the big first baseman who hit the long ball and played his position with hands like stones. Stewart was a smart aleck who approached the game casually. He was supposed to have feuded with Pesky. Drove the manager crazy with his laxity.

I ask Pesky about Dick Stewart.

"Everybody thought I didn't like the son of a bitch," Pesky says. "Nah, he was okay. We got along."

"Remember when he hit the inside-the-park home run?" says Malzone.

Pesky chuckles. "Jesus, yeah."

"Stewart?" I say.

"*Here,*" Pesky says. "Unbelievable."

"It hit Davalillo on the head," Malzone says.

"It hit the wall," Pesky says, "and bounced off Davalillo's head. Then it rolled *in*, along the foul line. It was the goddamndest thing."

"Everyone was laughin'," Malzone says.

"When I went over to Pittsburgh," Pesky says—the Sox let him go, and the Pirates hired him to coach third base—

"Stewart was traded to the Phillies. The first time I see him over there, he comes up to me and says, 'You know, I'm the reason you're a coach and not a manager.' " Pesky grins, slides his hand across his chin. "That night he made three good plays against us. I mean, fuckin' terrific. Goes to his right. Goes to his left. Beautiful. I couldn't believe what I'm seein'. Afterward I told him, 'You son of a bitch, if you'd done that in Boston, we'd both still be there.' "

Pesky beams, working his chaw around. Malzone smiles but says nothing. He is sitting hunched, gazing straight ahead. The smile may or may not have anything to do with Pesky's story. The old-timers listen to each other's stories wordlessly. It's hard to tell by looking at them whether they're even paying attention. I think they are, though. I think they drink in every word, and that there simply isn't any need for acknowledgment. Pesky, Malzone, Morgan, Cliff Keane. The stories flow and flow, as numerous as the days of their lives.

It's too bad for the Yankees they couldn't pull it out last night. Now, to win two out of three, they must beat the Rocket Man. Small chance of that. Clemens is eleven and two in his last seventeen starts. The earned-run average is 3.33 and falling inexorably.

The night is humid and warm. A nearly full moon looks mistily down over the shoulder of the Prudential Building. In the top of the first the Yanks lash out against Roger. Randolph singles, Mattingly singles, Winfield singles. Easler lifts one nearly over the wall; the ball hits a foot from the top, kicks down to Greenwell, who gets rid of it so fast Easler can only stop at first. Two runs are in. Clemens pitches out of it, and the Yanks never score again till the ninth. They don't get another *hit* till the ninth. Roger strikes out an even dozen.

The Sox scratch a run in the first. Greenwell drives it in with a hard, sweet single to left. What a kid. With one out in the fourth, nobody on, Rice kisses Hudson's first pitch flush, sends it arcing high into the screen, a vintage Rice home run. The game is tied. Hudson gets a new ball, which Benzinger promptly cracks on a line into the bull pen.

Clemens now is scything them down effortlessly, and it is too much for Piniella, who can see the championship slipping down over the horizon. In the sixth, Boggs dives flat to his left and gloves a hard ground ball stroked by Easler; Wade springs to his feet and guns Easler out. A splendid play, the fruit of all those hours of practice. It's close at first, and Piniella comes scampering out to yell at the ump, Larry McCoy. Piniella is doused in a groaning chorus of "Loooo . . ." He dashes at McCoy, sticks his face down in the ump's, and commences to holler. The crowd urges Piniella on, "Loooo," with a certain affection. Boston fans know the game, and Lou played smart and hard, a winner. It isn't his fault he's a Yankee. Piniella rants on, and McCoy throws him out of the game with a grand spin and wave. Piniella's answer to his ejection is to grab hold of first base, wrestle it out of the ground, and heave it into right field. McCoy watches this tantrum calmly, without moving. The crowd lets out a great happy cheer. They croon Lou's name again as he stamps to the dugout, muttering blackly over his shoulder.

Benzinger drives a double into the alley in right center in the sixth, though the Sox don't score. They score two an inning later. Greenwell, Rice, and Benzinger provide the hits. Todd is three for four, red-hot.

It is 5–2 after eight innings, and people begin streaming out of the ballpark. Imagine: the best pitcher in baseball is about to put the finishing touches to a win against the Yankees, and people with good seats are walking out of the ballpark. They miss a very small scare that in the end merely underlines Roger's brilliance. Mattingly hits a ground ball that takes a crazy hop off Boggs's shoulder. Winfield rolls one into left field, the ball trickling just past Owen's glove, slow enough to allow Mattingly to take third. First and third, nobody out. Roger fans Easler on three pitches. Pagliarulo chops an easy ground ball to Owen; Winfield is running, so Spike gets the out at first. Mattingly scores. Clemens strikes out Claudell Washington. He throws a fastball that pounds Marzano's mitt at about the time Claudell takes his big cut.

Afterward, light swims in Clemens's face. The deep-set eyes are sparkling. Happiness is beating the Yankees.

"You could see they were hungry," Roger says, still breathing hard, thick shoulders rising and falling. "You could see it in their eyes. They're goin' for it, all right. You aren't kiddin', I was pumped up. You have to get pumped up for these guys."

Benzinger, the hitting star, is grinning in the most contented sort of way. "There's no team I'd rather do well against than the Yankees." The grin widens. "Especially when they're five games out and fighting for their lives."

It *was* five games. Now it is six. The Yanks have been bumped out of the race, and it happened right here in Fenway Park.

Eleven

"I Still Can't Believe
We Lost the Sixth Game"

ON SEPTEMBER 21 THE DETROIT TIGERS ARE IN FIRST PLACE.
The Blue Jays are in second, a half game behind. The Brewers
have caught the Yankees; the two teams share third, eight and
a half games from the Tigers. The Sox by now have sunk eighteen games beneath first place. Even so, the old ballpark is full
night after night, and the crowds are happy. They're turned
on. Listen to the cheers.

Tonight, September 21, sums it up. The Sox knock the
Tigers out of first place, but that isn't it, exactly. Nor is it the
nature of the win, a 9–4 drubbing, sixteen base hits. Red Sox
fans are wise enough to savor a pitching duel. No, it's the kids
who make this night worth the trip to the ballpark. It's who
the heroes are.

Take the second inning. No score. Greenwell kicks it off
with a home run into the bleachers in right. After Evans grounds
out, Horn taps a line drive, base hit, into left. Now Benzinger
lifts a weightless fly ball to left center, which finally knocks against

258

the wall, hits the grass without being touched, and rolls half a mile, it seems, easy triple for Todd. Owen doubles, Marzano singles, and Ellis Burks drills the wall halfway up, a double. The explosion produces four runs.

Burks gets three hits, Greenwell two, Horn two, Benzinger two, and Marzano three. In the third inning Lou Whitaker strokes a hit to center field. Lou thinks he has a double, but Burks zooms in, scoops and throws, perfectly, to second, where Whitaker, who for some reason doesn't bother to slide, is out dead. In the fifth, Chet Lemon belts one into the alley in right center; Burks gloves it, whirls counterclockwise, and throws, all in a single fluid motion, a ballet on the outfield grass. Lemon is paying attention and brakes at first, settling for the single.

Knowledgeable baseball fans understand a transition period. They are patient with it. In the bright moments they read the future. The Sox are eighteen games out, but no one is counting anymore. They are watching Burks, Benzinger, Greenwell, and Horn. They are bearing in mind that their team has the best pitcher and the best hitter in all of baseball. Both are still young men. It is springtime in Fenway, springtime in September. Fifth place, who cares? Come see the future.

Dwight Evans is standing behind the batting cage waiting to hit. He chews gum rapidly, nervously. His forehead is furrowed. It always is. Dewey is a thoughtful man. A serious man. He's been with this team since 1973, longer than anyone else. Of course I have to talk to him. Ask him about his catch in the '75 Series. Tell him how much I miss seeing him out in right field.

He doesn't remember speaking to me long ago, before the exhibition game at Shea. He doesn't know me from Adam. Could he, sometime at his convenience, spare ten minutes?

A quick, short smile. "More like five." The voice, deep and rich, has a faint twang, an elasticity.

"I'm not opposed to talkin' to you," he says. "It's just

that . . . well, this is a big series, the Tigers and all. I don't want to have to be at the ballpark at any special time. I'm tryin' to relax a bit, spend more time with my family." He squints out to where the last of the sunlight is washing the steel-blue bleacher seats. "I want to start bein' a father for a change. Know what I'm sayin'?" He squints at me.

"Sure."

"This is kind of a bad time for me. A down time."

I wait, but he doesn't elaborate. It will be his best year ever, but Dewey has been slipping lately. The batting average is down to .316. He made a couple of errors at first base last night. He bounced a throw to Owen at second, and he booted an easy ground ball, double-play material. This is one of the best right fielders in the business. Stubborn man, McNamara.

"Look," Evans says, "we'll work somethin' in. I promise."

"I'll be here for the Milwaukee series," I say. This is the last weekend of the season, ten days away. "If you'd be more relaxed, we could talk then."

He nods vigorously. "Yeah, I definitely would be. Definitely."

"I'll remind you, okay?"

"Absolutely. We'll catch up, I promise."

"Thank you," I say.

I go sit in the dugout to jot some notes. The dugout is empty at the moment. I'm sitting there writing when Mc-Namara emerges from the tunnel, hands stuffed in his hip pockets. He stops by the bat rack, surveys the bench, sees only me. He doesn't say hello, doesn't nod. Nothing. He sends me an icy stare, then leans over and drops a splash of juice on the floor. He climbs the steps, his mouth stretched sourly, as if finding me in the dugout first thing has left a bad taste.

I feel a sudden swoop of depression. Same old disappointment, doubling back and hitting me one last time, this failure of mine to make friends with any of the ballplayers. I'm still invisible. Even the guys I interviewed, even the kids, don't know me. They seem to have no recollection of talking to me. Even Hurst, the nicest guy in the world.

But now Pesky and Morgan sit down with their fungoes.

"Fabian Gaffke."

"*Who?*"

"Fabian Gaffke," Morgan says.

"Outfielder, right here, you son of a bitch."

"You got it. And?"

"Right-handed hitter," Pesky says.

"Also played for Cleveland," Morgan says.

"That's right," Pesky says.

Sam Horn has finished taking ground balls and comes now to the railing to sign some autographs and chat with his admirers.

"Sam's a fan man, huh?" says Morgan.

"He'd talk to a fuckin' post," says Pesky.

Tonight, September 22, Wade Boggs is hobbling around with his left knee locked. Boggs hurt the knee in the big win last night. He'd hit a double near the bull pen and was trying for three. They got him at third on a close play, and Wade banged the knee as he slid.

Boggs is hitting .363, comfortably out in front of the league's second-best hitter, Paul Molitor, whose average is .350. Wade has one hundred ninety-eight hits. Since he has been in the big leagues, he has had two hundred hits every year but the first, 1982, when he played in only one hundred four games. (He batted .349.) Generally, two hundred hits is a measure of excellence. Two hits short of this resonant number, Boggs will be the DH tonight. The knee is bad. He can't play third.

Before the game he does a TV interview in front of the dugout. As usual, Boggs is matter-of-fact about his abilities. He speaks drily, with quiet conviction. Just stating the obvious.

"I'm hitting a quiet .363," he tells his interviewer. "Just

look in the papers and the media guide. It isn't played up. People expect me to hit .350 and above, and when I don't, that's when I make news."

The interviewer points out that there have been some cold spells in Boggs's season.

"I've had some rough stretches," Wade agrees. "I've had some one-for-eighteen stretches, which makes this an even tougher .363."

The Sox lose the game, 8–5, but even so, some notable things are achieved. In the first inning Burks slams one into the screen, his twentieth home run. Ellis has stolen twenty-five bases, and so becomes the third man in the history of this team to steal twenty bases and hit twenty home runs in a season. The others were Jackie Jensen, my childhood hero, and Carl Yastrzemski. Benzinger hits his seventh home run, a two-run blast. And Wade Boggs gets the two hits he needed, a double and a home run.

The double, hit number 199, comes in the fifth with the bases empty. Wade lines it off the wall and limps into second. In the seventh he whacks the home run, also to left, the opposite field. As Wade jigs around the bases, Josh Spofford announces that this is the fifth straight year that Boggs has had two hundred hits, which has been done by only three players since 1901. That year, Josh tells us, Wee Willie Keeler did it for the eighth time in a row.

Boggs is on his way down the dugout steps when all of this is printed out on the electronic scoreboard. It takes a few moments to sink in, and then the crowd rises and bestows an immense ovation on Boggs. The applause goes on: they want a curtain call. A moment of suspense—Wade, all business, isn't one for hoopla—and Boggs pops into view. The ovation swells. Boggs climbs to the top step. He lifts his cap high and slowly turns, rotating completely around. Enough: he clatters down into the dugout.

In the ninth, Boggs comes up with two men on, one out: a rally, tying run at the plate. A relief pitcher, Willie Hernandez, walks Wade on four pitches. McNamara sends Kevin Romine, a new arrival from Pawtucket, to run for Boggs. Boggs hobbles off the field to a grateful roar. No one dreams—except maybe Wade himself—that he is through for the year.

Hernandez, amazingly, gets Greenwell to scoop a high pop fly to Whitaker, the second baseman. Two out. It's up to Evans. "*Dooooh* . . ." moans the crowd, with love in its voice. Hernandez is a lefty, so the Tigers' venerable, big-hearted manager, Sparky Anderson, goes out to remove him. Sparky summons righty Dickie Noles, who joined the team a few hours ago in a deal with the Cubs. Noles is the quintessential journeyman, a hired hand who never stays long. Eight years in the big leagues, six teams, with occasional stopoffs in the minors. Lifetime earned-run average of 4.56.

A big moment: the Jays have shellacked the Orioles down in Baltimore, so the Tigers will tumble to a game and a half out if they let this one get away. Evans gets ready, the jaw outthrust, the bat dangling down over his shoulder. He looks at ball one. He hacks at the next pitch, raps the ball on one sharp bounce to Noles. Noles runs halfway to first with the ball, and finally lobs it over there, ending the ball game.

Boggs is a contented man afterward, and Evans is not. Dewey peels down to his gray T-shirt and those brilliant blue tights, and goes as usual to the buffet table for his pasta. There's none left. This is the last straw, and Dwight commences to flip dirty paper plates off the table. He flips over a plate that holds several wedges of pizza, a plate of sausages, a plate of hot dogs. No one pays the slightest attention except the equipment man, Vince Orlando, who drops to his knees and scrambles around picking things up almost as fast as Dewey sends them down. Orlando doesn't say anything to Evans, or look upset. He just wants to get the stuff off the floor. Evans returns without food to his locker and undresses. He wads each piece of clothing and flings it to the floor.

Boggs, on the other hand, is basking in a nimbus of TV lights, standing tall with his arms folded over his chest, face uplifted. Saint George. The reporters jam in, straining to hear him. Two hundred hits for the fifth year in a row:

"It's very special. Only three guys in the modern era have done it. When you can put that many years together, that many two-hundred-hit years, it's an achievement. It's certainly the biggest achievement of my career."

Boggs stops, reflects.

"You know one of the hardest things about it? The walks. If I didn't pride myself in getting so many walks, it'd be easy getting two hundred hits. I get a lot of walks, and that's a lot of swings I don't take, a lot of hits. People don't understand that."

Someone asks him about his knee.

"I'm running at about forty percent," Boggs says. "Seems like it always comes this time of year, doesn't it?"

A year ago he twisted an ankle and sat on the bench through the last weekend of the season, three games in Fenway with the Yankees. The Sox had wrapped up the championship. Mattingly was chasing Boggs for the batting title, and some people wondered if Wade was malingering, standing pat with his .357 average. Mattingly wasn't going to hit .357, but if Boggs slipped, Mattingly might have caught him. It was pointed out that with the play-offs and perhaps the World Series coming up, it would have been foolish to risk aggravating an injury in games that counted for nothing. Still, the ugly suspicion dogs Wade to this day.

At twilight it is raining gently on the ballpark. A few of the players wander out, squint appraisingly at the sky, and sit on the bench to wait out the rain. The western sky lightens a bit, turns creamy. The rain sifts down more gently.

Evans comes out, busy-looking as always. He bustles down the bench, past me, *not* past. He sits down beside me almost before I know it.

"Okay," he says.

I look at him. "Really?"

Now he looks at me with a start. "You *are* the one who wanted to talk?"

"Absolutely."

"I'm not mixin' you up?"

"No, no."

"I don't want to give an interview to someone who didn't ask for one."

"I asked," I tell him. "It's just that I wasn't expecting to get the interview till the Milwaukee series."

"This is fine," he says. "I got some time. What'd you want to talk about?"

"Oh . . . how 'bout the year you're having?"

"Well, I've said this again and again: I'd rather be hittin' .260 and be in the race. You know, this year I'm havin' . . ." He shakes his head, sighs. "I've never had a better year, but I've never been so disappointed. It's been a long year. It's tough for me now, I think I told you that. I'm having trouble concentrating. I'm tired."

I wonder if this extraordinary year has become a burden to him. He has called attention to himself, created new expectations.

"It's a down time for me," he says again. "Do you have kids?"

"Stepchildren."

"Then you know what it's like. You get a call from school. It might be good news, it might be bad news, but either way it takes time to deal with. I want to be a good father. There's a lot goin' on that people don't know about."

I remember hearing years ago that Evans was going through some great sadness with one of his children. The announcer—

this was on national television—didn't elaborate. Dwight's chiseled face is nicked with lines that hint at some private anguish.

"I miss seeing you play right field," I tell him.

He gives me the vigorous nod. "People have told me that. And I *do* miss it. I take a lot of pride in what I do out there."

"Do you have any choice where you play?"

"No," he says quickly. "None at all."

"Why did they decide to put you on first base?" I ask. "Whose idea was it?"

"It was my own idea, believe it or not," he says. "We were out in Kansas City. I'd pulled a hamstring and couldn't play right field. I went to Mac, told him I was hurt. I told him I could DH, but I didn't want to push it, because Don Baylor was our DH, that was his job. Then I said, just sort of off the top of my head, 'I could play first.' He says, 'Could you?' I said, 'Yeah, sure.' Just like that. Buckner had been hurtin', he needed some rest, so Mac sent me out there." A smile. "I didn't even know where to throw the ball during infield practice."

"Do you regret your offer?"

"Nah, I wouldn't say that. First base has its advantages. It's a lot easier on the body."

"Easier on the body?"

"Less wear and tear. Playin' right field I figure I run a mile every game just goin' on and off the field. That's not including the hard running after fly balls. I'm not even sure I could play the outfield now. I'm not sure I'm in *shape* for it."

I look out to right field, where the barrier bends around to the bull pen. The barrier is four, maybe five, feet high. In that epic sixth game of the '75 Series—the game decided by Carlton Fisk's home run—Evans made the most wonderful catch. The Reds' Joe Morgan, a strong lefty pull-hitter, drove the ball over Evans's head. Dewey spun, seemed to lose his balance, and lurched in a kind of staggering run toward the barrier, watching the ball over his shoulder. The ball sailed directly over his head; he took it with a stabbing lunge that seemed like blind luck. And yet you knew somehow it wasn't. A runner on first, never dreaming Dewey could catch that ball, was steaming into third. Evans found his balance, whirled, and flung the ball to first, double play. Tremendous.

Twelve years ago, and the play is as fresh in both our minds as yesterday.

"I caught the ball *here*," says Evans, showing me, reaching and spreading his fingers. His arm is slightly bent and extended exactly in front of his face, the hardest way to catch a fly ball. You need the angle, need to be converging on the flight of the ball, not running a congruent line. This way skews your balance, your vision, everything. "The ball didn't tail toward the line the way I expected it to," says Evans.

"You looked as if you didn't know where the wall was."

"I didn't. I didn't know if I'd hit it, or what."

"What are some of your other big thrills?"

"Well, my home run in the '75 Series. In a way that thrilled me more than the catch. To hit a home run in the Series . . ." He ponders. "My double in the seventh game last year, that meant something."

"That was a tough piece of hitting."

"It was," he says. "I was proud of it."

The Mets were leading, 6–3, and the heart had pretty much gone out of the Sox. In the eighth inning, though, Buckner and Rice pushed singles through the infield, and Dewey came up, the tying run. He smashed it to right center, a line drive that skipped deep enough to let both runners score. Evans cruised into second without sliding. Nobody out. One single, and the game would have been tied. They didn't get that single, because the fire had died in them. But not in Evans, the old pro, declaring himself in his final at-bat.

"You said you were tired," I say. "Is this part of aging?"

"Definitely. I'm not just tired; I *hurt*. I come out here every day and the first thing I do is run sprints. Well, it hurts. It hurts to run those sprints at this time of year. I'm on aspirin all the time."

"You're in good shape."

"You have to maintain," he says, and describes an elaborate conditioning program of lifting weights and using exercise machines. I have seen some of this machinery in a windowless room off the corridor to McNamara's office, massive blue contraptions of unimaginable use, all with moveable joints, some with bright silver chains. It looks like a torture chamber. "The guys say I'm crazy. They say I'm a fanatic. I never stop workin' out. You got to maintain."

Evans, by staying so fit, so young, and by playing so well, has created a dilemma for the Red Sox. Like Buckner, Baylor, and Rice, Dewey is in the autumn of his career, but unlike them—unlike almost any ballplayer at his age—he is playing better than ever. What to do with him? Trade him? Unthinkable. Trade Todd Benzinger? Unthinkable. The solution this year seems to have been to stick him at first base.

"I enjoy first base," Dewey says now, "but it's not as if I'm not capable of playing right field anymore. I was playin' a *good* right field when they moved me."

As it is to Boggs, Fenway is just a ballpark to Evans, nothing more, nothing less. "I don't know how many home runs I've lost on account of playing in this ballpark," he says wistfully. "Dozens, I guess. Dozens and dozens. I hit line drives off the wall a lot of times that would be home runs in other parks. They're rising, see, as they hit the wall. Then I lose home runs on fly balls to center field, all those three-hundred-ninety-foot fly balls." He looks out, points to left field and then to right. "Fenway'd be perfect for me if you reversed the dimensions. Put the wall in right."

The ballplayers' obliviousness to the charms of Fenway Park is one of the great surprises of the summer.

"When I was drafted," Evans says, "I didn't know who the Red Sox *were*. Growin' up in Hawaii and California, you know. When I heard the news I went out and bought a red jersey, that's how much I knew. I didn't even know what the uniform looked like."

The sky has continued, slowly, to lighten. It is now a shade of cream, but still weeping the gentlest of rains. Stanley has ventured out onto the slick grass in right to play catch with John Leister, another arrival from Pawtucket.

"This weather," Evans says, gesturing at the rain. "It's depressing. The East is so different from California. People out here, they don't get sun like they do out West. Everyone looks so pale and unhealthy all the time. They go around with bags under their eyes." He's half-kidding. He loops his index fingers to his thumbs, bags, which he holds under his eyes. I laugh. He smiles.

Here comes Hriniak, filling his cheek with tobacco.

"You ready, Dwight?"

"Soon's I finish with the gentleman here," says Evans.

"Go ahead," I say. "You've been great. Really."

"No problem," he says.

I watch him and Hriniak jog into the distance of center field, where Dwight has hit so many deep fly ball outs, home runs other places. They talk as they go, running easily, unhurriedly, through the rain.

"What can I do for you fellas?"

McNamara looks around at us, smiling. Ruddy and smiling. Happy. We are in the dugout.

We begin with a medical question: Crawford is hurt.

"Crawford," says McNamara, "is through for the season. He will be operated on next week."

Adios, Bombino.

Someone asks, "How you holdin' up, John?"

"The closer October fourth comes," says McNamara, smiling still, "the better I get."

Laughter.

Leigh Montville is standing in front of McNamara. Montville starts scribbling.

"Hey, don't print *that* shit," says McNamara.

More laughter. Montville smiles under his rusty mustache, not sure how to take it.

"Ah, go ahead and print it," says McNamara.

Montville, who is working up a column, says, "These guys are where you were at this time last year." He means the Tigers. "What do you think about when you look over there?"

McNamara frowns, but not angrily. "Over there is what it's all about," he says. "It's what we're all here for." A pause, and then he says, "You know, last year we were tied for second in the league in ERA, and this year we're next to last." You can't blame *that* on me, he is saying, and he's right.

Montville crosses to the Tigers' dugout, and I go with him. The dugout is full of people, and not just ballplayers. There are writers doing interviews, and several expensively dressed men who perch forward on the bench. These latter are watching the guys play catch on the grass out front and the reporters bustling up and down the dugout, interested in everything. Club officials, I guess, getting a taste of the excitement. The dugout is full of people, full of noise. The ballplayers all look happy. They bark jokes at each other, they laugh loudly. There's a happy tension in the air, an electricity you can feel on your skin. Montville selects another veteran named Evans—Darrell, the Tigers' first baseman—for an interview.

Darrell Evans is sitting on the bench in his windbreaker, a chaw bulging in his right cheek. He is quieter than his younger teammates, sitting back against the wall with his hands stuffed in his jacket pockets, working the chaw around and taking in the scene. Evans is forty-one. My age. He squints, regarding the world coolly, warily.

"Sure, it's enjoyable," he tells Leigh Montville. He speaks slowly, choosing his words. "You can't buy an experience like this, not for any price. This is everything."

Evans was a member of this team in '84, when they took the World Series. Montville asks him if it's different the second time around.

"There are no surprises," Evans says, "not after your first pennant race. I remember standing in the outfield in the second play-off game in '84, looking around at the crowd and the players scattered out in front of me, and for a moment I saw the thing as a whole. I saw how . . . *big* it was." He leans and squirts tobacco. "Before you taste it," he says, "you can't know what it's like. You can't have any idea."

The Tigers take the game, 4–0. Another bruising for Hurst. Horn bats third, Boggs's spot, and does nothing. Doyle Alexander, who came in a trade with the Atlanta Braves on August 12, throws the shutout. The Tigers' press release for this evening says, "Alexander has pitched very well for the Bengals." I'll say. He begins the game with seven wins, no losses, and a 1.61 earned-run average. Before the trade, he'd won five and lost ten. No one has been able to shed light on this rejuvenation, including Alexander, a veteran of seventeen years in the majors. The writers have taken to calling him Alexander the Great.

He's great tonight, all right. Burks and Barrett hit clean singles in the first inning, and the Sox don't get another hit. Owen walks with two out in the second, and Alexander pitches perfect baseball from then on. He does it with slow stuff and a medium-speed fastball that slides upward. The ascending movement has the Sox swinging just under the ball, lifting it harmlessly in the air.

Afterward I go to the winners' clubhouse, which is so jammed you can barely get around. The reporters are together in a tight clump—there isn't room to spread out—waiting for Alexander, who is, I assume, taking his sweet time in the trainer's room. The players are sitting around half-undressed, eating and drinking. Coke, beer, and the same greasy repast the home team feasts on. A TV sits high on the wall, and at this moment—strange but true—the cable sports channel is running a film on the '75 Series. The '87 Tigers, almost all of them, are raptly watching.

They sit in front of their lockers in a row along the wall, and around a table at the TV end of the room, gazing solemnly at the screen, saying nothing. The uplifted faces, slick with sweat, seem mesmerized. The film now is showing the big moments of the sixth game. Bernie Carbo's pinch-hit home run. Evans's catch. And finally, Fisk's home run. Pudge waves the ball fair, waves and waves, sees it slam into the screen, home run, and leaps straight up with his arms held high. Alan Trammell, the Tigers' superb shortstop, is sitting at the table under the TV. Trammell watches Pudge urge his home run fair, and as Fisk sports around the bases a smile spreads on Trammell's cordial, intelligent face. "That was a nice moment," he says softly.

The last time I saw my mother I showed her an autographed ball and bat Gary Carter had given me, and told her and my father all about the week I'd just spent in New York. My mother loved to hear her kids' stories. She got as big a kick out of our adventures as her own.

My parents had come to the island for the weekend. They came every other weekend, before my mother got sick, to my great-grandfather's house, theirs now. After the illness came they tried to keep to their schedule, every other weekend, but as often as not my mother didn't feel up to the trip. So you never knew. They'd call at the last minute to say they weren't coming. In the beginning this would alarm me, but then a week or two later they'd come, and she'd be looking pretty good. You went up and down, I decided, recovering from cancer.

My wife and I walked over that night in the light of a new, thin moon. The trees leaned up tall and skinny in the gray moonlight. Later I would think back and squeeze my memory for details, things I would have noted and stored up if I'd known what this evening was. But there was no way of knowing. So now I have pieced together that slice of moon, the bare oaks tilting up, and the gullied road twisting along faintly visible in its gray glaze. I was carrying the bat and ball. The ball had been signed by Carter and his teammates. A World Series ball. The bat was a new Louisville Slugger. What a pleasure to hold: thin handle, thick barrel, so smooth, so hard, light but with sock in that wide barrel. Above the label Gary had penned felicitations to me and my wife: *May I extend my best wishes to you both for continued happiness always. May the Lord's blessings guide you always.*

The dogs barked when we walked in. My mother was sitting to the left of the fireplace, with the dining table between her and my father. She looked very tired, but happy. She was, in that last year of her life, smaller. Not shriveled, not scrawny, just smaller. Nothing ugly happened to her; she had too much vitality in her, too much bounce. She just turned smaller. She'd lost a vocal cord in the operation, and her voice now was a light, airy purr.

I pulled a chair over beside her and presented, first, the ball. She laughed, shrugging up her shoulders, at these prizes of mine, at my schoolboy enthusiasm. She turned the ball over in her pretty hands and tried to read the scribbles. I imagined Gary circling the clubhouse with the ball, handing it down to the guys sitting half-dressed at their lockers. My mother held the ball and I pointed. "Dwight Gooden. Keith Hernandez."

She knew Gooden. She remembered Hernandez, sort of. She'd watched the Series with my father. There'd been good reasons to watch this year: the Red Sox, Gary Carter. "Darryl Strawberry," I read, and my father snorted up a derisive grunt. Strawberry had irritated my father during the Series with his sulking. Me, too. "Mookie Wilson," I said. I like to think now of those ballplayers' big young hands on the leather skin of that baseball—Carter's muscular paw, Hernandez's ropy sculptor's fingers, the iron claw of Strawberry—the ball coming away charged with the energy in those hands, and with the excitement of the clubhouse at World Series time, and in turn conferring this strength, pressing it back into the hands of my mother.

She examined the bat, holding it across her lap. She read Gary's inscription. With her fingers she traced the label, which was branded into the golden-brown wood. She hefted it with both hands.

I handed it across the table to my father. He had to get up out of his chair, cock the bat, swish it, draw a bead on an imaginary pitcher. There wasn't room to take a swing, but you could see he was itching to. He squinted out at that pitcher. When he lowered the bat he studied it another moment in a satisfied sort of way, as if he'd just used it to drive one off the wall.

An hour, an hour and a half, by the fire. A couple of drinks. What else happened? They wanted to hear all about New York. But the memory of myself talking is of no use to me. No use at all.

My mother's hair was red-brown. Rinsed. She wore it short, and it grew in abundant curls. I used to grab her head in both hands when I leaned over to kiss her hello and good-bye. Sometimes, to tease, I'd muss her hair, rubbing the curls around.

That night I spread both hands around the crown of her head in the old way. The springy coils of hair bunched against my palms. I bent over to kiss her in her chair by the fire. I didn't muss her hair; she seemed too fragile, too tired. Tired but happy.

" 'Bye, Mom."

"Good-bye, Child."

And the walk home, down through the woods, with the whiskey we'd drunk floating us along. People she loved, my mother called "Child," unless they were older than she was. My wife brought the ball, stashed carefully in her coat pocket. I carried the bat, pausing now and then to swing it in the moonlight.

It is the last weekend of the 1987 baseball season. October. The Sox finish the season in Fenway with the Milwaukee Brewers, against whom they opened out in Milwaukee.

I was at home on Opening Day. It was cold, they said, in Milwaukee; on Martha's Vineyard it was gray and cool. I have my own Opening Day ritual, which I observed as usual.

At game time I left the house with my transistor radio, followed by our male bull terrier, whose name is Bad Edward. I climbed into the old Ford stake truck and hauled the dog by his collar up and across my lap, and shoved him over amongst my equipment—bow saw, timber jack, sledgehammer, iron wedges. The truck is on permanent loan from our neighbor Harold Rogers, who, forty and fifty years ago, was doing similar favors for my great-grandfather. The truck is in retirement, but Harold keeps its sleepy old engine running. How he does this is a mystery. He is a tinkerer, a wizard.

I drove a quarter of a mile down a twisting dirt road to a field sloping down to swampy woods. The field was greening and beginning to stir. I backed the truck to the edge of the woods. Bad Edward took a flying leap as soon as I opened the door. He ran around sniffing the soft wet ground. I got out and set the radio on the decaying planking of the truck platform. I found the ball game.

A short distance into the woods, maybe twenty yards, there

was standing swamp water. Maples grew in the swamp, their roots lifting round islands of moss out of the water. The moss was beginning to brighten. Ferns were waking, pale green fiddleheads. A huge sassafras tree had fallen just inside the woods, short of the swamp. It had been dead a long time. Its roots had rotted, and the mucky earth had released the tree. It had crashed down into thickets of viburnum and had clubbed over a young locust tree. I calculated that the sassafras was sixty years old. It had been dead another ten years, which meant it had sprouted up out of the ground when Woodrow Wilson was President and Babe Ruth was pitching for the Red Sox. Nothing has changed here. The maples and sassafrases have been growing for centuries. For millennia.

After a while the spring peepers got used to me and the radio, and resumed singing in the swamp. I cut into the sassafras, soft wood that smells like root beer inside. Good firewood, hot and crackling, though fast-burning. Bad Edward found himself a hunky stick and brought it to me for throwing. I sailed it off into the thickets, and he went crashing after it. The peepers' sweet jingle floated and shimmered. I've never seen a peeper, but in April their song rings everywhere. I could hear the radio fine. The Sox went out easily in the first, and Bob Stanley promptly pitched into trouble. I sawed a firewood-length section of the dead sassafras, and heaved the big log out onto the field. I cut the tree up and split the pieces with the sledgehammer and wedges, listening to the peepers and the first game of another baseball season.

This final Friday is as cool as that April day, but burnished in golden, hazy sunshine. At four o'clock the vendors are setting up on Lansdowne and Yawkey Way, but otherwise the streets are empty. The crowds will build, but not as early as they did in June and July, when already the kids and their fathers would be sitting under the arches waiting for the gates to open, and the cops would be waving people aside on Van Ness Street as the players' cars whirled in. Right now there is no one to smell the sausages cooking on the vendors' griddles.

The clubhouse, too, is quiet. Greenwell sits with a writer, chatting in a low monotone. Big Sam sits alone by his stall. Benzinger is slowly pulling on his uniform. He pauses to sign a ball presented to him by the fat clubhouse boy. Todd returns the ball and pen with a courteous nod.

On the field Hriniak is throwing extra batting practice to Marzano. The shadow of the grandstand blankets left field and slants up the canvas-green wall. The scoreboard is all in shadow. Wind yanks the flags from right to left, blowing out for the hitters. Old Glory and the pennant, American League Champions, which will soon fly elsewhere.

Others come out, more of the kids, to listen to Hriniak, who seems not to know that it is October, and that everyone is about to disperse for the winter. Hriniak is as nervous and busy as ever. Rac Slider takes over on the mound, and Walt hurries in to preach. Benzinger has arrived, and the big Pawtucket first baseman, Pat Dodson. Kevin Romine, an outfielder, chugs out, and finally the rabbit-quick little shortstop, Jody Reed, who some think will have Spike Owen's job next spring.

"Maintain the head," Hriniak tells Marzano through the netting. "Maintain, *maintain*."

Dodson, Reed, and Romine gather round to hear a sermon about the swing of the Yankees, which is generally bad, except for Don Mattingly's beautiful ripple. Back in June Walt pointed it out to me: the Yanks jerk their heads up and away as they take their cut. The Sox have just been down in New York, so it is fresh in Hriniak's mind and, he hopes, his pupils'. He goes on awhile, hacking for emphasis with those knobby hands, and sums up:

"That's why guys hit fuckin' .220."

Benzinger goes in to hit. Hriniak studies him. He crouches, pops up, crouches again.

"Stay exactly with what you got, Todd," he says. "Don't change *nothin'*."

Benzinger nods and plants a line drive *clunk* against the wall.

What a game. *Oh*, what a game.

The Brewers' pitcher is Teddy Higuera, one of the best in baseball. Higuera won twenty last year, has won eighteen in '87. He is a stocky little lefty, almost plump, with a slow, fluid motion. A dancer. His mound opponent is Jeff Sellers. Sellers has won seven, lost eight, and is lugging a ponderous 5.60 earned-run average. He has promise, nevertheless. I like him because he's smart, and because he's forthright with the reporters. You'd think Higuera would have an easy win here, but after three innings the score is knotted, 1–1, and both pitchers are in a groove. Higuera has given up two singles and has struck out five. Sellers has given up four singles and whiffed four. Nothing, really, is riding on this game. Settle back, then, and enjoy it for its own sake.

Enjoy, for instance, watching Higuera operate on Sam Horn. Higuera at this stage knows too much, is too wise, for Horn. With Boggs gone, McNamara has promoted Sam to the third spot in the batting order. The first time he bats, Sam gets way ahead, three balls, no strikes. Higuera then tosses the slowball, a lazy little pitch thrown with the same smooth motion that produces Higuera's zippy fastball. Horn, of course, is assuming the fastball, and he swings viciously and misses by a couple of feet. Higuera tosses in another slow one, and again Horn sees a fastball in his mind's eye, and again swings way early. Nothing in Sam's experience has prepared him for what happens next. No one has ever fed him three straight slowballs—no one has ever dared—but that is what Higuera does, and Horn strikes out with a mighty hack, hunting the fastball to the end. In the third Higuera gets him one ball, two strikes, and now Sam is braced for the tricky stuff, the slow curve, the change-up. Instead, Higuera whips the fastball, and Horn swings and misses. Higuera's change-up does move a bit. It seems to jig, to shake itself, just in front of the hitter. In the sixth he strikes Horn out on three pitches.

In the fourth the Brewers' shortstop, Dale Sveum, steals a hit from Evans. Dewey sends the ball on the ground, hard, up the middle; Sveum snares it running full tilt and, still on the run, snaps a throw to first, just in time.

In the top of the fifth, Spike Owen matches Sveum with a lovely play on a ground ball hit by Robin Yount. Sveum is on first. Yount pulls the ball way to Spike's right; Spike gloves it backhand, spins, and chucks it to second like a quarterback throwing off-balance. Sveum is out at second.

Otherwise the outs are routine. Sellers has a decent fastball, a decent curve. Tonight he is putting them both exactly where he wants to, which makes all the difference. In the top of the eighth, none out, he walks Yount and gives up a single to B.J. Surhoff. Trouble. He needs ground balls, maybe get the double play. He's going to try to keep his pitches low, twist them down. Greg Brock bounces the first pitch he sees to second base, not fast enough for the double play. Barrett tosses to Owen at second. Runners at first and third, one out. Glenn Braggs takes a ball, then grounds one straight to Owen, easy double play. Neither ground ball was an accident.

In the bottom of the eighth the Sox get a run. Burks walks. Barrett doubles, Ellis stopping at third. Horn is next. He has fanned three times, and now he swipes and misses, strike one. But he finds the next pitch, slaps a ground ball to Brock at first base. Burks is coming home, Brock throws, Ellis slides, safe. The out looked easy; Burks flashed home, greased lightning. Higuera pitches free of further trouble.

In the top of the ninth, Ernest Riles singles up the middle. He takes second on a sacrifice bunt. Sellers fans Rich Manning, but Sveum lifts a fly ball into the wind, which has helped nobody till now. Greenwell follows it back, fading a step at a time, figuring he's got it in his pocket. But the wind chases it, till Mike is at the wall. He leaps; the ball grazes the wall a few inches above his glove, caroms back, a double for Sveum, and a tie ball game. The dangerous Molitor is next, and Sellers strikes him out with three straight fastballs, pouring them in there as if angered by the double. Higuera gets the Sox easily in the bottom of the ninth, and we go into extra innings.

Sellers dispatches them one, two, three in the tenth. Nothing is hit out of the infield.

In the bottom of the tenth, Higuera does the same.

Sellers gives up two singles in the eleventh, then pitches out of it.

Higuera puts them down in order in the bottom of the inning.

Wes Gardner prances in to pitch the twelfth. He gets Molitor and Yount on fly balls. Surhoff walks. Brock rolls a ground ball to Owen.

Higuera comes out to pitch the twelfth. It is his last game of the season, and he must badly want that nineteenth win. Eddie Romero makes him work. The count stretches full, then Romero hits an easy fly ball to the left fielder. Higuera throws two strikes past Owen. He teases Spike with the slowball, outside, and Spike lets it go. The next pitch is up, perhaps inside. Little Spike sees the mistake and pounces. A crisp, hard swing, a fly ball, high, riding the wind, riding and riding, disappearing over the wall.

The ball game is over.

"I never hit a game-winning home run," says Spike afterward, smiling the biggest smile. His cheeks are pink. "It's somethin' you always dream of," he says. He hit a slider. "It was a *hangin'* slider, out over the plate." A mistake, Higuera's only one in eleven and a third innings. "I was just tryin' to put the ball in play," Spike says modestly.

Sellers, who had left the game and therefore doesn't receive credit for the win, talks to us in his usual brisk, easy way. Both his arm and shoulder have ice packs strapped to them, the Ace wrappings bulging out grotesquely.

"I've always known I could pitch," he says.

"Hey, Jeff." It's Evans, interrupting, calling across the room from his chair. Sellers turns. "How old's your kid?" Evans says.

Evans is sitting in his blue tights smirking at a little boy who stands there staring at him.

"Why?" Sellers asks. "What'd he say?"

"He doesn't *know*," Evans says. "He doesn't know how old he is."

"Yeah, he does," Sellers says. "Tell him how old you are."

The kid sends his father a sly look, then resumes staring at Evans.

"Tell him how old you are," Sellers says. "You know how old you are."

"No, he doesn't," says Evans.

"Will you tell him how old you are?" Sellers sounds exasperated.

"I don't think he knows, Jeff," says Evans.

"He *does* know," says Sellers.

The kid stares at Evans.

You can hear the showers' hiss and splash, and voices echoing on the tile. "Two more games," someone bellows. *"Two more fuckin' games."*

Saturday is warmer. Softer. Clouds have moved in, and the mellow light has faded. Boggs is in the ballpark this morning, hobbling around on a stiff left leg. His knee has been operated on, but this has not quite silenced speculation that he could have played out the season and given Molitor a chance to catch him. Eddie Andelman, who has a nightly radio sports talk show on one of the big Boston AM stations, has been giving Wade the treatment. Boggs is "jaking it," says Andelman.

Wade is wearing designer jeans and a white polo shirt with the logo of the Seattle Seahawks pro football team stitched on the pocket. He looks cheerful. He gimps gingerly down the dugout steps and is accosted by Mike Ross, an expatriate baseball worshipper who publishes a newsletter called the *Transatlantic Baseball Bulletin* in London. It is, I gather, for Americans living abroad. Ross has just come over from London. He lifts a photograph out of his shirt pocket and shows it to Boggs.

"I took this in Yankee Stadium in June," he says. "You remember that?" He has a peppery way of talking, a shade British.

"I don't remember a picture being taken," Boggs says. The eagle eyes look away from Ross, to the outfield.

"Not the picture," Ross says, "the conversation. Lou Piniella was talking to some of his guys about hitting the outside pitch. You were listening."

"I remember," Boggs says.

"Well, did you pick anything up? Did you learn anything?"

Boggs's gaze swings coolly back to Ross. "I already know how to hit the outside pitch," he says. "I just wanted to see if Piniella was tellin' it right."

It is a little after eleven, and McNamara is shooting the breeze with Cliff Keane and Bob Ryan of the *Globe*. Ryan covers the Celtics and seldom writes baseball, which may be why McNamara seems to bear him no ill will.

"I picked Detroit a week ago," McNamara is saying. The Tigers and Jays are playing each other this weekend for all the marbles. "Toronto has the best personnel in the American League, but Detroit has the chemistry. Of course, what chemistry is, I don't know."

"Is the home field a big advantage?" Ryan asks.

"No. The only advantage to the home field is, you get to bat last."

Keane says, "Clemens gonna get the Cy Young Award?"

"He should get it," says McNamara. "He should have it before he even walks out there tomorrow."

Clemens, with nineteen wins, is pitching the finale tomorrow.

McNamara remembers something that makes him smile. "You know who hit the home run last night, Cliff?" Cliff must know, but McNamara tells him, relishing the memory, "That fuckin' little pisspot shortstop." McNamara shakes his head, lighting up with admiration for little Spike.

Talk drifts this way and that. I could sit forever in this dugout and listen to the men talk baseball. Last time I was here, the Detroit series, Al Kaline and George Kell, who broadcast Tigers games on television, came over to say hello to Pesky. Of course, they got swapping stories. Recollections of Dizzy Trout and Prince Hal Newhouser. I could listen forever.

McNamara now is remembering the year he managed winter ball in the Dominican Republic. "One day—I'll never forget it—Pedro Borbon's pitchin' against Andujar. They're both fuckin' crazy, of course. Borbon was a little wild that day, so Andujar comes up to bat and stands like *this*." McNamara gets off the bench to demonstrate. Andujar wasn't standing at all; he was squatting on his haunches. Chuckling, McNamara sits back down. "Then Borbon comes up, and *he* does it. He squats way down just like Andujar did, but Andujar throws two strikes by him. So with two strikes, Borbon—he's been batting left-handed—goes around to the other side and squats down *right*-handed."

"It's crazy down there, huh?" says Keane.

"Christ, I'll tell you. People light newspapers and throw 'em down on the field."

Ryan wanders away. McNamara glances up and sees that they've printed out his starting lineup on the electronic scoreboard. He's turning loose three of the Pawtucket kids today: Leister pitching, Dodson at first, Jody Reed at short.

"How do you like that lineup, Cliff?" McNamara says.

Keane studies it. "I like the shortstop," he says.

"I like the shortstop who played last night," says McNamara.

"The kid's better," Keane says.

"Bull*shit*," says McNamara. "He hasn't proved it yet." He isn't angry, though. He'll take it from old Cliff.

Rice comes out.

" 'Lo, Jimmy," says McNamara.

"How you doin'?" Rice asks him.

"I feel better every hour," McNamara tells him.

Rice chuckles and bounds up the steps. McNamara falls silent. Keane, too.

"Well, it's almost over, John," Keane says finally.

McNamara turns to him. "You know," he says, "I sit here thinkin', and I *still* can't believe we lost the sixth game of the World Series. There's a part of me that just doesn't believe it."

"Yeah," Keane agrees.

"One fuckin' out," McNamara says. "That's all we needed. One fuckin' out."

Keane says nothing. He's right; there's nothing to say.

Leister gets belted around in the first and sixth innings, and the Brewers win handily. Todd Benzinger goes three for four with two doubles. Burks hits three singles and steals a base. Greenwell swats a double.

There are nearly twenty-two thousand people in the ballpark. The Sox lose, 8–4, but no one seems disappointed.

Twelve

A Player for a Moment

IT IS AS IF BASEBALL HAD OVERSTAYED BY A DAY. LAST NIGHT a cold rain pounded the city. The rain has slackened, and a mist is coming down, steady and cold as snow. The first thought is Clemens. He is to win number twenty today, and put an end to any notions that anyone else deserves the Cy Young Award. In the contract settlement, the club agreed to pay Roger $150,000 if he won the Cy Young. Today, in one swoop, Clemens can win his twentieth, put a lock on the Cy Young Award, and shrink his earned-run average below 3.00. Clemens has nothing to prove; it will be, rather, a day of affirmation. But the mist slants down, and a wind begins to gust, chasing it against the sides of the city buildings.

I go early, ten-thirty, on this final day. The clubhouse is full and noisy. Vince Orlando is yelling at both clubhouse boys, the fat one and the gangling one. The boys are circulating with baseballs, getting autographs. Boggs hobbles around, chatty. The ballplayers are emptying their cubicles. They are folding clothes and dropping them into the maws of their big duffel bags. They examine letters, the season's accumulation, stick some into their duffels and toss others into trash cans. Spike Owen asks Bill Fischer if he'll be able to catch a five-twenty flight out of Logan; Fish says he will. A couple of writers now have Boggs at bay by his stall. Wade stands, one more time, with his arms clamped over his chest, looking out beyond his interrogators. I miss the question but not Wade's answer, which is delivered in the usual decisive way, but with a bit more heat.

"Eddie Andelman," Wade says loudly, "can kiss my ass."

Music to the ears of Pesky, who winks, chuckles, and invites me to sit down. "I'll give you some bullshit," he promises.

The adjacent chair is empty but belongs to Mike Greenwell. Sit in Greenwell's chair?

"Sid*down*," Pesky says, and I do.

There won't, of course, be any batting practice, so Pesky isn't getting into his uniform. He's just sitting, puffing on a cigar, watching the season end. There's nothing left for him to do. I ask him about the clubhouse, how it has changed, and he points to where a wall used to be, and to the area that used to be the trainer's room. In the old days it was much smaller. I ask him where Williams's locker was, and Yaz's. Ted's was over there, out in the open, and Yaz dressed in the corner where Stanley and Crawford hide out.

I remember the question I haven't asked Pesky. It's now or never. I haven't wanted to trouble him, but with time running out I decide to take the plunge. So many people have asked me about it: *What does he say about the '46 Series?* I put them off. I haven't asked him yet, I tell them.

"John," I say, sitting in Mike Greenwell's chair facing Pesky. "I hate to bring this up, but I got to ask you about one thing."

"The play," he says.

The play. Forty-one years later, and the moment floats atop his consciousness; it is at the tip of his tongue.

"Yeah," I say. "Do you mind?"

To recapitulate, the score was tied in the bottom of the eighth inning of the seventh game. Enos Slaughter was at first. There were two outs. Harry Walker hits a single to left center; the relay throw comes to Pesky, who whirls, sees Slaughter rounding third, and throws home, too late. Slaughter has scored what turns out to be the winning run. Pesky, history says, held the ball while Slaughter scored.

"Hell," he says, "I'll talk about it. First of all, Slaughter was running with the pitch. He's practically at second when Walker hits the ball. It's a base hit, left center. Now, Dominic had gone out of the game. He'd come up lame. The kid who was out there might have been a little slow gettin' to the ball. I went out for the relay, of course, and I got out farther than I realized. I didn't know Enos was tryin' to score. I was surprised; that was the hesitation. Some of the Cardinals said afterward that Doerr and Higgins should have hollered to me, let me know Enos was going home. No one said a thing to me."

It has seemed painless enough, but as Pesky describes himself out there—deeper than he realized, everything up to him as Slaughter sped home—his eyes widen and his face turns quiet. It was a lonely moment. I think of Buckner after Mookie's ground ball had gone through. The loneliness.

Owen clatters past us, headed out with his bat. He'll hit with Hriniak under the bleachers.

"Go get 'em, Spike," Pesky says.

"Hey, Johnny," Spike says cheerfully.

Pesky shakes his head. "Jesus Christ," he says, his old self again. "Last day of the season, and he's takin' fuckin' hitting. What's this game coming to?"

———

I'll probably never see the inside of this dugout again, and so at eleven-thirty I go clanking down the tunnel and sit awhile, watching the mist blow down over the field. The silver-gray tarpaulin blankets the infield. The tunnel breathes thick, stale heat into the dugout. It's cold, though. They've sold a lot of tickets—Clemens—and a couple hundred hopeful people are scattered in seats under the grandstand roof. And believe it or not, there are kids at the railing by the dugout. They are dressed in raincoats and yellow slickers, and they've got their pens and baseballs. Benzinger pops out of the dugout, carrying his bat, and the chorus goes up. *"Todd! Todd can I have your autograph pleeeeze? Come on Todd, pleeeeze. . . ."*

At noon McNamara opens his door, and the writers, who have nothing else to do, sift in to chat. McNamara has his uniform on. There are five or six writers, not many, and we all find chairs.

"What are your immediate plans, John?"

"I'm goin' to the Series."

"Are you going to keep Evans at first base next year?"

"It depends on what happens."

"John, what are some of the things that have pleased you this year?"

McNamara looks disgusted. "Shit, I don't have to enumerate those. You can see what's goin' on. The *kids* have pleased me, what do you think has pleased me? And Roger comin' back like he did after the slow start."

These sharp answers always bring things to a temporary halt. McNamara waits for the next meat-head question. But the next question will probably be a gift, something McNamara will be happy to discuss. It will patch things up, get us rolling again.

So someone says, "John, can you talk a little about Ellis Burks?"

"Well," says McNamara, "I'll be honest with you. When

we brought him up, I wasn't sure he was ready. I didn't know."
Odd. A month or two ago McNamara was saying that he believed in Ellis right from the start. He said it emphatically. "I
think the key with Ellis has been sittin' him down when he
wasn't goin' well. Knowing when to sit him down, when to put
him back in the lineup."

The Associated Press guy, Dave O'Hara, strolls in. O'Hara
is a reedy veteran. On McNamara's desk is a vase of flowers,
and as O'Hara lowers himself into a chair he nods at the flowers
and says, "Someone sending you condolences?"

Laughter sputters around the room, but not from Mc-
Namara, who sends O'Hara his steeliest look. "*Jesus Christ*," he
says finally, loudly. "Did you go to church today?"

O'Hara chuckles. "I couldn't resist it," he says.

A photographer comes in, aims, clicks a shot of Mc-
Namara.

"*Hey*," snaps McNamara. "No pictures in here."

April to October, nothing has changed.

The photographer backs out of the room, mumbling an
apology.

Mike Ross of the *Transatlantic Baseball Bulletin*, who apparently hasn't seen enough of McNamara to know any better,
asks a question guaranteed to rile the man. Shaughnessy, in his
Sunday column, noted that Dave Smith, a relief pitcher for the
Houston Astros, plans to become a free agent, and let the im-
plication dangle that the Sox ought to consider bidding for his
services.

Ross, who looks British with his gray curls and long skinny
feet, says, "Is there anything in the speculation that the Red
Sox might get Dave Smith?"

You can hear a pin drop.

McNamara looks as if he just had his first and last taste of
fish ice cream. He gazes at Ross, sizing him up, and tells him,
"I don't know *what* you're talkin' about."

"Dave Smith, the relief pitcher?"

McNamara just stares.

"Dan Shaughnessy in the *Globe* today," Ross staggers on, "he was saying . . ."

Bob Ryan is sitting next to Ross. Ryan to the rescue. Ryan of the *Globe*. "*All* he said," Ryan puts in, "was that Smith's a free agent. *Period*."

McNamara appears to have decided that none of this is worth bothering with. He watches Ross balefully. Let it not be said that McNamara is afraid to look a man in the eye.

Ross isn't quite willing to be slapped down. "He didn't *just* say that."

"That's *all* he said," intones the dapper Ryan.

"I just thought . . ."

"Don't blow it up," Ryan tells him.

". . . maybe he had some inside angle."

"There wasn't any angle," huffs Ryan.

Ross shuts up.

But after McNamara dismisses us Ross takes it up with Ryan in the clubhouse. Mike just wants to explain. He doesn't want anyone mad at him. Ryan, still ruffled, says there's enough bad feeling between McNamara and Shaughnessy already, and why toss more fuel on the fire? Why give McNamara one more thing to hold against Shaughnessy?

"So," I say to Ryan, "you were protecting Shaughnessy?"

"There's enough irrationality on *both* sides," he tells me. "Let's keep a lid on it, huh?"

On the last day of the season, a new moral dimension in the clubhouse.

The mist does stop falling. The wind rises, scouring the ballpark, drying the grass. They roll up the tarp; the infield is damp, but it can be played on.

I eat my last meal in the lounge, enveloped in the usual baseball talk and old-boy conviviality. I look once more at the pictures. Yaz, Williams, Williams and DiMaggio, the sweaty, grinning Parnell. Pesky, the kid, stopping a ground ball for the photographer. At quarter of one I cross the miniature alley to the press box. The windows are shut, and the heaters blow, filling the long room with too much warmth. I go down past the little bar and pick up the press releases and stat sheets laid out in stacks. I sit down at the blue Formica counter and open my score book.

Many of the ticket holders have stayed home. This is easily the smallest crowd of the year, maybe twelve thousand people scattered around. Yellow slickers spatter the grandstand. The wind straightens out the flags, pulling them left to right. It rolls them and snaps them. A pitcher's wind. Clemens is throwing in the bull pen, wheeling and bending down hard in the distance. The players fidget up and down in the dugouts. Organ music swirls through the ballpark. I'm going to miss this. *Boy, I bet you're sick of baseball,* people have been saying. Oh, no. Not of this.

The pitchers finish warming and come jogging in their windbreakers across the rain-darkened outfield. The crowd greets Clemens, calling to him by his first name. Roger knows what he's going to do this afternoon, and so does the crowd. Twenty wins, the Cy Young Award. Affirmation. If I had a taker, I'd empty my wallet on this blue counter, sixty bucks, and bet it all on a Clemens shutout. The Brewers are a hitting team. A *good* team. It won't matter today. Sixty dollars.

The Sox take the field, exploding out to a burst of organ music. Clemens charges to the mound.

The Brewers are going to be lucky to get a hit.

Molitor leads off. Someone in the press box has done some calculating on a pocket computer: If Molitor can go five for five, he will overtake Boggs and win the batting championship. Molitor had a big day yesterday, three for three with a pair of walks. Five for five—bet your life against it.

It is easy to forget, because he throws the great fastball, that Clemens is a control pitcher. Molitor doesn't forget it. He swings at the first pitch, knowing it is probably as good a pitch as he will see, and bounces it to Romero at third. The crowd greets this first out with a shrill, electric roar. Clemens strikes out Robin Yount, who takes the third one, a fastball, and walks away without complaining. Surhoff taps a ground ball to Barrett. Clemens charges in.

Let's not dwell on the Sox' offense. They knock out the starting pitcher, Chris Bosio, in the seventh. They score three in the fourth. Greenwell unloads a triple. Marzano comes through with a single. They score one more in the seventh, finishing Bosio's season. The relief pitchers then shut the door.

The tale today is the Rocket Man.

In the second inning he strikes out Brock, Sveum, and Riles, in order.

In the third, Mike Felder leads off, and with two strikes punches a fly ball to left center, midway between Greenwell and Burks. The ball bounds once, hits the wall, a double. A nervous quiet dips down over the grandstand. A leadoff double isn't in the libretto; could we all be wrong about Roger today?

No.

He strikes out Rick Manning on four pitches. Manning can't get the bat off his shoulder on the third strike. The fastball freezes him. Clemens strikes out Juan Castillo, swinging. Now we have Molitor, with that runner still at second base. Roger throws ball one, then drops two hard curves, or maybe sliders, over the outside corner, strike one and strike two, Molitor taking. This is a .350 hitter, remember. Now Roger leans back and hurls his best fastball, which Molitor has to swing at and does, late, strike three. Roger pounds his fist in his glove and runs for the dugout.

No strikeouts in the fourth, but Clemens puts them down easily, three straight. A pop fly and two ground balls. In the fifth he whiffs Sveum with his high fastball; Sveum takes a short snappy swing, pecking at the ball, trying to adjust to this impossible fastball. Riles hits a fly ball to Greenwell. Clemens strikes out Felder, who hit the double, with the fastball. It has begun to seem as if the Brewers' swings and Roger's pitches are only vaguely related to each other. There is the pitch, and then a swing, which occurs at some random-seeming point in the fraction of a second the fastball is in the air. Swing and miss, swing and miss. The fastball is too fast. Swing and hope for the best.

In the sixth, Manning falls behind, two strikes, but does manage to pop the ball in the air to Barrett, swinging late. Castillo takes a third strike without moving a muscle, standing there stock-still as if in admiration for the speed of the ball flashing by. He remains so a moment, motionless with the bat on his shoulder, then rouses himself and walks briskly away, no argument with the umpire. This is Clemens's tenth strikeout, his ninth ten-strikeout game of the season, a new team record. Roger held the old one of eight, he and Gentleman Jim Lonborg. Molitor takes ball one, then gets a pretty good swing and chops one off the grass halfway to the mound; Roger, who isn't built for jumping, springs straight up, arching his body, and lands like a big cat with the ball in his glove. He tosses Molitor out. The cheering seems to beat back the wind.

No strikeouts in the seventh, but the Brewers go down on seven pitches. Yount and Surhoff hit ground balls, and Brock lifts one into the wind to Ellis Burks. Brock's fly ball is the third that has made it to the outfield, including Felder's double.

Leading off the eighth, Sveum, who bats left, swings late and pushes a ground ball that dribbles over third base and rolls to the barrier. It knocks against the barrier and dodges Greenwell. Sveum has a leadoff double. Here we are again, except that it is the eighth inning, and Clemens has given a whale of a performance, no matter what should happen now. They say that when the first man reaches base, the chances that a run will result are fifty-fifty. Surely the odds increase when the leadoff man reaches second. The only question remaining in this game—the Sox are leading, 4–0—is the shutout. A little luck either way may decide it. Clemens fans Riles, who flails helplessly at a very high fastball. Now the luck: Felder hits a ground ball, hard, to the left side; Romero slashes sideways, lands on his belly, snares the ball, has it so instantaneously that it takes the brain another half second to register it. Romero scrambles to his feet, uniform smeared with wet dirt, and whips the ball neatly to first, in time. The crowd heaps a cheer on Romero. Manning grounds out to Barrett, and the inning is history.

The ninth. Roger leads his teammates onto the field, springing up out of the dugout and running hard to the mound. His appearance ignites a prolonged cheer, and everyone stands, cheering, yelling his name, smiling. They remain standing. They stand in the cold, in the coming darkness, outshouting the wind as Roger fans Castillo on three pitches.

Molitor. One of the best, but it won't matter. Not today, not at this pont. Molitor tries to slap the first pitch to right and skips it to Barrett, easy out. A cheer is building. Yount takes a strike, then swings and misses. Celebration. Noise. Clemens pours the fastball, and Yount, a superb hitter, manages to put his bat on it, to dump it into right field, not deep, where Benzinger waits and gloves it, ending the season.

The crowd still stands, cheering and beating their hands together, and a chant goes up. *"Rah-ger! Rah-ger!"* The players swarm around Clemens, grabbing his hand, and the pack moves quickly to the dugout, to warmth. *"Rah-ger! Rah-ger!"* They begin to leave, pouring down the ramps, bringing their chant, singing as they go. *"Rah-ger! Rah-ger! Rah-ger!"* It fills the deep cave under the grandstand roof, and twines itself up the steel bones of the old ballpark. It shakes the place.

Out they stream into the gray afternoon and cold wind, all

happy. On my way to the clubhouse I pause to look down at the corner of Van Ness and Yawkey Way. The vendors are all in place, bundled in wool parkas. The people coming out of the ballpark are taking their time, loitering. Already a crowd is gathering at the gateway to the players' parking lot. The crowd is as big as ever. Bigger, maybe. People clutter Yawkey Way, indifferent to the cars trying to fight through. The mood down there is festive. It is as if they, too, had finished their work for another season, and champagne were being served in the streets around Fenway.

McNamara looks weary, sitting back with his can of beer, his silver-gray hair dripping down. He answers the questions dully, tired of it all.

Is Clemens the best pitcher in the game?

"There's no question in *my* mind."

Will he win the Cy Young Award?

"He *should* win it."

In the clubhouse Clemens is giving a television interview. A white towel wraps his neck, Roger's postgame trademark. He is smiling. His blue eyes shine. He says the usual things: he did what he set out to do, he put the numbers up there. The white light snaps off and the writers converge, jostling me back too far to hear the Rocket Man.

Marzano, who caught him, is telling a reporter, "He's hard to hit when it's ninety degrees outside, never mind today. They didn't have a chance."

"This team has a new look," Mike Greenwell is saying. He stands, I notice, like Boggs, arms folded over his chest. "This is a different type of team than the Red Sox ever had. We got speed now."

A writer asks him gingerly if he has considered the possibility that he might be traded. Someone's going to be, unless they want to embark next year with the same bull pen crew.

Greenwell nods, unsettled by the question. "Yeah," he agrees, "one or another of us may go. I just hope if they do make a trade, it isn't me." He flashes a boyish smile. "I like being a Red Sox."

Evans is having words with a little boy—his son, obviously, same dark hair and tawny beauty. The boy is crying. His dark eyes are tear-swollen, his cheeks glistening. He looks like a little gypsy.

"There's nothin' I can do about it," Evans is telling him. "One of the writers took it. Or a player, I don't know. But it's gone."

The boy says something, squeaky-voiced from crying.

"There's nothin' I can do," Evans says. "It's gone."

Boggs is holding forth to an audience of reporters. "It's hard being in the situation I'm in, this year with the knee, the injury last year at the end of the season. You got people out there like Eddie Andelman puttin' out this stuff about me. This was my best year, and Eddie Andelman's still poppin' off. He still wants me traded, still wants me out of here. He says I'm jakin' it. Eddie Andelman can just kiss my ass."

Evans sits down with a paper plate of food. The little boy has detached himself from his father and from everybody else. He stands apart, looking at the floor, crying silently. No one is paying attention. I go to him, touch his shoulder. He raises his wet face.

"What did you lose?" I ask.

"A ball." He snuffles. "Autographed."

"Who autographed it?"

"The whole . . ." His mouth trembles, and he starts to cry again. ". . . the whole . . . *team*."

"And someone stole it?"

He nods.

Jesus, I think, but there's nothing I can do.

His father, meanwhile, is eating pasta shells and meat sauce, slowly eating, slowly talking; talking in a low voice with the reporters all leaning down to hear through the noise of the clubhouse. Dewey is exhausted. He wears the dull, vacant look of a man who is plain worn out.

"The front office knows what they have to do," he says. "They know what's wrong with this ball club. They'll do what they have to to fix it." He stares awhile at nothing. "Better times are ahead of us," he says.

Eddie Romero, who has showered and dressed, is going around the room saying good-bye. Romero whacked three hits today and saved Clemens's shutout. He whisks up to Evans, grabs his hand.

"So long, Eddie," says Evans.

"Take care, man," says Romero. "We'll win."

The concourse sweeps around empty and chilly from the wind coming down the ramps. Hot dog wrappers litter the blackened concrete floor. Squashed Dixie Cups, napkins, peanut shells. The crowd has swirled through like a river, laying down its detritus. The ramps lead up to squares of leaden daylight. I choose one and walk up.

First-base side, over toward the plate. Good seats. The grandstand curves empty around the ball field. It looks frozen in time, a picture taken years and years ago. How is it that an empty ballpark looks so much smaller than a full one? Especially little Fenway. Crowds swell the place. I sit down in a red seat. Too many times I have had to sit in the distant sections overlooking right field. I buy my tickets months in advance, and still they put me out in right field, where I have trouble seeing. Who gets the good seats, I wonder? My aunt and I sat out there on the Sunday afternoon when she brought me to my first game. Years later, in 1979, my aunt and I came back to Fenway together, and again we had to sit in deep right field. It was a gray August afternoon, and in the third inning rain began to fall. Freddie Lynn, still in his prime, robbed somebody of a triple, sliding on his belly in a spray of rainwater to make the catch. At the end of six innings the umps stopped the game. My aunt and I were sitting out of the rain under the grandstand roof. The umpires hadn't decided yet whether to call the game, and so my aunt opened her pocketbook and sent me down for beer and hot dogs. My aunt would never eat a hot dog anywhere but here. We ate and drank, and then I went down for two more beers. The beer was thin and foamy—ballpark beer, the best in the world. I know from memory and photographs that my aunt was a stunning woman that day in 1955 when she led me by the hand into Fenway Park. In '79 her long hair was stone-gray, and the skin was pinched tight against the fine bones of her face. We talked about my writing and a woman I thought I might be in love with—matters on which she'd always counseled me. We talked and watched the rain come down on the ballpark. They waited more than an hour before calling the game. We were sorry not to see more baseball, but neither of us felt cheated.

The scoreboard on the left-field wall is still plastered with today's numbers. MIL for Milwaukee, and then the long row of zeros, Clemens's shutout. BOS for the Sox, a three and a one interspersed among the goose eggs. The other American League games are posted: score, inning, current pitchers by their uniform numbers. Red lights for outs and strikes, green lights for balls. Sherm Feller turns the lights on and off, flicking toggles in his booth. People inside the scoreboard hang the numbers by hand, dropping them out through slots.

There's a color photo of Ted Williams, bright in my memory, standing in front of the scoreboard during a game. There's a lull, a change of pitchers, perhaps; Williams stands with his hands on his hips, a knee canted out, head dipping over as if he were thinking momentarily of something else. His long body is slack. He looks tired. It is late in the day; he throws a shadow behind him.

I asked Jim Samia if I could walk out on the ball field sometime; and with no fuss, as usual, Jim turned me loose one afternoon before batting practice. It was a late summer's day. A couple of the guys were playing catch in front of the Sox' dugout. I walked out across the first-base chalk line, across the sticky dirt of the infield, and out into the fan-shaped valley of center field. The wall and the bleachers loomed, but looking the other way I felt unenclosed. The sky spread huge, acres of sky with white and pale violet clouds sliding along. The grandstand squatted low, like a bandstand or country ballpark with its flat roof.

I roamed to the wall, the famous left-field wall. It rose like a cliff. I could hear the swish of traffic on the Turnpike below Lansdowne Street. The base of the wall is cushioned so you won't break a bone when you slam against it making a great catch. I went to the scoreboard. I was surprised, for some reason, to discover it was made of steel plates, riveted like the hull of a battleship. The steel was pocked with hundreds of round dents, as if it had been pounded by cannonballs: nearly a season's worth of line drives.

The left-field grandstand juts sharply, a ship's bow plying the outfield. It isn't high, and I could imagine it loaded with people, who would be close enough to yell clearly down to you. You could converse with them. Rice doesn't. I doubt Williams did, or Yaz. But one night I saw an Angels' left fielder named Leon Wagner spend the entire game bantering with the people up there. They would yell down, and he'd laugh and say something back. It went on all night, till they began cheering him each time he trotted out there.

When I was sure I'd looked at all there was to see, I circled back to right field. Evans's spot. I went to the barrier where Dewey made his catch off Morgan in the '75 Series. He'd been running straight back, looking for the ball over his right shoulder; the ball hadn't faded, and he'd had to find it directly overhead. It was then that he'd staggered. I went to the barrier, looked up, searching the sky for a whizzing baseball. Evans told me the ball would have found the seats; I think so, too. A few feet from the wall he thrust the glove up, snared the ball as it came whistling over his shoulder, and finally regained his balance. I turned. It was a long way to first base, a long throw. But the runner never dreamed I'd catch Morgan's drive, and was almost at third by now. The crowd had let loose a screeching din, and in the excitement, and in the lung-bursting joy of having made the catch, I whirled and hurried the throw. It flew way to the right of first, but it didn't matter. There was time. Doyle was there to meet it; he threw accurately to Cooper at first. Double play, and the game was saved. The crowd rose, and the noise shook the ground.

I get up and take a last, long look. I walk down the ramp, through the empty concourse, and out onto Yawkey Way.

The wind is blowing harder. It has chased away the crowds. It hurtles up Van Ness Street between the brick factory buildings. I unlock my car door and pull it open against the shove of the wind. In the old days players used to walk to the ballpark from their hotels and rooming houses, and in the lightless afternoon I can see Babe Ruth, tall and broad in a fur coat and tweed touring cap. A grin cuts his face, and he's smoking a fat cigar.